AF662907

ASEAN CALLING

Development of India's North-East through Sub-regional Cooperation

Editors

Ujjwal Kanti Paul
Gurudas Das
C Joshua Thomas

ASEAN STUDIES CENTRE
ICSSR-NERC NEHU, SHILLONG

PENTAGON PRESS

ASEAN CALLING: Development of India's North-East through Sub-regional Cooperation

Editors: Ujjwal Kanti Paul, Gurudas Das and C Joshua Thomas

First Published in 2017

Copyright © ICSSR-NERC, Shillong

ISBN 978-93-86618-02-3

All rights reserved. No part of this publication may be reproduced, stored in a retrieval system, or transmitted, in any form or by any means, electronic, mechanical, photocopying, recording, or otherwise, without first obtaining written permission of the copyright owner.

Disclaimer: The views expressed in this book are those of the authors and do not necessarily reflect those of the editors.

Published by

PENTAGON PRESS
206, Peacock Lane, Shahpur Jat
New Delhi-110049
Phones: 011-64706243, 26491568
Telefax: 011-26490600
email: rajan@pentagonpress.in
website: www.pentagonpress.in

Printed at Aegean Offset Printers, Greater Noida, U.P.

Contents

Foreword

I am delighted to present the book, *ASEAN Calling: Development of India's North-East Through Sub-Regional Cooperation,* which is an outcome of the national seminar organised by the National Institute of Technology, Silchar in collaboration with the ASEAN Studies Centre, Shillong, on 18-19 April, 2017.

The ASEAN Studies Centre is a unique regional think-tank designed to generate ideas and academic research on how to enhance engagement between North-East India and ASEAN, spanning the political, economic, developmental and socio-cultural domains.

The volume captures the key themes of connectivity, policy restructuring, infrastructure development and potential of convergence between the North–East and ASEAN, which were deliberated upon during the seminar.

I trust that the publication will serve as an important piece of literature on India's Act East Policy and North-East India, and that policy makers, researchers and the general public will find it of relevance.

Ms. Pooja Kapur
Joint Secretary (ASEAN Multilateral)
Ministry of External Affairs
Government of India, New Delhi

Preface

Why do certain areas, social groups and economic institutions of a nation remain underdeveloped while others advance and prosper? This subject has fascinated and consumed the attention from scholars in fields as diverse as anthropology, history, sociology, economics and political science. Even developed countries like Canada, Great Britain, France, Italy and United States are also no exception to the universal phenomenon of uneven development. While uneven development is considered to be an essential feature of the capitalist economy, the socialist nations also face similar problems. For instance, the Yunnan province in Southwestern China in which minority nationalities comprise over one third of the population lags far behind than other provinces in most of the socio-economic indicators.

The neoclassical theories advocate for laissez-faire or free market economy to deal with regional disparities. These theories assume that the factors (e.g. capital, labour and technology) are perfectly mobile and react to market signals in an instantaneous manner. Therefore, the disparities in income and productivity level tend to converge and the regional economies that start out poor eventually grow faster. Since convergence is the natural tendency, there is no need for any government intervention to prop up poor regions because such action might prolong rather than cure interregional differences.

However, the assumption of perfect mobility of factors in response to market signals faces severe criticism (Shaoguang and Angang 1999), even as the quality market signal is itself a matter of debate. The market signal in peripheries i.e., the regions which are far from core areas and main markets usually remains weak (Day and Schoemaker 2005) and due to the weakness of market forces to bring about a convergence in the incomes and wellbeing of heartland and hinterland, Friedmann

(1966) argues in favour of a government intervention to ensure such convergence.

Nevertheless, state-led development suffers from a *built-in* bias against the peripheries mainly due to two reasons. Firstly, 'scorched earth' policy—keeping the borders deliberately underdeveloped so that enemy forces cannot make any sweeping progress at times of war—keeps the government from committing large scale investment in peripheral areas. Secondly, the limited bargaining power of the inhabitants of the peripheral areas who often belong to the minority group and have insignificant representation in the democratic structure (Das et al. 2013).

This paradox of peripheral development has given to spurt in regionalism (began in 1950s and faded away in 1970s) and subsequently new regionalism (emerged in the mid-1980s). New regionalism comprises a 'combined approach', with a focus on development for 'the excluded'. Today, virtually all countries in the world are members of at least one regional group, with many belonging to more than one. As an 'Alternative Development Theory' new regionalism aims at convergence among regions along the dimensions of economic development, security, political regimes and culture through a natural or politically steered or most likely a mixture of the two processes. Currently, numerous regional groupings like EU, ASEAN, APEC, CEMAC, GMS, SIJORI, OECD, SAARC, SAFTA etc. are functioning all over the world.

Originally designed as an anticommunist organization, the ten-member Association of Southeast Asian Nations (ASEAN 10) is the driver of this new regional movement in Asia. ASEAN+3 comprising ASEAN plus Japan, China and South Korea periodically indicate the formation of an East Asian Community as a long term goal. India's relation with ASEAN has grown rapidly from a sectoral dialogue partner in 1992 to a full dialogue partner in 1995 and further as summit level partner in 2002. From India's point of view, ASEAN is a decisive platform which could influence its strategic and economic status in the Asia-Pacific region and bring to fruition its "Act East Policy. ASEAN too realized the importance of India as the third-largest economy in Asia and an emerging regional power, significant for its political and economic ambitions. Moreover, India, with the largest naval forces in the Indian Ocean and nuclear capabilities, is perceived by the ASEAN countries as a strategic partner to balance China's growing power in the region (Anand, 2009). The bilateral trade between India and ASEAN reached to US$58.5 billion in the year 2015 constituting nearly 3 percent of ASEAN's total trade with the world. During the same period, over 3 million Indians visited ASEAN.

The thin corridor comprising the seven north eastern states—Arunachal Pradesh, Assam, Meghalaya, Manipur, Mizoram, Nagaland, Sikkim and Tripura—connects India to ASEAN through land route. This connectivity is important for the flow of trade, investment, tourism and cultural and social exchange between India and ASEAN. A number of cross border infrastructure projects such as The Trilateral Highway, Kaladan Multi-modal Project, Asian Railway Network encompassing the region have been undertaken to improve its connectivity with ASEAN. However, it is not clear as to how the north eastern states that are blessed with abundant water, forest, fertile land, oil and gas, and strategic geographical location would reap dividend from this improved connectivity? What kind of opportunities and challenges would surface after connectivity improvement? What policy restructuring is required to enable NER to benefit from the infrastructure development? How NER can contribute to the growth of ASEAN? What are the potential areas of convergence between NER and ASEAN?

The book attempts to answer some of the questions raised above. It is the outcome of a national seminar titled "ASEAN Calling: Development of India's North-East through Sub-regional Cooperation organized by the Department of Humanities and Social Sciences, NIT Silchar, held during April 18-19, 2017. We are thankful to ASEAN Studies Centre Shillong for sponsoring the event and NIT Silchar for providing the necessary space. We would like to thank all the participants and support staff—contributors, resource persons, commentators and others—for making it such an intellectually stimulating meeting.

Ujjwal Kanti Paul
Gurudas Das
C Joshua Thomas

Contributors

A. Pushpalata Singh is assistant professor, Department of Economics Cachar College, Silchar. singha.pushpu@yahoo.co.in

Akshay Jyoti Sarma is assistant professor at Omeo Kumar Das Institute of Social Change and Development, Guwahati, Assam. ajsarma.86@gmail.com

Bidhan Barman is assistant professor Department of Political Science, Radhamadhab College, Silchar. bidhanbarman@yahoo.in

Dipon Ghosh is assistant professor of Economics at Rabindra Sadan Girl College, Karimganj, Assam. dipon86@gmail.com

Gurudas Das is professor of Economics at the Department of Humanities and Social Sciences, NIT Silchar. gurudas.nit@gmail.com

H Srikanth is professor of Political Science at the Department of Political Science, North East Hill University, Shillong. hskant@gmail.com

Jajati. K. Pattanaik is associate professor at the Department of Political Science, Jomin Tayeng Government Model Degree College, Roing, Arunachal Pradesh. pattnaik.jajati66@gmail.com

Konthoujam Sarda is research associate at the ASEAN Studies Centre, Shillong. sarda_kont@hotmail.com

Malabika Das is assistant professor of Economics at East Calcutta Girls College, Kolkata. malabi_das@yahoo.co.in

Monalisa Das is researcher in the Department of Economics, Assam University, Silchar. monalisa.das17@gmail.com

N.B Singh is assistant Professor, Department of Humanities and Social Sciences, NIT Silchar. nbsingh.597@gmail.com

Niranjan Roy is dean at the Mahatma Gandhi School of Economics and Commerce at Assam University, Silchar. roy_niranjan@yahoo.com

Subodh Chandra Das is researcher at the Department of Humanities and Social Sciences, NIT Silchar. dsubodh30@gmail.com

Subroto Chowdhury is faculty at Department of Humanities and Social Sciences, NIT Silchar. subroto.nits@gmail.com

Surat Basumatary is assistant Professor, Department of Education, Radhamadhab College, Silchar

Suwa Lal Jangu is assistant professor of Political Science at the Department of Political Science, Mizoram University. suwalaljangu@gmail.com

T Chandra Devi is researcher at the Department of Humanities and Social Sciences, NIT Silchar.

Tanuj Mathur is researcher at the Department of Humanities and Social Sciences, NIT Silchar. tanujmathur10@gmail.com

Ujjwal Kanti Paul is faculty at Department of Management Studies, NIT Silchar. ujjwal.paul@gmail.com

List of Figures and Maps

List of Tables

SUB-REGIONAL COOPERATION FOR DEVELOPMENT OF THE PERIPHERAL AREAS

1

Sub-Regional Cooperation: An Overview of the Global Best Practices

Tanuj Mathur

Introduction

Development of the peripheral regions has been a major challenge faced by big countries. Landlockedness, remoteness from mainland markets and complex geographical positioning are some of the barriers that impede the growth of peripheral regions. Similar challenge is being faced by the China's south west and India's north eastern region (NER). Scarce job opportunities, poor health care intuitions, shortage of power, lack of industries and poor road infrastructure predominantly seizes the development in these two regions. Moreover, nation states find it difficult to address the development need of such peripheral regions through the strategy of national development. In this discourse, sub-regional development cooperation can be viewed as a reasonable strategy for the growth of the peripheral region. Much of the credence for taking up this strategy pervades from the experiences of other sub-regional groupings in the world. In this endeavor, we attempt to review some of the international regional groupings in details in order to sketch what could precisely be the basis of the cross cultural sub-regional cooperation that embraces the development of NER.

Greater Mekong Sub-region (GMS)

In 1992, with the assistance of Asian Development Bank (ADB) six countries: Cambodia, the Lao's People Democratic Republic (PDR), Myanmar, Thailand, Vietnam, Yunnan and Guangxi Province in the region of People's Republic of China (PRC), came together to form a sub-regional cooperation around the natural economic area of Mekong River. The Greater Mekong Sub-regional (GMS) as it is better known is an activity based economic cooperation that enables the landlocked regions to integrate with the external markets in order to facilitate development of regional infrastructure and reduce the cross-border obstacles to reap the social and economic benefits to the fullest. To achieve its agenda of growth and development of the sub-regions, the GMS program has adopted a three-pronged strategy (3Cs):

(1) Increasing *connectivity* through transformation of transit corridors and development of physical infrastructure,
(2) Improving *competitiveness* by efficient trade facilitation mechanism and,
(3) Building a greater sense of *community* through program that addresses social and environmental concerns (ADB bulletin, 2015).

Over the past two decades, substantial progress has been made by the GMS countries in areas of transport, energy, telecommunications, environment, human resource development, tourism, trade, private sector investment, and agriculture. The trade between the GMS member countries has grown significantly from US$5 billion (1992) to US$413 billion (2014). Moreover the bilateral foreign direct investment (FDI) inflows have also seen threefold increase from US$8.49 billion (2001-2006) to Us$23.49 billion (2007-2012). In fact, among the entire GMS partner, China has been the lead investor followed by Thailand and Vietnam (table 1.1). The GMS program has contributed

Table 1.1: Percentage share of GMS FDI inflows

Year	*2001*	*2005*	*2010*	*2012*
GMS (USD million)	229	6379	12012	2706
PRC	7	2	79	67
Thailand	93	98	19	12
Vietnam	0	0	2	21
Cambodia	0	0	0	0
Lao PDR	0	0	0	0
Myanmar	0	0	0	0

Source: Report on Greater Mekong Sub Region Statistics on Growth, Infrastructure and Trade.

significantly in enhancing the per capita GDP for all member countries post its formation which on the average rose from US$1714 (1992) to US$8314 (2014) level (GMS Report, 2016).

Further, a considerable drop in the procedural delay to export and import goods has also been noticed among the partner countries. For instance, in Lao PDR to export goods, minimum time required to comply with necessary procedures was about 55 days in 2005 but because of improved trade facilitation measures it has come down to 23 days in 2014 (GMS Report, 2016). More evidently three countries (China, Thailand and Vietnam) under the GMS grouping in the year 2014 were ranked among the top 50 countries of the world in the overall logistic performance indices, showcasing remarkable improvement in their trade facilitation process (GMS Report, 2016).

The rapid improvement of logistical services between GMS member countries has drastically changed the orientation of global economy. In fact, the growth in the GMS countries has also opened the trade with rest of world economies. The trade-to-GDP ratio reflecting the countries integration into the world economy has increased in all GMS countries in the last two decades (figure 1.1). Beside trade, satisfactory progress has been made by GMS program in the energy sector in past two decades. Integration of large scale high-volume grids systems, expansion of power generation capacity,

Figure 1.1: Trade to GDP ratio (in percent)

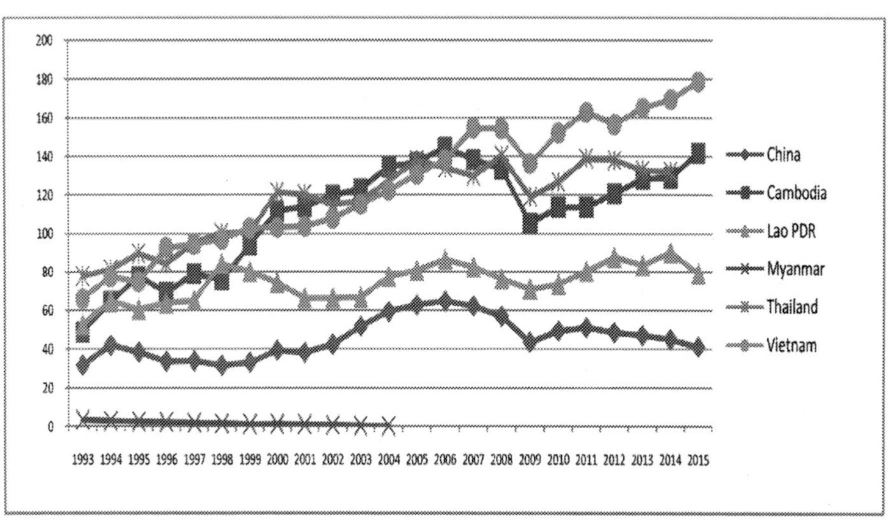

Source: http://wits.worldbank.org

alternative means of power generation systems and strengthen control of energy consumption has been the prime focus of the GMS energy sector program. Several projects have been undertaken by China to increase Cambodia's hydro power installed capacity from 20 MW to 3,045 MW by 2024[1]. Similarly, substantial investments have been made by Chinese and Thailand firms in Myanmar which nearly holds a potential 40000MW of hydro power on its northeast and southeast borders (GMS energy sector report, 2013). In addition, Thailand is even expected to supply 3800 MW of electric connection to Lao PDR by 2017 and about 400 MW and possibly 1900 MW to Myanmar and Cambodia respectively in the coming years (GMS energy sector report, 2013).

Therefore, opening of transit corridor, improvement in the regional connectivity and policy and institutional reforms has complemented well in enhancing the trade and commerce among the GMS member countries. While the increase in trade has raised the GDP of all GMS member countries, this growth has even resulted in ensuring better living standards for its native citizens. Increase in government revenues and higher spending on social sector over the last decade precisely reflects the benefits the member countries have reaped from this cooperation (Table 1.2).

Table 1.2: Socio-economic factors

Year	*1998*		*2008*		*2014*	
	Government revenue as % of GDP	*% Employed population*	*Government revenue % of GDP*	*% Employed population*	*Government revenue % of GDP*	*% Employed population*
Cambodia	8.7	40.6	12.6	49.9	15.6	54.2
China	11.7	55.8	19.5	56.3	22.1	56.5
Lao	8.6	0.0	13.9	0.0	18.3	0.0
Myanmar	7.3	NA	15.8	NA	28.5	41.2
Thailand	15.5	49.4	17.0	56.8	17.5	56.8
Vietnam	19.6	47.0	26.3	54.6	21.8	58.1

Source: https://www.adb.org/publications/key-indicators-asia-and-pacific-2015.

Central Asia Regional Economic Cooperation (CAREC)

CAREC emerged as a regional forum by the initiatives of Asian Development Bank (ADB) in the late 1990's to promote economic cooperation between the countries of Central Asia. This forum brought together ten member countries (Afghanistan, Azerbaijan, People's

Republic of China, Kazakhstan, Kyrgyz Republic, Mongolia, Pakistan, Turkmenistan, Tajikistan, and Uzbekistan) and six multilateral institutions (ADB, European Bank for Reconstruction and Development, International Monetary Fund, Islamic Development Bank, United Nations Development Programme and World Bank) with an aim to achieve principal goal of development through cooperation as embodied in its motto "Good neighbors, good partners, good prospects". Over the past 10 years, CAREC attracted substantial regional investments and technical assistances primarily from several multilateral funding agencies in the areas of transport, trade facilitation and energy sectors. Since 2001, CAREC has mobilized US$27.7 billion of investments and 166 projects, to which a sizeable share have gone to transport (79 percent) and the rest to the energy (19 percent) and trade facilitation (2 percent) sectors.

CAREC identified six priority transport corridors spanning across the Central Asia's east to west and north to south with a prime aim of reducing cross border bottlenecks and to improve transit and logistical arrangements. The consistent investment and procedural improvement has brought considerable reduction in both the time and cost of movement of goods. The Corridor Performance Measurement and Monitoring (CPMM) Report (2015) has shown marginal reduction in the border crossing time by 9.3 hours which is a 6 percent improvement year-on-year while the average border crossing cost (i.e. fees) has come down from US$186 to US$161 between 2010 and 2015. Moreover, the costs incurred to travel a corridor section per 500-km per 20 tons has fallen from US$1467 (2013) to US$1323 (2015) and the road and train speed has increased by 1.3 percent and 20 percent respectively in comparison to last year.

The infrastructural improvement has favorably impacted the trade and commerce between the member countries. There has been a phenomenal increase in the trade between the member countries which increased from US$6.34 billion (2000) to US$115.42 billion (2014). Among all the member countries, China occupied the major share in total trade, followed by Kazakhstan and Pakistan (see table 1.3 and figure 1.2). China has been the biggest exporter of durables, capital equipments and machinery, while Kazakhstan, Mongolia and Kyrgyz Republic have been prime exporter of agricultural goods, minerals and animal products. Although, the CAREC program has been able to improve the trade between the member countries but somehow remained slow in transforming energy and social sectors. However, in 2005 an energy sector coordinating committee (ESCC) meeting was held in Bishkek (Kyrgyz Republic) to discuss the issues and prospects related with development of regional electricity market in Central Asia, following which a moderate increase in the number of energy projects has been observed.

Table 1.3: Export and Import Trade among CAREC countries (in USD Million)

Year	*2000*		*2014*	
Country	*Total Exports to CAREC Countries*	*Total Imports from CAREC Countries*	*Total Exports to CAREC Countries*	*Total Imports from CAREC Countries*
Afghanistan	NA	NA	203.87[c]	2366.12[f]
Azerbaijan	44.52	95.94	474.50[d]	959.48
China	1570.18	1765.74	40557.21	27689.79
Kazakhstan	1039.47	311.38	13074.89	9094.78
Kyrgyz Republic	188.06	191.99[b]	NA	1788.63
Mongolia	268.02[a]	118.37	5076.40[e]	1736.37[g]
Pakistan	NA	NA	4185.90	10001.61
Tajikistan	111.24	367.53	NA	NA
Turkmenistan	146.82	122.68	NA	NA
Uzbekistan	NA	NA	NA	NA

Source: http://wits.worldbank.org, NA = Not available *Note:* (a): Export figures to: Afghanistan, Azerbaijan, Kyrgyz Republic, Tajikistan and Turkmenistan not available. (b): Import figures from Mongolia not available. (c): Export figures to: China and Pakistan are only available. (d): Import figures from Afghanistan not available. (e): Export figures to: Afghanistan, Azerbaijan, Tajikistan, Turkmenistan not available (f): Import figures from Azerbaijan, Kazakhstan, Kyrgyz Republic, Mongolia, Tajikistan and Turkmenistan not available. (g): Import figures from Afghanistan, Tajikistan and Turkmenistan not available.

Thus, CAREC, by and large has remained as an action-oriented and pragmatic alliance of countries. Its success has resulted from the mutual understanding and consensus building through work by its technical and senior official committees. Moreover, participation of countries technical ministries (transport, energy, finance etc.), engagement of multilateral funding agencies for resource mobilization and priority sector approach has benefitted enormously in strengthening Central Asian market.

Figure 1.2: Volume of approved CAREC-related projects, by sector, cumulative since 2001

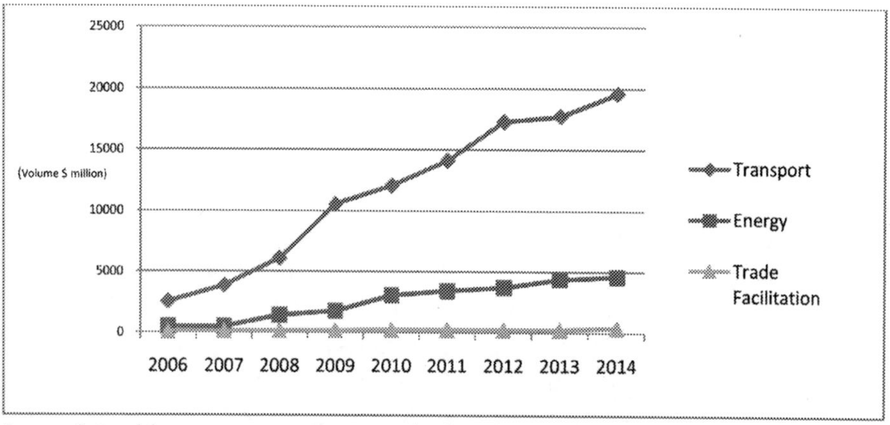

Source: http://www.carecprogram.org/index.php?page=carec-projects

Greater Tumen Initiative (GTI)

Initiated by UNDP in 1991, Greater Tumen programme was set up to strengthen the regional interaction between the four provinces of China: Heilongjiang, Inner Mongolia, Jilin and Liaoning; three provinces of Mongolia: Hentii, Dornod and Sukhbaatar; Eastern port cities of Republic of Korea (ROK): Busan, Ulsan, Gangwon-do and Gyeongsangbuk-do; and Russian eastern territory of Primorsky. Although, the GTI program during its commencement phase does encountered few functional, institutional as well as spatial challenges, but it was able to successfully resolve them and establish itself post 2005. The member countries took the full ownership of the program by making greater financial contribution to the common fund, setting-up legal institutional frameworks and initiating development projects.

GTI programme attracted significant regional interests among the countries in the regions. China was first to realize the importance of this cooperation in boosting the growth of its north eastern provinces which otherwise lagged behind on several economic and social indicators in comparison to other provinces. Similarly, both Mongolia and ROK showed great interests in becoming member, as the former's economy is largely under-developed and was expecting to reap economic benefits with utilization of their abundant untapped natural resources, while the latter faces huge industrial and energy resource constraints that can be addressed through this mutual cooperation.

Russia on the other hand shown its eagerness by looking at the prospect of resolving its oldest problem related with financing and building of infrastructure and technology in order to access Siberia's vast mineral base. At this outset, a Strategic Action Plan (SAP, 2006-15) was envisaged in 2005 that identified five priority sectors: transport, energy, environment, trade and investment, and tourism to increase the interaction with the local governments of these Northeast Asian (NEA) regions.

As far as the intra-regional trade is concerned among the NEA countries, it has risen even though at a slow pace but the volume of business has seen a threefold increase from US$470.18 billion in 2003 to US$1388.94 billion in 2012. During 2003-12, the exports have grown at an annual average rate of 14.4 percent and imports have grown annually at average rate of 13.4 in the same period (Adhikari, 2015). This boost in trade has been an outcome of several initiatives taken-up by the GTI members with a purpose improving the transport corridors (See Table 1.4). In fact, GTI SAP (2006-2015) clearly stated to "achieve a ten to fifteen per cent increase in the cross-border cargo through the Tumen ports between the Greater Tumen Region (GTR) and the wider world through lowering the transportation costs and improving the infrastructure".

Table 1.4: Transport sector project proposed in 2007

1.	NEA Ferry Route Infrastructure Framework
2.	Modernization of Zarubino Port
3.	Mongolia-China Railway Construction
4.	Resuming Hunchun-Makhalino Railway
5.	China Road, Harbor Project in the border between China and North Korea.

Source: Koo et al., (2011)

Besides trade and transport sector, in 2007 an Energy board was set up to develop energy related infrastructure and facilitate energy trade among the GTI member countries. To supply stable and secure power to the Tumen region, "Small Ring" initiative was taken up in Energy Action Plan 2010-2011, to connect the electric power systems of – China, North Korea and Russia. Moreover, China in order to meet its future energy demand initiated project in Mongolia to generate power through Uranium, while Republic of Korea has also signed an inter-governmental agreement in 2011 to set up thermal power station.

Tourism has attracted the attention of the members and had in fact rolled out few projects such as sustainable development of Mt. Baekdu in the Changbai Mountains, tourism development in eastern Mongolia regions and tourist trips from Beijing, China to North Korea.

GTI emerged as the only major multilateral cooperation that aimed at integrating the regions of NEA. So far GTI has achieved substantial growth in terms of trade and transport. In fact, a study by Tochkov (2015) exhibited that provinces under each member countries have converged at a decent pace over the past decade. More specifically, GTI's success can be attributed to the initiates undertaken in the transport and trade facilitation sectors. Although its deliverables through energy, tourism and environment sectors is yet to offer tangible benefits to the region but the proposed projects in the list does provide adequate support for the success of this cooperation in the near future.

The Sub-regional cooperation an answer to India's Northeast Problems

Sub-regional cooperation is a possible antidote to abridge wide disparities in India's NER. In fact, before the partition of the Indian subcontinent in 1947, NER was linked with the mainland of India through present-day Bangladesh as well its trade linkages with other neighboring countries were much integrated. Following partition, these traditional channels of communication got disrupted making NER a landlocked territory. Besides NER being rich in resources, such as hydrocarbons, forest resources, hydroelectricity and other minerals, the high transportation costs, less governmental focus and discontinuous neighboring relations did not allow it to grow according to its comparative advantages. These complexities have made the region perpetually underdeveloped and politically unstable.

It is startlingly to see that, despite Myanmar shares the land border with NER and been a longtime member of ASEAN, did not spearheaded any concrete efforts to improve regional ties with India. Moreover, the majority of trade that is flowing between ASEAN countries and India largely happens through the sea routes, which benefits the coastal states leaving the landlocked areas of NER to remain incessantly underdeveloped. In fact, the government-led development process that pursued in India during pre-and-post liberalization periods has even not succeeded in invigorating economic growth in the NER.

As geographic isolation of NER have perennially kept them away from economic development process, a strategy closely linking up the markets across its borders can act as a plinth to economic growth. A formidable sub-regional cooperation would provide NER with the opportunity to showcase its geo-economic advantages by establishing cross-border connectivity and enhancing access to markets of neighboring countries such as Myanmar, China, Thailand etc., thereby making production and marketing cost effective. Thus, sub-regional cooperation could be an effective strategy for the development of NER rather than accomplishing the same through the framework of national growth. Apart from economic advantages, a sub-regional cooperation could make the neighboring countries partners in the developing the region of northeast. This might facilitate the resolution of conflicting territorial disputes in some parts of NER by the different players across the borders and restore tranquility between the disturbed states.

Conclusion

Sub-regional cooperation is a mechanism through which NER's potential can be harnessed to promote growth. Whether it is a trade and transport, or a project based route, or a synchronic mix of each route, what is more crucial is to utilize the competitive advantage of each neighboring state to promote growth. For example, China could provide the manufacturing inputs, Bangladesh could provide the corridor, and Myanmar and northeast India could provide natural resources. The mobilization of these cross-border synergies is destined to make an economically vibrant zone that could transform the landlocked NER into land-linked areas through the development of cross-border connectivity. The sooner this regional cooperation comes into being, the better it would be for economic wellbeing of all neighboring partners.

END NOTES

1. https://energypedia.info/wiki/Cambodia_Energy_Situation.

2

Sub-Regional Cooperation: Changing Contours of India-ASEAN Experience

Konthoujam Sarda

Introduction

In international relations it is widely accepted that regionalism embodies regional consciousness, promoting a regional identity and an urge for a regional political and economic order in a particular geographical area. The concept of regionalism is complex because of its essentially contested and flexible nature. Regional cooperation has assumed greater significance and has motivated states to cooperate with each other to resolve common problems or achieve certain objectives beyond the capacity of individual national attainment (Weigall, 2002). Joseph Nye defines regionalism as 'the formation of interstate groupings on the basis of regions' and defines international region as 'a limited number of states linked together by a geographical relationship and by a degree of mutual interdependence'. Regionalism is defined as a form of inter-governmental political collaboration whose principal objective is to foster economic cooperation among participating states (Ravenhill, 1995). Jagdish Bhagwati distinguishes two waves of regionalism since World War II, the first began in the late 1950s and lasted until the 1970s; the second began in the mid-1980s (Bhagwati, 1993). Significantly while old regionalism was characterised by selectivity in its tariff liberalisation process, the new regionalism is more universal (Devlin and Estevadeordal, 2001).

According to Björn Hettne, "The new regionalism is a multidimensional form of integration which includes economic, political, social, and cultural aspects and thus goes far beyond the goal of creating region-based free trade regimes or security alliances" (Hettne, 1999). The liberal school of thought argues that cooperation at the regional and international level is possible with institutional structures and regimes whereas the realist school rejects the idea. The neo-liberal theory focuses on absolute rather than relative gains through institutional structures and regimes unlike neo-realism which espouses that even though countries cooperate, it is bound to disintegrate as there is no central authority to enforce decisions of cooperation (Brook, 2006). The neo-liberal approach to new-regionalism says that it not only benefits the member countries economically but also politically. Economically, when member countries sign formal trade agreements and politically, when member countries come together for regional sovereignty and collective security. "The notion of collective security comes from the liberal argument that by attacking a trading partner you are actually hurting yourself. As regionalism is intended to increase trade links between nations within the bloc, it can be seen as fostering liberal collective security" (Brook, 2006). The neo-liberal framework of new regionalism can be used in understanding India-ASEAN relations in the contemporary context.

From the economic perspective, ASEAN-India Free Trade Agreement (FTA) in goods came into force on 1st January 2010 and ASEAN-India FTA in Services and Investment came into force in 2015. ASEAN is projected to be the fourth-largest market after the EU, US and China by 2030, supported by an increasingly well-educated human resource, natural resources and strategic location. ASEAN is India's fourth largest trading partner. From the political perspective, India's engagement with ASEAN have evolved to even more significant with the changing regional economic and security architecture constructed with US-China competition for regional supremacy. This can be seen in the India's enhanced maritime pursuits, connectivity and trade, traditional and non-traditional security cooperation. This has played an important role in India's rebranding its Look East into Act East. In the domestic front the Act East policy is also pronounced in projecting the northeast of India to be the gateway to South-East Asia through connectivity and infrastructural development.

India's Act East in Context

The three C's of Culture, Connectivity and Commerce has been the foundation of India-ASEAN relations. India-ASEAN relations have evolved, progressed and metamorphosed from Look East to Act East with the Prime Minister's announcement in the East Asia Summit held at the Myanmar's capital Nay Pyi Taw in November 2014. 2017 will mark the completion of 25 years of India's dialogue partnership with ASEAN, 15 years of summit level partnership and 5 years of India-ASEAN strategic partnership. This defines a dynamic trajectory for India-ASEAN relations.

Bilateral trade between India and ASEAN grew from $3 billion in the early '90s to $12 billion in 2003 US$21 billion in 2005-06 to US$65 billion in 2015-16. Prime Minister Narendra Modi has stressed the importance of India's north eastern states to be the gateway to the South-East Asian countries. At the India-ASEAN Summit in Kuala Lumpur in November 2015, Prime Minister Narendra Modi announced a Line of Credit of US $1 billion to promote projects that support physical and cultural connectivity between India and ASEAN which signaled the primacy of 'connectivity, culture and commerce'.

During the 20th ASEAN-India Summit held in New Delhi on 21st and 22nd December 2012, India and ASEAN formally upgraded their relationship into a strategic partnership. It committed both the sides to fostering greater security cooperation to further address traditional and non-traditional security challenges including transnational crimes and international terrorism. The Act East Policy signals India's renewed focus to its South-East Asian neighbours in the context of maritime and strategic cooperation, economic, connectivity, etc. It is also been projected that trade between India's northeast and southeast Asia through Cambodia, Laos, Myanmar and Vietnam (CLMV) has tremendous potential. India's total trade with CLMV countries has grown tenfold over the past decade, from $1.1 billion in 2004 to $11.9 billion in 2014.

"Act East" has geo-historical, economic-commercial-trade and cultural engagements bolstered by very strong overseas Indian presence from northeast and south peninsular India of the Coromandal coast (Lawrence, 2017). India's role in the region is expanding in terms of how its presence and partnerships could shape the Asian security architecture that has important strategic implications. Another important perspective is C Raja Mohan's *Samudra Manthan: Sino-Indian Rivalry in the Indo-Pacific* which offers interesting insights into the amalgamation of the Indian Ocean and the Pacific Ocean into a new region, the Indo-Pacific which predicts that Sino-Indian rivalries will eventually spillover from land to the maritime domain as both India and China are rigorously pursuing to modernise their navy by 2020 and 2022 respectively (Mohan, 2012). Amitav Acharya in his book, *Constructing a Security Community in Southeast Asia: ASEAN and the Problem of Regional Order,* analyses the different challenges that ASEAN as a regional organization namely the Cambodian invasion of Vietnam in 1978, the Asian Financial Crisis, and expansion of ASEAN as important milestones in testing the durability of ASEAN's regionalism (Acharya, 2000). S D Muni and Vivek Chadha in *Asian Strategic Review 2015: India as a Security Provider* assesses India's capabilities and limitations as a security provider in Asia in the context of India's immediate neighbourhood, Indo-Pacific and West Asia and underscores India's stake in the evolving strategic contours (Muni and Chadha 2014). Unlike regional development in the past, the India-ASEAN sub-regionalism is characterised by 1) centrality of ASEAN way and institutional arrangements challenged by an aggressive China and US in the regional institutional experiment; 2) US and China's competition for regional supremacy in the sub-region.

What is at Stake?

An important milestone in ASEAN's history is the establishment of the ASEAN Community which was formalised on 31st December 2015. The three pillars of the ASEAN Community are: (a) ASEAN Security Community (b) ASEAN Economic Community and (c) ASEAN Socio-Cultural Community. The ASEAN Economic Community is projected to be the seventh largest in the world with a combined GDP of over US $ 2 trillion. Economically, ASEAN is projected to be the fourth-largest market after the EU, US and China by 2030, supported by an increasingly well-educated human resource natural resources and strategic location (ASEAN's Bright Future: Growth Opportunities for Corporates in the ASEAN Region, 2017).

Strategically, ASEAN's major contribution in Asian regionalism has been the socialisation of China and its involvement in Asian regional institutions which further led to China's wider international cooperation (Acharya, 2010). China's approach to the South China Sea territorial dispute which might have been more uncertain and less cooperative if not for the socialisation process. The various ASEAN based free trade agreements with China, Japan, South Korea, Australia, New Zealand and India, and also the ASEAN plus arrangements points to ASEAN centered Asian economic integration. However, centrality of ASEAN arrangements and the "ASEAN Way" is questioned in the case of South China Sea dispute as China has objected to ASEAN's proposal of resolving the conflict multilaterally through dialogue and consultation.

The Asian Financial crisis exposed the loopholes in regional mechanisms of its inefficacy in regenerating resources and failure to serve the region's interest which led to the idea that an exclusive Asian regional grouping should be formed. It is said that India and China's lack of capacity and the US's lack of legitimacy resulted in the failure of early regionalisation in Asia which led to ASEAN led regionalisation process in Asia (Acharya, 2012). However, after the Asian Financial crisis, China has systematically developed a new sphere of influence through mechanisms such as the Shanghai Cooperation Organization (SCO), ASEAN Plus Three, the ASEAN Plus China Summit, the ASEAN and China Free Trade Area, the East Asian Summit, and the Boao. Economic Forum points out that China strives to become the leading player in the process of Asian regionalism.

The Indian Ocean region and South China Sea, has become economically, strategically and politically important for all the powers. The Chinese media has referred to it as the second 'Persian Gulf' because of its oil resources. It is one of the world's busiest international sea lanes as over half of the world's merchant fleet sail through it. India is seen to be focused on greater maritime involvement with other regional maritime powers such as Japan, Australia, and Vietnam along with improving India's naval prowess in the strategically located Andaman. India's participation in the inaugural meeting of the ASEAN Defence Ministers Meeting Plus (ADMM-Plus) in 2010 was in explicit recognition by Southeast Asian states of the rising importance of India as an indispensable and durable player in the new regional security architecture.

The Question of ASEAN's Unity

The US–China competition for regional supremacy is increasingly referred to as the 'New Great Game' with an 'East Asia twist' and is said to have further implications for global and regional politics (Yang, 2012). This constructs a complex scenario for India and ASEAN. This could be seen in the Annual Regional Ministerial meeting at Phnom Pehn in July 2012 where ASEAN could not come up with a joint declaration over the issue of South China Sea. India urged both countries to exercise restraint and resolve the issue diplomatically according to principles of international law (PTI, 2014). It is pertinent to note that in the ASEAN Regional Forum, 2014, in Myanmar US's call for a freeze in South China Sea issue was met with a cool response (Paul and Lesley, 2014). The Philippines, Thailand and Vietnam have welcomed the US repositioning in Asia; countries such as Indonesia and Malaysia have given measured response. It is well known at Southeast Asian countries which are in direct territorial conflict with China having been doubtful of China's regional aspirations. Though it has been in ASEAN's interest to position itself at the centre of Asian integration through East Asia Summit, ASEAN Regional Forum, ASEAN Defense Ministers Meeting Plus, and ASEAN has not faced a dilemma before of this intensity in accommodating big powers. In this context it can be said that China's economic diplomacy is paying dividends. For example, when the tribunal of the International Court of Justice delivered their verdict on July 12, 2016 constituted under Article VII of the UNCLOS in favour of the Phillipines against China in the South China Sea dispute, the newly elected President Rodrigo Duterte had declared that he is willing to enter into negotiations with China for joint development of South China Sea. This marks a distinct departure from the policies of the previous government, which had been extremely critical of China's assertive claims in the South China Sea.

ASEAN in India's Strategy

It is interesting to note that China's GDP is nearly 9 times that of all of ASEAN. India's GDP is around the same as that of ASEAN but it has twice the population of ASEAN. China is ASEAN's largest trading partner. This explains why India has placed its primacy in ASEAN in its Act East Policy. The ASEAN Economic Community (AEC) as a single market and production base has combined Gross Domestic Product (GDP) values of $2.4 trillion as against India's GDP of around $2 trillion and China's around $9.96 trillion. India also has the opportunity to become a part of ASEAN production network and it is necessary for India to have a well-functioning infrastructure to aid economic development to be in tune with Prime Minister Modi's 'Make in India Policy' of making India a manufacturing hub. In 2016-17, the World Economic Forum in its Global Competitiveness Index Report places India in the 68th position (out of a total sample of 138 countries) when competitiveness is measured in terms of infrastructure development (World Economic Forum Report, 2013). The report also cited lack of infrastructure as the key bottleneck for global business. The Modi government has advocated a 'Look East, Link West Policy' pointing to a broader Indo-Pacific conceptualization of India's region. Border trade between India (through the north eastern states) and CLMV countries (through Myanmar) is said to have a trade potential of US$10 TO US$ 22 million (Export-Import Bank of India Report, 2013). For India, ASEAN is at the core of its Act East Policy mainly because economic and strategic reasons. India and ASEAN are thriving trade partners as bilateral trade between India and ASEAN grew from $3 billion in the early '90s to $12 billion in 2003 US$21 billion in 2005-06 to US$65 billion in 2015-16. ASEAN is India's fourth largest trading partner. Strategically as more than $5.3 trillion of global trade passes through South-East Asian waterways each year the proposed Chinese Maritime Silk Route from the southern China's ports to South China Sea, the Straits of Malacca, to Indian Ocean to the Persian Gulf, Red Sea and Gulf of Aden encompasses Asia, the Middle East, East Africa and Europe. It also implies shrinking India's strategic space.

It is often argued that India does not have a coherent strategic approach (Bajpai et al., 2014), however the present developments give India with an opportunity of diplomatic leverage to engage with China, ASEAN and the US and chart a grand strategy combining the tools of geo-politics and geo-economics in its foreign policy. This is a unique opportunity for India to prove itself as a serious regional player to shape regional economic and security architecture. For starters, India must be willing to effectively engage, participate, and contribute in the regional developments such as the negotiation of Regional Comprehensive Economic Development, Bangladesh-China-India-Myanmar Economic Corridor and China's One Belt One Road Policy. India cannot afford to ambiguous as these developments is bound to have strategic implications in the future.

SCOPE FOR COOPERATION

3

Synchronizing Internal Economic Development Initiatives and External Opportunities in India's North Eastern Region

Niranjan Roy

Introduction

The colonial rulers in India did not pursue any plan or strategy for a balanced development of the country. It resulted in regional imbalances, and group identities. Unfortunately, despite planned development, the independent India witnessed the rise of regionalism, linguism, separatism, etc. Both intra and inter regional disparities or imbalances refer to wide differences in per capita income, literacy rates, availability of health and education, industrialisation, etc. There are enormous imbalances among the regions on various accounts in India. In fact regional imbalances and disparities are a major cause of regionalism in India in recent times. The situation has more aggravated during the period of globalisation.

An overwhelming evidence seems to suggest that many of competing firms adopt similar technologies, that life styles are homogenous all over the industrialised world, whereas the globalisation and sophistication of financial markets do tend to synchronise national economies It may converges in three distinct forms, viz., economic, social and precise institutional settings.

Globalisation of finance, labour, technologies and products would be so developed that each nation would now resemble to a small or medium size firm in an ocean of pure and perfect competition. Secondly, convergence is to be traced back to the collapse of authoritarian regimes, and their replacement by more democratic constitutions. Thirdly, the interactions of political and economic interests can take a multiplicity of configurations according to the precise balance between market and democracy and the mix between public regulations, associations, private and public hierarchies, and finally markets (Boyer, 1993). In fact globalization has diverse effects across nations and within nations. Within nations it may lead to both economic and social divergence leading to instability and create regional disparities which result in acute suffering to a particular region. This argument is presented in Figure 3.1.

Figure 3.1: Impact of globalisation

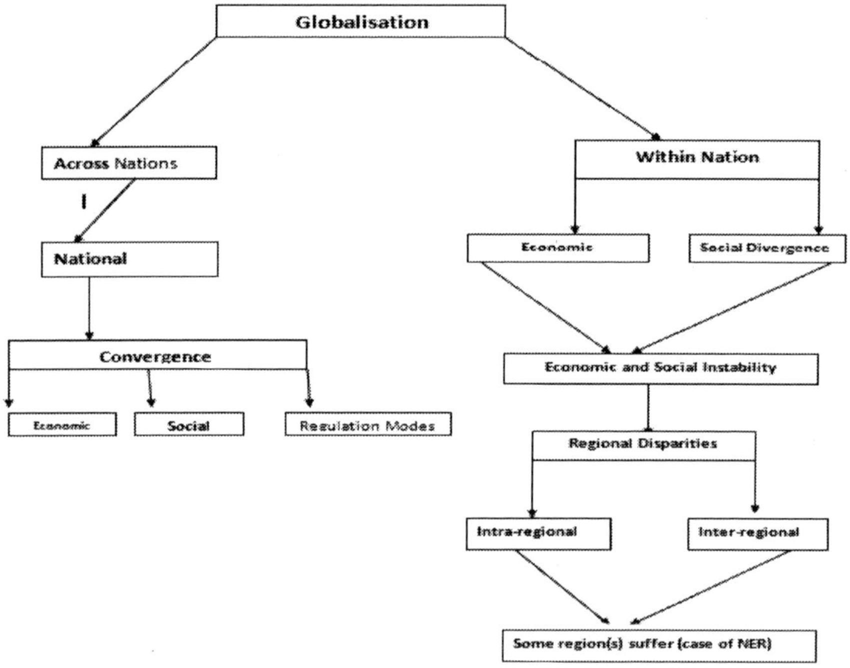

Source: Author's conceptualization

The present study is confined to the north eastern region (NER) of

India consisting of eight states viz. Assam, Arunachal Pradesh, Meghalaya, Mizoram, Nagaland, Manipur, Sikkim and Tripura. The region is covered with 98% of border with neighbouring countries with small corridor (Chickens neck) connecting mainland India. The total population of the region as per 2011 census was 45.8 million and predominantly rural with more than 80 percent of population live in the villages. The basic objective of the study is to analyse the status of economic growth, sectoral composition and comparative performance of north eastern region with other regions of India in the context of globalization and external opportunities. The research question taken for the present study is: Whether the north eastern region of India able to gain from external sector linkages through harnessing internal economic strength during the period of liberalization.

Region and the Issues of Regional Development

In regional studies broadly three approaches are found to the definition of a region, viz, homogeneous regions, nodal region and planning and programming regions. Economists, by and large have emphasized the homogeneity aspect in defining a region. Yet different economists seem to base their interpretation of homogeneity on different factor. North (1955) considered the existence of an export base as the unifying cohesive force of a region. Isard (1955) takes into account output and production processes in determining this. A nodal region is a spatial organization consisting of a node with its hinterland areas functionally tied to it. Though many consider these to be real or natural regions, however, the boundaries of a nodal region are difficult to define. In the Indian context, (Chatterjee, 1965) divided the entire country into physiographically homogeneous regions without regard to administrative boundaries. Similarly states can be looked upon as regions for many a purpose (Bhattacharya, 1973). The question of economic progress of a region may be dealt with in the context of realisation of its economic potentialities like physiographic, economic, socio-cultural, political and neighbourhood. However, all these factors do not work in isolation. Interwoven in a systematic structure, they prepare the ground for a region to take off. On the other, the problem of regional development may refer to the rate of economic progress of a particular region compared to the same in other regions (Roy and Bezbaruah, 2002). The argument is depicted in Figure 3.2.

Figure 3.2: Region and its potentialities

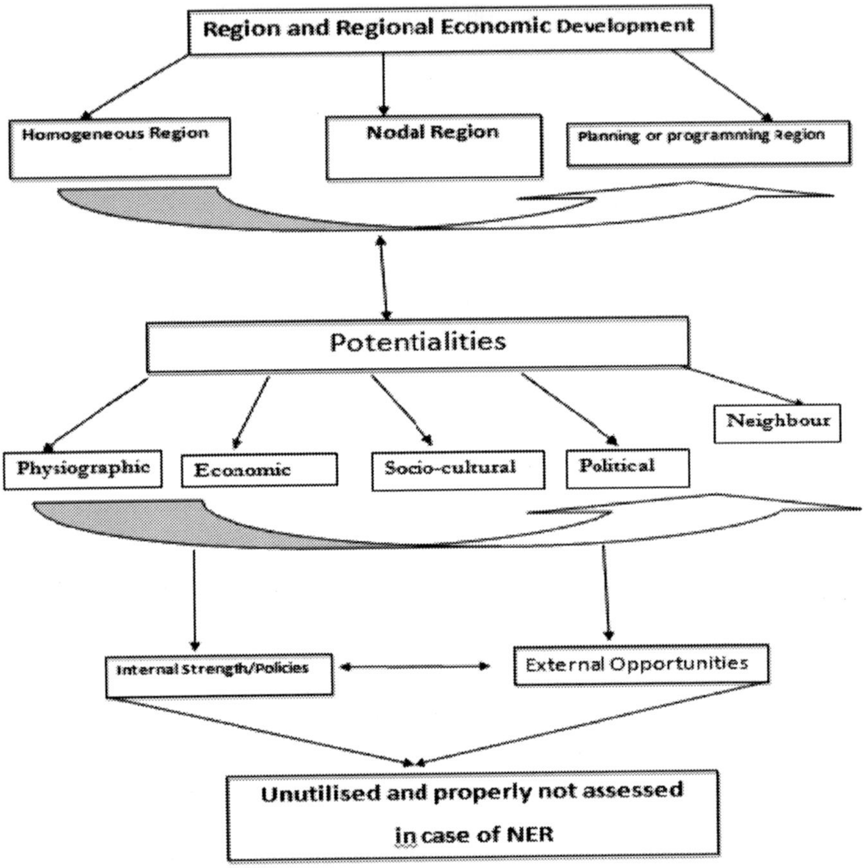

Source: Author's conceptualization

In the present study the entire country is divided in to six regions combining the states, namely, (i) northern region (ii) southern region (iii) central region (iv) eastern region (v) north eastern region and (vi) western region in line with the approach adopted by National Health and Family Welfare Survey of the Government of India.

Database and Methodology

The data for the present study for NSDP for the period 1980-81 to 2014-15 has been collected from Handbook of Statistics on Indian Economy published by RBI. The data were provided for different series, viz., at constant prices 1980-81, 1993-94, 1999-2000 and 2004-05. In order to obtain a consistent set of data on SDP the usual procedure of linking the indices by changing the base of constant prices is followed. In order to study variation in growth experience of the state economies by sectors, SDP data has been classified in to three parts viz., agricultural sector SDP, industrial sector SDP and service sector SDP. The agricultural sector consists of agriculture and allied activities, fishery, and forestry. The industrial sector includes mining and quarrying, manufacturing, construction, and electricity, gas and water supply. The service sector comprises the rest of the sub-sectors. The data for area, production and yield of different crops have been collected from the Directorate of Economics and Statistics, Government of India.

The growth rate of a variable in period t over period t-1 has been estimated using the following method:

$$g_{t-1,t} = \left\{ \frac{Y_t - Y_{t-1}}{Y_{t-1}} \right\} \times 100 = \left\{ \left(\frac{Y_t}{Y_{t-1}} \right) - 1 \right\} \times 100 . \qquad (4.1.1)$$

Here is percentage growth/change in variable Y from period t-1 to t. The one period growth rate has been used to measure annualized growth of a variable.

Growth of NSDP and Its Sectoral Composition in NER

It is seen from Table 3.1 that during the post reform period the growth rate of north eastern region is lower than pre-reform period. Interestingly average growth rate of north eastern region during pre-reform period was comparatively higher than other regions in India. But during the post reform period except Central and Eastern region the growth rate was lower than all other regions. Significantly there is wide diversity among different states in the region in growth rate both in pre and post reform period. The performance of the states like Arunachal Pradesh, Assam, Nagaland and Sikkim was better during pre-reform period as compared to post-reform period. On the other hand the state of Tripura has performed well during post reform period followed by Meghalaya and Manipur. In fact performance of Tripura is higher than almost all regions except Western region.

The disaggregated growth rate of NSDP on primary, secondary and tertiary sector separately across different regions in India is shown in Table 3.2 and Fig 3.3(a), 3.3(b) and 3.3(c). It is observed that the north eastern region could prevent downfall in agricultural sector during post-reform reform like that eastern region. Interestingly except north

Table 3.1: Growth rate of NSDP (at constant 2004-05 prices) (in percentage)

States/Region	*Pre-Reform (1981-1991)*	*Post-Reform (1992-2014)*	*Deviation*
Northern Region	5.98	6.62	0.64
Southern Region	5.18	6.88	1.70
Central Region	4.96	4.35	-0.61
Eastern Region	4.09	5.97	1.87
Western Region	6.17	8.26	2.09
Arunachal Pradesh	9.09	6.49	-2.60
Assam	4.14	3.94	-0.20
Manipur	4.74	5.10	0.36
Meghalaya	5.49	6.68	1.19
Nagaland	8.61	6.71	-1.90
Sikkim	10.81	7.97	-2.83
Tripura	5.52	8.20	2.67
NER	**6.91**	**6.44**	**-0.47**

Source: Compiled from Handbook of Statistics, RBI.* Mizoram is not included as data prior to 2000 is not available.

eastern region all other regions in India gained higher growth rate in service sector during post reform period. Like north eastern region many other regions in India experienced lower growth rate of industrial sector during post reform period.

Table 3.2: Growth rate of agricultural, industrial and service sector NSDP (at constant 2004-05 Prices)

States/Region	*Pre-Reform (1981-1991)*			*Post-Reform (1992-2014)*			*Deviation*		
	P	*S*	*T*	*P*	*S*	*T*	*P*	*S*	*T*
Northern Region	5.47	10.81	6.07	2.63	8.26	7.96	-2.83	-2.54	1.88
Southern Region	3.90	7.10	6.24	2.69	5.55	8.75	-1.21	-1.55	2.51
Central Region	4.15	9.18	5.58	3.21	6.05	6.79	-0.95	-3.13	1.21
Eastern Region	3.02	5.57	5.56	3.05	5.60	7.80	0.03	0.03	2.24
Western Region	6.50	8.28	6.99	5.95	9.02	9.19	-0.56	0.74	2.20
Northeast Region	4.72	9.34	7.47	4.74	8.39	7.78	0.02	-0.95	0.31

Note: 1. Figures for UP, MP and Bihar have been calculated after adding corresponding figures for Uttaranchal, Chhattisgarh and Jharkhand respectively. 2. We have not included Mizoram because figure for this state is not available at source prior to 2000. P—Primary sector, S—Secondary sector, T—Tertiary sector.

Source: Compiled from Handbook of Statistics, RBI.

Figure 3.3 (a): Growth rate of Agricultural NSDP during Pre and Post-reform period (2004-05 prices)

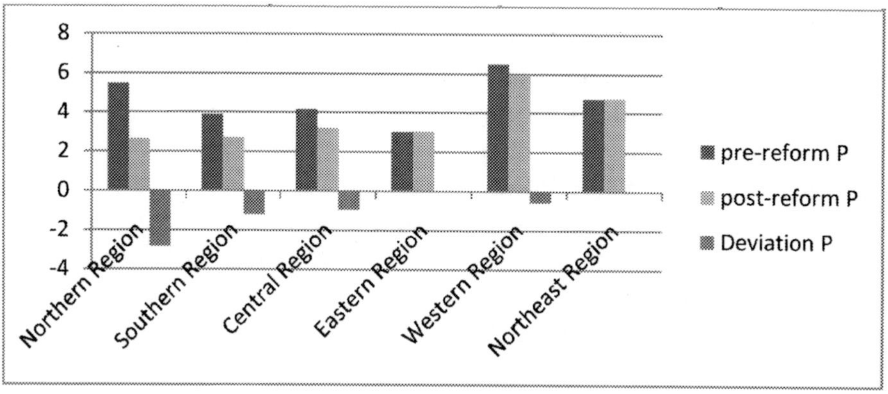

Figure 3.3 (b): Growth rate of industrial NSDP during pre and post-reform period (at 2004-05 prices)

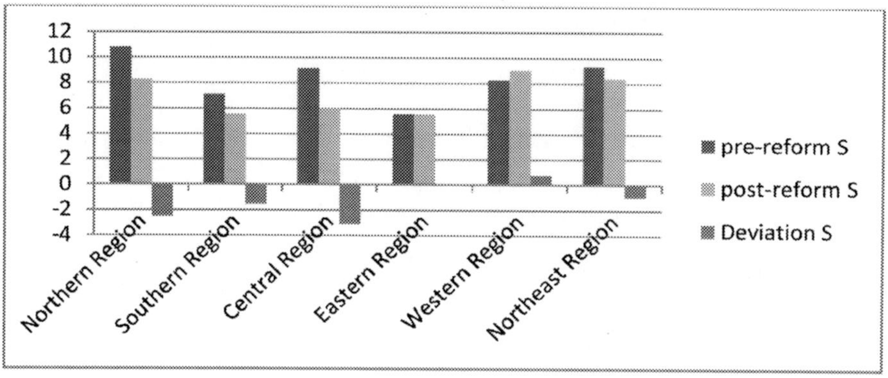

Figure 3.3(c): Growth of service sector NSDP during pre and post-reform period (at 2004-05 prices)

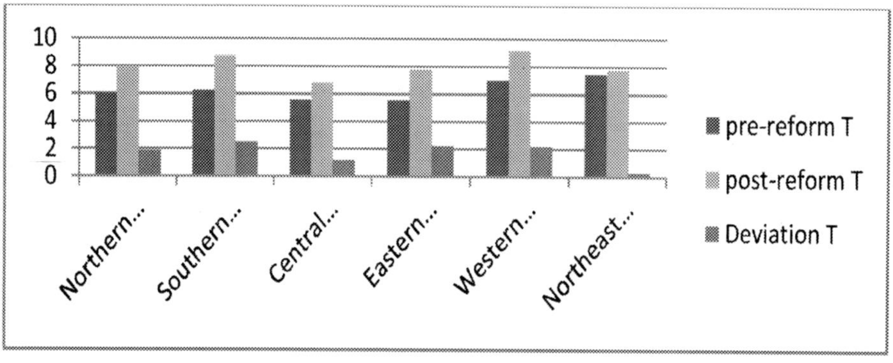

Inflow of FDI in Different States in India

Foreign Direct Investment (FDI) inflow has become a panacea for economic development in the post liberalization period. There are many studies carried out on the effects of FDI inflow in economic growth of a nation. Many of them observed positive impact of FDI on host economy towards enhancing economic growth including Indian context (refer (Barrel & Pain, 1996; Sharma, 2000; Johnson, 2005; Agrawal, 2005). The collapse of Soviet Union and the pressure on India's domestic economic liberalization force to rethink its relations with East and Southeast Asian nations in the form of new Look East Policy in 1990s of Government of India. The essential philosophy of India behind the Look East Policy is to forge closer and deeper economic integration with the eastern neighbors' i.e. with ASEAN countries. Consequently India became a sectoral dialog partner in March 1993, a full dialogue partnership in 1995, a member of the ASEAN Regional Forum in July 1996 and finally to a Summit level partnership in 2002. For the development of sub-regional cooperation, in the year 1997, a sub-regional economic grouping called BIST-EC (Bangladesh-India-Sri-Lanka-Thailand Economic Cooperation), comprising Bangladesh, India, Sri Lanka and Thailand was established with a view to strengthen and reinforce India's Look East policy (Sarmah, 2015).

The Cumulative FDI inflows as depicted in Table 3.3 for the period April, 2000 to December, 2016 shows skewed distribution across different states in India. The picture for north eastern region appears to be very gloomy with share of only 0.03% of total inflows in India during the period as mentioned.

Another important aspect of FDI inflow in host country is its sectoral distribution. It is found that service sector attracted highest FDI in India accounting to 18% of total inflows followed by Construction, Telecommunications, computer software hardware etc. during April, 2000 to December, 2016 (refer Table 3.4).

The meager FDI inflow in north eastern states during 2000 to 2016 indicates weak external sector and the region failed to attract foreign investment even during second decade of adoption of liberalization in India.

Table 3.3: Cumulative FDI Inflows in different states in India (April, 2000 to December, 2016) (in million US$)

Sl. No.	*RBI's— Regional Office*	*State covered*	*Cumulative FDI inflows*	*Percentage to total inflows*
1	Mumbai	Maharashtra, Dadra & Nagar Haveli, Daman & Diu	100,165	31
2	New Delhi	Delhi, Part of UP and Haryana	66,994	21
3	Chennai	Tamil Nadu, Pondicherry	22,647	7
4	Bangalore	Karnataka	21,938	7
5	Ahmedabad	Gujarat	16,003	5
6	Hyderabad	Andhra Pradesh	13,209	4
7	Kolkata	West Bengal, Sikkim, Andaman & Nicobar Islands	3,983	1
8	Guwahati	Assam, Arunachal Pradesh, Manipur, Meghalaya, Mizoram, Nagaland, Tripura	95	0.03

Source: RBI as available in http://dipp.nic.in/English/Publications/FDI_Statistics/2016/FDI_FactSheet_OctoberNovemberDecember2016.pdf

Table 3.4: Sectors attracting highest FDI inflows in India (April, 2000 to December, 2016) (in million US$)

Ranks	*Sector*	*Cumulative inflows*	*Percentage to total inflows*
1.	Services Sector*	58,345	18 %
2.	Construction Development: Townships, Housing, Built-up Infrastructure	24,287	8 %
3.	Telecommunications	23,921	7 %
4.	Computer Software & Hardware	22,832	7 %
5.	Automobile Industry	16,518	5 %
6.	Drugs & Pharmaceuticals	14,537	4 %
7.	Trading	13,873	4 %
8.	Chemicals (Other than Fertilizers)	12,683	4 %
9.	Power	11,437	4 %
10	Metallurgical Industries	10,149	3 %

*Services sector includes Financial, Banking, Insurance, Non-Financial / Business, Outsourcing, R&D, Courier, Tech. Testing and Analysis.

Source: RBI as available in http://dipp.nic.in/English/Publications/FDI_Statistics/2016/FDI_FactSheet_OctoberNovemberDecember2016.pdf

Sectoral Composition in North Eastern Region

From the data available on sectoral composition of NSDP in the different states of north eastern region it is found that agricultural sector contributes 21.3%, industrial sector 11.2% and service sector 67.6%

during 2014. There are wide variations among different states in the region in respect of sectoral contribution to NSDP. For instance in the state of Arunachal Pradesh agricultural sector contributed 32.7%, industrial sector 6.2% and service sector 61.2%. The contribution of agricultural sector amounted to 21.3% in NSDP for the region is much higher than 13.2% for the country as a whole during the same period. As per 2011 census 55.4% of total working population is directly dependent on agriculture in the region.

Table 3.5: Sectoral distribution of NSDP in north eastern region (at 2004-05 prices) (in percentage)

State	*1981*			*1991*			*2001*			*2014*		
	P	*S*	*T*	*P*	*S*	*T*	*P*	*S*	*T*	*P*	*S*	*T*
Arunachal Pradesh	64.4	2.4	33.2	62.2	3.0	34.3	51.6	4.50	43.9	32.7	6.2	61.2
Assam	46.2	13.6	40.2	37.8	19.9	42.3	31.9	16.2	51.9	22.2	9.5	68.3
Mizoram	NA	NA	NA	NA	NA	NA	28.5	4.6	66.9	18.9	3.8	77.3
Manipur	42.9	9.4	47.8	30.7	16.3	53.0	26.8	9.6	63.7	20.3	9.1	70.7
Meghalaya	45.0	5.7	49.3	31.9	11.5	56.5	25.7	11.7	62.7	16.5	10.9	72.6
Nagaland	29.3	6.6	64.1	19.2	37.7	43.1	32.7	2.7	64.6	26.5	2.7	70.8
Sikkim	26.0	38.7	35.3	24.5	32.2	43.3	16.5	24.0	59.5	10.4	42.4	47.3
Tripura	52.9	17.7	29.5	46.4	8.5	45.2	26.4	10.3	63.3	22.7	4.9	72.4
NER	43.8	13.4	42.8	36.2	18.5	45.4	30.0	10.4	59.6	21.3	11.2	67.6

P—Primary sector, S—Secondary sector, T—Tertiary sector.

Source: Compiled from Handbook of Statistics, RBI. Data for Mizoram not available prior to 2001.

During the post green revolution period in India negative growth of food grains area was compensated by higher growth of area under non-foodgrains and yield growth. No such trend is visible in the north eastern region as evident from the agricultural SDP growth and its sectoral composition.The region failed to participate in the green revolution technology package programme for enhancing higher productivity of both food and non-food crops initiated in India in mid 1960s. While the green revolution technology has led to significant change in per-capita availability of foodgrains assuring food security in the rest of the country, there has not been any substantial change in the north eastern region. Similarly per hectare consumption of fertliser (N+P+K) in NER was 45.2 kg in 2009-10 and 51.7 kg in 2012-13 as against 133.2 and 128.3 for the country as whole, which itself is lower than in China, Japan and other ASEAN countries. In the tribal dominated states in the region, viz, Arunachal Pradesh, Meghalaya, Mizoram and Nagaland, where there are higher concentrations of shifting cultivation, per hectare fertiliser consumption is even lower, at between 1-2 kg per hectare.

Conclusions

The study examined the issue of regional growth dynamics in the context of north eastern region economies in India both in the pre and post-reform period. The region could not be benefitted from global investment climate in terms FDI led industrial and service sector growth in the post liberalization period. Despite having both internal potentialities and in built external opportunities due to significant geographical locations, the region could not utilize its strength in transforming the traditional economy. While the majority of the agricultural sector confined to traditional practices, there is hardly any effort for transforming the agricultural sector by utilising green revolution technology. However, the service sector growth in NSDP has not been encouraging during the post reform period. The meager share of FDI in the region speaks about under utilizations of immense external opportunities. There is a wide opportunity for cross border trade in goods and services. This calls for creating enabling environment to attract FDI in the region.

Going by the sectoral composition of growth it can be argued that the region could not utilise its potentialities in increasing agricultural productivity and service sector growth through sustaining manufacturing sector as experienced in other parts of the country during the post liberalisation period. This raises concern about significance and implications of post liberalisation development agenda in a backward area like north eastern region. Thus co-ordinate efforts required for harmonizing internal economic strength mainly in agriculture and service sector and external opportunities in terms of cross border trade paradigm for the region.

4

'Development Regime' in India's Northeast: The 'Look (Act) East Policy' Perspective

Akshay Jyoti Sarma

Introduction

The stake of northeast India in the 'Look East' turned 'Act East' Policy has been still in great confusion and with lot of ambiguities. The role of the north eastern region (NER) has neither been specified nor been directed towards any goal or objective. However, a massive advancement of development projects can be observed in recent decade, which this paper argues – 'development regime' in the northeast. The developmental initiatives in the region are merely concentrating on the building physical infrastructure – mainly the communication infrastructure which aims at easing transnational connectivity between India and South East Asia. These initiatives have been pursued without taking cognizance of certain basic infrastructure gap within the region. However, a transnational connectivity will hardly succeed to improve the growth rate of this peripheral region of northeast. The paper tries to argue that the Look (Act) East Policy framework lacks a proper roadmap for development of the region. The paper tries to analyse some of the basic questions – what role to be played by the region in India's Look (Act) East Policy and whether the region identifies itself with the broader objectives of the Policy.

There is a need to critically examine the existing 'development regime' – whether 'development' of the region will remain political rhetoric.

In the post-Cold War international system, transnational market interests govern the priorities of individual countries where no countries could remain independent especially on economic matters. The economic and trade policies individual countries are now directed by the International Financial Institutions (IFI) such as IMF, World Bank and WTO. Under such a backdrop, countries have aggressively initiated the process for regional cooperation and economic integration to cope with the newer challenges of economic globalisation. Mutual trade cooperation became the primary objectives of the countries and formation of regional trade blocks and organisations has become prominent. The dismantling of the Soviet Union and penetration of neo-liberal economy in a globalised set-up, global political economy took new directions, one leading to mutual interdependence at the global level in the tune of economic globalization and another as the regional cooperation – countries relied on simultaneous bi-lateral and regional block consolidation on economic grounds. Indian policymakers have responded to the emerging global economic challenges since the mid-1990s by proclaiming a 'Look East' policy, targeting greater interaction with what China considers its immediate neighbourhood: the ASEAN (Association of South East Asian Nations) countries (Alamgir, 2009; Shahin, 2003).

India's Look East Policy was evolved following the country's economic reforms in the beginning of 1990s. It has been observed that the Policy is spurred by economic motivations and by the conviction of a large section of Indian elites for strengthening ties with the countries of the 'Asian Miracle' – countries of East and Southeast East Asia (Chakraborty and Ray, 2014). This development was itself a paradigm shift in the foreign economic policies of the country. The initiative was to have closer ties with the South East Asian neighbours. It has been a matter of fact that, India could not ascertain an amiable relation with the countries of East and Southeast Asia despite having cultural and historical proximities. This was because of the existing global political scenario and the Cold War polarisations (Naidu, 2008; Haokip, 2015). Traditionally, India's engagement in regards to international trade and commerce was Europe and West centric. Soviet Union and the Eastern European states were at centre of India's foreign trade (Racioppi, 1994; Ganguly, 2015). The 'Look East' Policy has altered India's approach to the international trade and cooperation and the East and South East Asia received prominence in India's economic objectives.

In a changing global order, India clearly needed to adapt to some changes in its economic and foreign policy orientations. Further, the changes in the global order and rising China in the East Asia also contributed towards India's 'strategic shift' – Look East Policy (Ranganathan, 2011; Gupta, 2007). Former Prime Minister Manmohan Singh once stated that Look East Policy 'was not merely an external economic policy, it was also a strategic shift in India's vision of the world and India's place in the evolving global economy' (Singh, 2006). The policy was an attempt to diversify India's diplomacy as well as realize its new post-liberalization economic engagement with its 'extended neighbourhood' in Southeast Asia (Singh, 2007). Nevertheless, India has to develop far greater expertise in geo-economics, an area which has not received the requisite attention. In this regard, India has to aggressively thrive for its space in the established regional project such as the East Asia Summit (EAS), ASEAN and BIMSTEC. India's stake in such forums will be important for re-structuring Asia's future role in the global order (Sundaram, 2013).

India's interests in the South East Asia became a natural choice and more significant as the initiatives for regional cooperation in the South Asia – the SAARC (South Asian Association for Regional Cooperation) could not yield much in terms of economic cooperation. The Southeast Asia on the other hand is an existing economic space with a vibrant regional experience of ASEAN. The ASEAN and the East Asia comprising of China, Japan and Korea are considered as an expanded 'regional market' and regarded as a 'playing field of global finance' (Chakraborty and Ray, 2014). There has been a steady growth in terms of trade between India and ASEAN which accounts almost 10 (ten) percent of India's total international trade. With the growth of economic strength and scope, India became a partner with ASEAN, called as 'summit partner' which took the India-ASEAN relationship into a new height. The free-trade agreement with ASEAN has already been signed and is in the process of implementation.

Look (Act) East Policy and India's Northeast

With Myanmar getting the ASEAN membership in 1997, India got a surface connection to the South East Asia through country's eastern peripheral region – the northeast. Following that, the north eastern region became a point of reference so far connecting India with South East Asia is concerned. Consequently, the region started receiving attention at the national policy circles. Discovering the possibility of a surface connectivity to the South East Asia through India's northeast, there has been a push for development in the region.

The north eastern region of India which is surrounded by the five countries – Bangladesh, Myanmar, China, Bhutan and Nepal with a 5437.15 km long international border[1]. The geo-strategic significance of the region coincides with 'huge' economic potentialities. However, the region remained at the periphery and could not grow in terms of 'development' and economic prosperity. The partition of India transformed this region into a land-locked territory hindering the prospect for international trade which was vibrant during the colonial period. The northeast India became a victim of many post-colonial developments as Sushil Khanna (2002) observed, 'there is no doubt that the disruption of trade and commerce and communication due to the partition of the country, as well as India's import substitution strategy of industrialisation and gradual erection of barriers to international trade, have disrupted economies that till 50 years ago were well integrated, and deprived the region of the gains from trade based on comparative advantage'. The region remained untouched in the national policy discourses on development until the late 1990s. The developmental gap in the region has also manifested in popular resentment against New Delhi in many of the occasions creating distance between the mainland and the northeast. Former Prime Minister once stated in a speech, 'when people in New Delhi think of the northeast, they usually think of the geographic distance, which translates itself into mental distance. When people in northeast think of New Delhi, they usually think of the developmental distance, which translates itself into emotional distance' (Vajpayee, 1998). Nevertheless, the adoption of Look East Policy and the proposed opening of international border towards South East Asia initially infused hope and aspirations among the people of this region that such initiative will be beneficial for the region and the region will get clear dividends from international trade and cooperation which will lead to prosperity and economic development of the region. There are hopes and aspirations among the people of the region that 'economic integration could bring about a spurt of economic activities' and will open up 'new economic opportunities' for the region (Baruah, 2005). However, the Look East Policy remained a political rhetoric and policy hype in the last two decades so far as the prospective benefits to the north eastern region.

However, the mainstream understanding towards the north eastern region has changed in the recent decade. The peripheral region has started becoming a talk-point in the national policy circle when the possibility of continental connectivity through the north eastern region was unveiled. As Subir Bhaumik (2009) observed, "India's Look East Policy sees the northeast not as a periphery anymore, but as the centre of a thriving and integrated economic space linking two dynamic regions (South East Asia and South Asia) with a network of highways, railways, pipelines, transmission lines criss-crossing the region" (Bhaumik 2009:21). One can see the unanimity about the prospect of the northeast states and its vitality in any arrangement in the South and South East Asian Region.

The northeast, being the only Indian region geographically proximate to the South East Asia with international border with five countries, can play a promisingly vital role especially in India's economic aspiration in the South and South East Asia. Northeast can claim a natural stake in many of the regional and sub-regional developments where the geo-strategic advantage of the region can be pivotal. The natural stake of the region can be understood beyond India's engagement with the ASEAN. Other multilateral regional initiatives such as Bay of Bengal Initiative for Multi-Sectoral Technical and Economic Cooperation (BIMSTEC), Bangladesh-China-India-Myanmar (BCIM) Economic Corridor, Mekong-Ganga Cooperation etc have created more space for the northeast to be engaged in transnational economic cooperation and market integration. The question unaddressed here is that the region could not make any breakthrough in terms of its capability to cope with the challenges of such transitional economic activity. The economic viability of the region has been established which can be developed in the line of a transnational market. However, it has been a matter of fact that the possibility of making this region economically vibrant has not been promoted seriously.

'Development Regime' in India's Northeast

The north eastern region received numerous attentions for development which the paper argues – induced by the broad objectives of India's Look East Policy. The trend of developmental push has become visible since the dawn of the new century. The initiatives for development have come mainly in terms of physical infrastructure – roadways and railways, aimed at making transnational connectivity viable. However, question remains unaddressed here as what for this infrastructure and what purpose such 'development' would serve for the region. Moreover, the role of the region under India's Look East Policy has not been defined clearly and therefore, current phase of developmental initiatives could not and will not augment the desired benefits for the region.

The shift in the policy approach towards the development of the northeast in the last two decades can be understood from the growing importance of the region in India's thrust for regional cooperation and economic integration primarily with the South East Asia. However, the policy level endeavour has not yielded much for the region as the implementation of developmental activities has not displayed similar rigour. The 'infrastructure' that has been regarded as the 'stumbling block' in the part of India's northeast, has yet to be adequately addressed. However, the 'Look East' policy has been renamed as the 'Act East' policy giving an action oriented twist in 2014 to rejuvenate India-South East Asia relations and also fasten the process of development in the northeast. Although, there has been massive growth in the developmental initiatives in the region but the internal connectivity in the northeast remained abysmally poor and in some cases it hardly exists. It has been a question that how far the 'Look East' turned 'Act East' Policy has accomplished in its desired objectives so far as India's northeast is concerned as one can see more rhetoric than substance in the policy.

So far the Look East Policy (LEP) is concerned, scholars argued that that there was lack of political vision to make use of or give space to northeast India in the initial decade of LEP (Chakraborty and Ray, 2014; Sundaram, 2013). Ironically, it was only in 2008 that north eastern region appeared in related policy formulation with the launch of 'North Eastern Region Vision Document 2020'. It was emphasised that the focus of the Look East Policy should shift so that South East Asia begins with northeast India and to this end, it is necessary to build the bridges – diplomatic and infrastructural.[2] Since the dawn of the new century, the 'development push' in the northeast is thriving for bridging the infrastructure gap in the region.

The driving force of the Look East Policy was to expand the market economy. The geographic proximity of northeast India with Southeast Asia has amplified its relevance as a prospective economic zone hitherto been in the periphery of the economic activity. Looking at the prospects of the region, government took several policy measures to create conducive business environment and to attract foreign direct investment to the region – incentive packages for investment in different sectors including tax subsidies, land grants and allowing use of local resources (Chakraborty and Ray 2014; Haokip 2013). However, these initiatives over last one and half decades could not achieve the 'conducive business environment' in the region. It is a matter of fact, Chakraborty and Ray (2014) demonstrated that the Look East Policy has changed the perception of northeast India from 'an anthropologist paradise' during colonial era and the 'security perception' in the post-colonial era to the 'gateway for trade and cooperation' with Southeast Asia in the contemporary era of globalisation.

As discussed above, there are numerous developmental initiatives for the region in the last one and half decade. Most of the initiatives are aimed at improving physical infrastructure in the region. As per the Government information[3], the policies and programmes for development of the region are directed towards a comprehensive development of infrastructure, entrepreneurship skills, markets and providing flow of credits to the entrepreneurs. We can discuss the nature of the 'Development Regime' in India's northeast as follows:

Institutional Arrangements for Development

The inception of an exclusive Ministry in 2001 – Ministry of Development of North Eastern Region (MDoNER), which is responsible for the matters relating to the planning, execution and monitoring of development schemes and projects in the north eastern region. The Ministry is working as nodal ministry for development of the region.

The North Eastern Council (NEC), once envisioned as the regional planning board has become a part of the Ministry of DoNER. However,

NEC remained the nodal agency for economic and social development in the region. The role of the Council is crucial in identifying and addressing the critical infrastructural gaps in the region that impair the prospects of economic growth and development. Similarly, some other organisations under the MDoNER such as North Eastern Development Finance Corporation Limited which is instrumental in promoting industrial and infrastructural base in the region. Government of India has also established the National Highways and Infrastructure Development Corporation Limited (NHIDCL) to fast track the road building activities. It has also undertaken up-gradation of neglected, but critical inter-state roads in the region.

Other institutional arrangements for the development of the region are – the North East Industrial and Investment Promotion Policy, 2007 under which industrialisation has been promoted in the region by providing various incentives such as investment subsidy and exemption from different duty and tax. However, this policy is currently under suspension. There are other institutional arrangements for funding development in the region. The provision of earmarking at least 10 percent of Gross Budgetary Support (GBS) by the Central ministries/departments for development of the north eastern states and the provision of a Non-Lapsable Central Pool of Resources (NLCPR), a fund accumulated by the unspent amount of 10 Percent GBS of different ministries and departments. These special provisions for establishing exclusive fund for the region have manifold implications so far the development of the region is concerned. The NLCPR is used for priority projects such as economic infrastructure, provisioning of drinking water and sanitation etc. However, future of these provisions is not known following the abolition of the Planning Commission.

Infrastructure Development Projects[4]

With a renewed seriousness, the Government of India has taken up several projects for improvement in roadways, railways, air connectivity, communication and telecom network in the region.[5] Through numerous infrastructure development projects focusing on the connectivity issues, a 'development regime' has been promoted in the region. The roadway has been the major and in most cases the only connectivity in the region, yet the capacity and condition of road remained abysmally poor. After the renewed emphasis on connectivity – internal and transnational, the road connectivity has become the most important feature of developmental intervention that northeast can see today. Although, there are issues in implementation of these infrastructure projects such as unprecedented delay, issues of compensation etc. The delay, which is amount to corruption in the system, costs heavy for the people of the region. However, the development regime has changed the approach towards development of the northeast that one can see the rigour and vigour in building physical infrastructure of the region.

The 'development regime' in the region became visible with initiatives for developing road connectivity in the region. There are various schemes and programmes through which the road connectivity has been prioritised in the region. The National Highway Development Project (NHDP)[6] is one of such schemes. Under different phase of this project a total of 980 km of National Highways have been targeted for up-gradation in the region. The most important developmental programme which is called 'Special Accelerated Road Development Programme for North East' (SARDP-NE)[7], that covers the region with a length of 10141 km of road which includes two phases of SARDP-NE projects and also the 'Arunachal Pradesh Package' with 2319 km. Apart from these road development programme, roads are being constructed under different heads and schemes.

Table 4.1: Road development under NLCPR in the northeast[8]

State	*No. of Projects*	*Approved cost (in lakhs)*	*Utilised amount (in lakhs)*	*(%) of utilisation*
Arunachal Pradesh	71	97964.76	35889.65	36.6
Assam	215	135954.20	62009.50	45.6
Manipur	24	21801.96	12904.11	59.2
Meghalaya	36	28648.35	13426.27	46.7
Mizoram	23	17326.52	9346.57	53.9
Nagaland	57	83260.32	53172.06	63.7
Sikkim	68	22974.42	13719.40	59.7
Tripura	28	29631.99	20566.00	69.4
Total	**522**	**437535.52**	**221033.56**	**50.5**

The NLCPR which is an exclusive fund for the developmental activities in the northeast has been one of the significant sources of road development in the region. It is evident from the table 1 that during the period of 2004-12, an amount of Rs. 437535.52 lakhs has been approved for development of critical roads in the region. However, only 50 percent of the sanctioned amount has been utilised.

Similarly, the NEC has also been engaged in developmental intervention in the region. For construction of infrastructures such as roads, bridges, bus/truck terminuses etc, NEC has sanctioned Rs. 252396.20 lakhs and released Rs. 111203.48 lakhs in a period from 2004 to 2012 to each of the state of the northeast.

The scheme called PMGSY (Prime Minister Gram Swarak Yojna) has also an important role in connectivity infrastructure in the region. There were 2,09,507 km of new rural road constructed under the scheme which is only 56 percent of the requirement (demand or eligible).

So far the railway connectivity in the region, only Assam and Nagaland's Dimapur are in the existing national rail network and some parts of Arunachal Pradesh and Tripura have been recently added to the national broad-gauge network. However, massive works are going on to make rail network effective and viable for internal as well as external connectivity of the region. A total of 1885.41 km of construction of railway is currently undergoing in the region as part of the 'development regime'.

Promotion of Industry and Investment

Promotion of Industrialisation and investment in the region has been another significant aspect of the 'development regime' in northeast. The region remained underdeveloped in terms of industrial base and in receiving capital investment until the late 1990s. There was hardly any initiative for industrial growth in the region during that period. The inherent difficulty of the region in terms location, physical infrastructure, political disturbances, insurgency etc have been always hindering its prospects of economic growth and development of an industrial base in the region. However, some initiatives were advanced to create conducive business environment for industrial development and by promoting incentive-oriented industrial investment in the region.

One of such initiatives was the North Eastern Industrial Policy of 1997[9]. Under this policy, Industries located in the 'Growth Centres' would be given capital investment subsidy at the rate of 15% on plant & machinery, subject to a ceiling of Rs. 30 lakhs. There was also provisions for exemption of income tax and excise duty for a period of 10 years. Certain high growth potential industries have also been given the tax-free status irrespective of the location in the northeast. An interest subsidy of 3% on the working capital loans would also be provided for a period of ten years after the commencement of production.

According to a press release dated March 21, 2007 of the Department of Commerce, Government of India, Rs 1067 crores were invested to set up 681 industrial units in the region during 1999–2004. However, Sharma and Bezbaruah observed, 'many of these units in reality were little more than packaging units of goods manufactured outside. Such units were obviously set up only to take advantage of the fiscal and other incentives and they cannot contribute significantly to real industrial development in the region' (Sharma and Bezbaruah 2009).

In 2007, a new industrial policy for the northeast came – The North East Industrial and Investment Promotion Policy (NEIIPP)[10]. Under this new policy, the industrial investment was further incentivised. However, tax exemption regime continued in the new policy and capital investment subsidy was enhanced from 15 percent to 30 percent with an increase in the ceiling from 30 lakhs to 150 lakhs. The policy also extended the scope of investment to service sector, bio-technology industry and power sector. The NEIIPP, 2007 has been obsolete now and the region is waiting for a new policy regime. However, efficacy of such incentive driven policy regime has to be critically evaluated.

Apart from the policy incentives, Government has also tried many other means to promote micro, small and medium enterprises throughout the country including north eastern region through various schemes and programmes. The major schemes/programmes include Prime Minister's Employment Generation Programme (PMEGP), Credit Guarantee Scheme, Credit Linked Capital Subsidy Scheme (CLCSS), National Manufacturing Competitiveness Programme, Cluster Development Programme, International Cooperation Scheme etc.[11] There are emerging sectors such as plastics and polymers, tourism and hospitality, information technology, food processing, aromatic and medicinal plants, sericulture, horticulture and floriculture, handlooms and handicrafts and bamboo processing etc. where entrepreneurs are being motivated[12].

Despite having State interventions in developing industrial base and required infrastructure, the region has not been in a position to stand itself in the competitive market environment. The 'development' that has been pushed forward by different policy regimes what we argue as under broad policy objectives of India's Look (Act) East Policy has not augmented benefits to the region. Whether capability of the region has been strengthened over the last one and half decades – remains a question unanswered.

Critical Gap in the 'development' approach: Thinking beyond Rhetoric

Most of the literatures that analyses the fate of northeast India under the Look (Act) East Policy argue about the possible benefits from the proposed India-South East Asia trade relations. However, challenge remained – whether capability of the region has developed to that end. Further, to claim such a stake, the region lacks adequate infrastructure, maintenance of law and order, efficiency in terms of human resource etc.

The 'development regime' that we discussed above, has been looking at the addressing only the physical infrastructure gap. However, such initiatives lack rigour in terms of addressing diversity within the region. The diversity within the region in terms of physical infrastructure, existing production base and trade complementarities, ethnic and cultural preferences, intra-regional connectivity etc have not been adequately considered. The physical connectivity will not be sufficient for the region because not only the local capability and popular aspirations vary from state to state but also regulatory mechanism and policy perspectives are different in every state of the region. When a common market policy could not be achieved in the region, how the region will make a space in an international trade regime. The 'development regime' has been silent on the trade-complementarities within different state of the region and also with the neighbouring countries. The Challenge for the region remains here to develop its own strength in tradability in order to sustain in the globalised market.

The massive interest on the issue of trans-national connectivity in the South East Asia to connect India and China through rail, road and other connectivity sources can only help the competent market actors in the process. Such interest was generated, which was also evident from the recent developmental push in the region, 'by the interests of multilateral organisations and advance countries with a stake in the globalised market' (Baruah, 2005:30). Sanjib Baruah (2004; 2005) further stressed that apart from the pressures from the globalising economic forces, geo-political changes have also pushed the process of connectivity and trans-national linkages.

The 'development regime' that has been pushed in the region seems to be aimed at making the region a part of the transnational linkages. But stressing only on the connectivity part, the region will misplace other opportunities to engage in the transnational processes of economic cooperation and market integration. In such a context, the region will be in the receiving end unless there is a parallel stress for internal capability and competency.

So far as locating northeast India in the Look (Act) East Policy is concerned, there is a serious disconnect exists here. Most regrettably, there has not been a single meaningful and positive outcome of the enhanced engagement with neighbouring countries in India's north eastern states. Scholars are of the view that north eastern region has been insufficiently articulated in the policy objectives (Gupta, 2011; Bhatia, 2011). It was also agreed in the policy circles that unless we use LEP to accelerate economic development of northeast, LEP will not be able to realize its full potential. The basic question – the role of the region in the country's engagement with South East Asia remained unanswered. Under the existing 'development regime' the stake for northeast India remained with ambiguities – whether the region is just a trade-corridor between India and Southeast Asia or there is a central role of the region to play in the process.

Moreover, identifying the strength of the region, there is a need to work for – a) enhancing tradability and internal capability of the region, b) an innovative and sustainable industrial base based on the local strength, c) a seamless connectivity among the states of the region, d) a common market policy in the region, and e) a comprehensive approach to development of the region, which would be based on beyond the existing framework. Finally, the 'development regime' would definitely improve the physical infrastructure in the region but to play the central role in the context of transnational economic cooperation between India and South East Asia, the approach towards the region has to be drastically altered.

END NOTES

1. Ministry of Development of North East Region, Government of India, (http://www.mdoner.gov.in/node/202)
2. Views expressed in the 'North Eastern Region Vision 2020' prepared by North Eastern Council under the Ministry of Development of North Eastern Region, Government of India, published in 2008.
3. Ministry of Development of North Eastern Region Press Release, Press Information Bureau, Government of India, 28 July, 2016.
4. The figures used in this section have been calculated from the information available in the Ministry Website (http://www.mdoner.gov.in/), Ministry of Development of North Eastern Region, Government of India.
5. Ministry of Development of North Eastern Region Press Release, Press Information Bureau, Government of India, 28 July, 2016.
6. NHDP was initiated in 1998 to improve the condition and up-gradation of National Highways across the country. The Project is running in phases in different parts of the country.
7. The SARDP-NE is a special road development programme for the North East. Under this programme, up-gradation of National Highways connecting state capitals, roads connecting district headquarters, improving road in the strategic borders, and improving connectivity to the neighbouring countries are targeted. Recognising the special need, a separate 'Arunachal Pradesh Package' has been created for improving internal connectivity in the state.
8. Figures are based on the 2012 information available in the Ministry of Development of North Eastern Region. (http://www.mdoner.gov.in/node/1266)
9. Office Memorandum, Department of Industrial Policy and Promotion, Government of India, dated 24 December, 1997. (http://www.dcmsme.gov.in/schemes/NESPLCY.htm)
10. Offiece Memorandum, Department of Industrial Policy and Promotion, Government of India, dated 1 April, 2007. (http://dipp.nic.in/English/Policies/NEIIPP_2007.pdf)
11. Ministry of Development of North Eastern Region Press Release, Press Information Bureau, Government of India, 28 July, 2016.
12. Ministry of Development of North Eastern Region Press Release, Press Information Bureau, Government of India, 28 July, 2016.

5

Act East Policy and Development of India's Northeast: Opportunities and Challenges

Jajati K. Pattnaik

The Look East Policy which was transformed into Act East Policy under the present political dispensation led by the Prime Minister Narendra Modi has entailed an action oriented approach to attain India's economic interest in its Eastern neighbourhood. The piecemeal approach was replaced by a proactive one to steer the course with a renewed spirit to secure tangible results in geo-economic perspective. Contextualised in India's northeast, the policy has remained a mere rhetoric; yet the recent stride has generated a lot of optimism among the academia, policy-makers and other stakeholders in the region for a relook at the policy with a new paradigm.

Development of India's' Northeast

The Union Government applied several paradigms to steer the trajectory of development of India's northeast. In the aftermath of India's independence, cultural paradigm was applied to preserve the cultural milieu of diverse tribal populace of north eastern region. The tribal ethno-space of the colonial period defined as excluded, partially excluded and frontier areas were put under the sixth schedule[1] of the Indian constitution which granted them autonomous districts and autonomous regions with elected councils to manage their customary laws, administer justice and control the land. To resonate the argument, the approach of the Union Government, christened as Nehruvian policy towards North East Frontier Agency (NEFA) could be cited here as an example that was 'determined to help the tribal to grow according to their own genius and tradition without any intention to impose anything on them (Elwin, 2007:56). The logic behind this paradigm was that their culture was pristine and it was to be shielded from the perils of 'big bad wolf called economic development' (Ramesh, 2005). No doubt, the political discourse during this period gave them wider cultural space to preserve their uniqueness minus industrial development.

In the subsequent period, the security paradigm emerged in the wake of Chinese invasion of India in 1962 and the region became strategically significant in the grand geo-politics of India's location in the East and South East Asia. Thus, northeast was perceived as a strategic frontier which became dominant discourse of thinking reflecting the policies of the Government towards the region (Ramesh, 2005). During seventies, the region witnessed transformation in shifting towards politics paradigm entailing political representation through pluralistic parliamentary democracy and participation in mainstream political process. It was envisaged that many of the problems of the region would be resolved through the instruments of participatory democratic politics (Ramesh, 2005).The exercise was made to reinforce the political system incorporating the modern political institutions which was interpreted from the viewpoint of political development as 'cultural diffusion, adaptation, fusion and adjustment of old patterns of life into new demands' (Pye, 1966: 33-34) and state building process which created new political structures in order to draw legitimacy from the people (Almond and Powell, 1966:35-36). Towards eighties, the 'development paradigm' was thrust in the region to get rid of the problems of identity and ethnic assertion. However, neither of those models could bring in development nor could they mitigate the problems on ethnic lines by experimenting parliamentary democracy.

The neo-liberal paradigm[2] was thrust in comprehending the geo-economic importance of India's northeast in an era of increasing regional and global cooperation (Pattnaik, 2015). The Shukla Commission Report observed that 'with the softening of geo-political rigidities following understandings with China, then Myanmar and, most especially, with Bangladesh, the northeast is no more burdensome peripheral region somewhere out there, but is poised once again to resume its dynamic role as a bridge to the booming economies of Southeast Asia and Southwest China for mutual benefit. No surprise that proposals to construct a Trans-Asian Highway and Asian railway have been revived (Planning Commission, 1997). The High Level Commission Report to the Prime Minister on 'Transforming the North East' found the resource-rich region of northeast as a national asset. The hydroelectric, oil, gas, coal, bio-diversity and agro-silvicultural potentials 'hold out promise of national solutions through regional development' and 'will add immeasurably to national security in every respect' (Planning Commission, 1997). Despite its potentialities, the region lagged behind development as compared to other regions of India. Thus, the northeast dimension was incorporated in India's Look East policy in a meeting between the External Affairs Minister, Shri Pranab Mukherjee and the Chief Ministers of the north eastern tates in October 2007 taking into account the geo-spatial connectivity of the region across the neighbouring countries to bring in development. Subsequently, the policy became an integral part of North Eastern Region Vision 2020[3] – 'a roadmap for development of the Region' in July, 2008. Since then, both the Union Government and the State Governments of the north eastern region have been focusing on the Look/Act east policy to reap rich dividends for the region. But the ground realities are far different from the policy formulations. So, the present situation demands a paradigm shift by identifying the opportunities as well as challenges for the northeast.

Opportunities

The Act East policy offers immense opportunities for the northeast needs to be tapped in a systematic manner for the development of this region. The region is abundant with natural resources such as oil, natural gas, coal, limestone, forest products, tea, rare herbs and medicinal plants. It is one of the hotspots of global biodiversity constituting near about half of the country's total bio-diversity. The region holds one fifth of the country's total hydrocarbon reserves and is highly affluent in hydropower reserve. There is tremendous potentialities in the northeast to develop industries based on agricultural, horticultural and plantation products; handicrafts and handlooms; pharmaceutical and herbal industries, hydro energy projects; electronics and IT industries; mineral and food processing industries; engineering and allied Industries. It is quite relevant to mention that the region shares near about 98 percent of its land boundary[4] with Bangladesh, Bhutan, China, Nepal and Myanmar. So, the land border potentialities of India's northeast at Moreh (Manipur), Champhai (Mizoram), Kibithoo (Arunachal Pradesh), Nathula (Sikkim), Dawki, Borsora, Dalu, Mahendraganj and Baghmara (Meghalaya), Agartala, Srimantpur, Old Raghnabazar, Manu, Khowaighat (Tripura) and Sutarkandi, Mankachar and Dhubri (Assam) could be effectively tapped to augment cross border trade and commerce (Pattnaik, 2016 a).

Trade in services is another possible area between ASEAN[5] and the northeast. Health care, hospitality, education, and tourism sectors provide tremendous potential for cross border cooperation. Further, this sector through backward linkages can generate trade in transport, communication and other related services. Once the rules are softened for the free movement across the borders, there is every possibility that the patients from Myanmar, Laos, and Cambodia will flow to the hospitals in Guwahati, Dibrugarh, Shillong and Imphal to get quality health care services at a cheaper price compared to their domestic hospitals in Yangon and adjacent regions. It is relevant to mention here that the Seija hospital of Manipur having a rich pool of trained doctors is already taking a lead in providing affordable quality health care services to the Myanmarese cross the border. Once the demand from across the border becomes apparent, then necessary health infrastructure for providing such services will come up in northeast as well. In addition to this, tourism potentialities of the region such as nature/eco tourism, cultural tourism and rural tourism will attach tremendous importance to cross border cooperation. In specific sense, Buddhist circuit of tourism can be developed to restore cultural linkages with the ASEAN.

The Act East policy would promote regional and sub-regional cooperation in South and South East Asia. It would enable India's northeast to collaborate with the Association of Southeast Asian Nations (ASEAN), Mekong–Ganga Cooperation (MGC)[6] and Bangladesh–China–India–Myanmar (BCIM)[7] forum for regional/sub-regional cooperation in the field of trade, transport, technology, automobiles, machineries, electronics, petrochemicals, pharmaceuticals, herbal, fertiliser, polymer, agro–horticulture, culture, tourism, education, banking, investment and tourism by harnessing their respective software and hardware resources for a meaningful bilateral or multilateral venture. The policy would generate growth triangles in the region. Growth triangles are formed on the basis of different comparative strengths of contiguous regions by capitalising their natural resources, technology, finance and human resources. This concept was unveiled by the first Deputy Prime Minister of Singapore Goh Chok Tong in 1989 in the form of Singapore–Johor–Riau (SIJORI) Growth Triangle which coalesced the technology and finance of Singapore with that of the land, labour and natural resources of Ria Island of Indonesia and Johor of Malaysia (Pattnaik, 2016b). Hence, there could be possibilities of similar growth triangles such as (a) Eastern Bangladesh, India's northeast and Western Myanmar (b) Eastern Bangladesh, Western Myanmar and South-West China, and (c) Myanmar, India's northeast, and Thailand etc. based on amalgamation of their comparative advantages quite akin to the SIJORI Growth Triangle.

Challenges

There are inherent internal and external challenges to the Act East policy in the context of India's northeast. Of course, they need to be removed to usher development in the region. A prime apprehension is that in case the Act East policy is materialized, India's northeast will be swamped with cheap Chinese goods. This kind of economic threat perception cannot be denied given the nature of easy flow of Chinese goods into the Indian markets. It is also pertinent to mention here that China has already spread its tentacles in the South East Asian countries through several road and rail corridors having deeper economic engagements with them. So, India can dispel such Chinese threat perceptions through increasing cross border trade and connectivity with the ASEAN, and thereby rightly balancing our national interest in South East Asia vis-a-vis China. In this connection, it would be noteworthy to point out that special economic zones (SEZs) should be developed in the northeast and potentialities of the region as mentioned earlier in pharmaceuticals and petrochemicals; hydro, herbal, horticulture, handicraft and handloom; tradition, technology, trade and tourism should be explored by tapping cross-border synergies. The indigenous entrepreneurial culture is conspicuous by its absence in the northeast and it has given rise to proxy transactions in business resulting in crony capitalism. The educated youth are mostly dependent upon the white collar government job. Thus, the need of the hour is to break the jinx by harnessing productive human resource by upgrading professional and techno-managerial skills to generate employment as well as entrepreneurship. In this context, both the government as well as civil society organizations would have to make conscious and sustained efforts to generate pro-investment climate and entrepreneurship culture to reap the dividends in case of cross border trade in the region.

Inner line regulations[8] implemented since 1873 are still continuing in Arunachal Pradesh, Nagaland and Mizoram without any modification and their extension is proving counterproductive to the industrial development of the region. It is significant to mention here that the Inner line regulations were promulgated to protect the British colonial interest rather than protecting the rights of indigenous population of the then NEFA. Alternatively, their rights can be safeguarded through protective measures as being practiced in the state like Sikkim. The outsiders do not possess land rights in Sikkim. But they are encouraged to setup industrial bases and evolve as well as train a human-power which would be globally competitive. The state has outpaced most of the northeastern states in terms of industrial development and employment opportunities, while the latter having similar geo-political space have not yet explored their optimum potentialities. Next question is how to address the concerns or redress the problem of minoritisation of the locals due to influx of outside population. No doubt, migration poses challenge to the identity of local population which is often trapped in the arithmetic of electoral democracy. In order to sustain their legitimacy, the political elites might use vote bank politics and garner the support of the outsiders. There is a possibility of being marginalization of locals as against such majoritarian politics. Of course, this apprehension can be removed through protective measures for indigenous groups. Citing one of the examples, Pradip Phanjoubam wrote, 'Even it is conceded that demographic protection is needed for Manipur, this protection does not have to be by the antiquated inner line system. A similar system of protection already exists in the hill districts of Manipur, what is being sought now is for such a provision to be extended into the valley districts as well. The question is, should it be one-size fit all approach to such a law, or whether it should be modeled, calibrated and designed contextually, accepting variations to suit the purpose and time in the best and just way possible. I would argue there is no option to the latter approach' (Phanjoubam, 2013).

Current land holding system poses a challenge to the agro-horticultural and industrial development in the state. Land holding in the tribal areas is more a community right, than an individual right. Neither there has been any cadastral survey of the land nor any attempt to register the land through land registration system. The recently introduced land settlement registration only legalizes the customary rights over such occupied lands. In the cities or in urban areas, mostly the customary rights of holding landed property are also manipulated to the interests of local leaders/influential/moneyed persons. In the process, the occupied land, later legalized through the land settlement registration system, is used either as a rent accruing mechanism given on rent to the migrant workers or bargained as a medium of compensation during the commissioning of any mega industrial/ road corridor project. This rentier mode of economy does not suit to the genuine economic development of the state. Moreover, this is not a sustainable form of development. So, the need of the hour is to have a through cadastral survey of the land and identification of genuine land holders for the acknowledgement of their individual land rights for the real economic development of the state.

Governance crisis is to be addressed both at the institutional as well as civil society level as the systemic leakages and fund mismanagement have marred the process of development in northeast India. Subir Bhaumik has attributed governance crisis to four factors: (i) 'a near total dependence on the centre for funds and even for decades for ideas on programmes for development'; (ii) 'unacceptable levels of spending on non-productive government employment and lack of investment in development of infrastructure that can sustain growth and generate higher volumes of employment in the long run'; (iii) 'siphoning off of funds through corruption and mismanagement, causing huge leakages and failure to develop trade and business links within the region and neighbouring countries' (Bhaumik, 2015). To get rid of corruption, the institutions are to be decentralized from bottom to top approach instead of top down bottom approach to ensure popular participation in the delivery mechanism while endowing the citizens with the responsibility of managing their own affairs at the grass root level through people's initiatives. Moreover, the process of development is to be continuously monitored through civil society activism and social auditing for effective and good governance.

Insurgency remains a major challenge to realise the potentials of Act east policy. India's northeast shares border with the insurgency ridden north west Myanmar—a safe haven for the northeast insurgent groups in Myanmar. The major groups are: United Liberation Front of Asom (ULFA), Anti Talk/Independent, National Democratic Front of Bodoland (NDFB), Assam; National Socialist Council of Nagaland-Isak and Muivah (NSCN-IM), National Socialistic Council of Nagaland-Khaplang (NSCN-K), National Socialistic Council of Nagaland-Reformation (NSCN-R), Nagaland; People's Liberation Army (PLA)/ Revolutionary People's Front (RPF), United National Liberation Front (UNLF), People's Revolutionary Party of Kangleipak (PREPAK), factions of Kangleipak Communist Party (KCP), Kanglei Yaol Kanba Lup (KYKL), Manipur People's Liberation Front (MPLF), Manipur; All Tripura Tiger Force (ATTF), National Liberation Front of Tripura (NLFT), Tripura; Hynniewtrep National Liberation Council (HNLC) and Garo National Army (GNLA), Meghalaya (MHA 2015). There is a section of intellectuals who think that how can cross border cooperation sustain through this insurgency infested region? They have skeptical views about this corridor being hostage to the militants. On the other, a few academics also opine that the problems of insurgency will be automatically resolved, once the highway and allied infrastructural developments take place. The Highways/corridors will create job opportunities bringing substantial changes in the social and economic aspects. As a sequel to this, the disgruntled youth would remain away from the unlawful activities and participate in the process of economic development. As noted scholar Samir Kumar Das observed: "The economic affluence that is bound to result from this economic integration will liberate the north east from its present landlocked state and make it prosper whether in terms of infrastructural development or in terms of generation of employment for the vast unemployed youth. Economic prosperity of the region is likely to bring down insurgency and violence as unemployment and denial of economic opportunities are believed to have been responsible for the easy availability of fresh young recruits for the insurgent groups. Economic prosperity will be the magic wand that is expected to wipe out the scourge of insurgency from the region" (Das 2010). Besides this, the problem can be resolved through multipronged strategies. In this respect, both India and Myanmar should try to secure peace constituencies across the border lands which are afflicted with insurgencies. They should also create congenial atmosphere through back channel methods and sustain the dialogue process with their respective insurgent groups to bring them back into the social mainstream. Moreover, the academia and civil society organizations through engagement paradigm should intensify their efforts for the peace building process (Pattnaik, 2015). Then, efforts should be channelized to generate confidence among disgruntled youth and then wean them away from the path of insurgency by addressing their legitimate grievances with adequate rehabilitation packages. Lastly, geopolitical borders should be transformed into potential economic opportunities to flourish trade and development in the region, so that the unemployed youth will not be allured to join the ranks of insurgency.

There is an apprehension that drugs and small arms might sneak into NER jeopardizing the peace and stability of the region. Myanmar, located in the opium producing golden triangle, acts as the land bridge to such regional/sub-regional cooperation and in the event of cross border trade, it may be transformed into a potential drug corridor. It is reported that the drug cartels use about thirty trafficking routes. Some of these, marked by the Indian Narcotics Control Bureau (NCB), are: Behiang-Singhat-Churachandpur-Imphal, Behiang-Singhat-Tipaimukh-Silchar, Mandalay-Tahang-Imphal, Tamu-Moreh-Imphal, Homalin-Ukhrul-Jessami-Kohima, Mandaly-Tahang-Tiddim-Aizawl-Silchar, Homalin Khamjong-Shangshak Khullen-Ukhrul–Imphal, Myitkina-Maingkwan-Pangsau Pass-Nampong-Jairampur-Digboi, Putao-Pashighat-Tezpur-Guwahati, Tamanthi-Noklak-Kohima-Dimpur, New Somtal-Sugnu-Churachandpur-Imphal-Kohima-Dimapur, Tahan-Tiddim-Melbuk-Champhai-Aizawl-Silchar, Tohan-Vaphai-Khawlailung-Serchip-Aizawl, Tahan-Falam-Ngarchhip-Khawlailung-Serchip-Aizawl, Falam-Dawn-Thingsai-Hnahthial-

Lunglei-Demagiri-Chittagong Hill Tracts-Chittagong, Falam-Lungbun-Saitha-Chittagong Hill Tracts-Chittagong, Churachandpur-Ngopa-Aizawl-Phuldungsei-Jampui Hills-Agartala-Chittagong (Bhaumik, 2015: 193-194). In this context, the potential threats emerging out of these drug corridors cannot be easily overlooked. It is also pertinent to mention that the state-run Chinese arms manufacturing company, China North Industries Corporation (Norinco) of Yunan, which shares its border with the Indian states of Arunachal Pradesh, Nagaland and Manipur, supplies unlawful weapons to the buyers ranging from the African dictators to the Asian rebels (Uninathan, 2011). Subir Bhaumik observed, "There is growing evidence of connivance between Chinese intelligence and ordnance establishments, as well as evidence of paybacks to Burmese military commanders who allow the weapons to pass through Burmese territory from Yunan to Northeast India" (Bhaumik, 2015: 189). Unless this unlawful smuggling of arms is stopped, it would be quite difficult to materialize any sub-regional cooperation or cross border synergy in the region. Yet, this problem can be can be addressed specifically by India and Myanmar by reinforcing joint surveillance mechanism through information and communication induced technology and intensifying border patrolling to check illegal entry of drugs and small arms. No doubt, the Memorandum of Understanding(MOU) signed between India and Myanmar for sharing intelligence information, synchronizing patrolling across the international border, exchanging information to combat insurgency, arms smuggling and drug trafficking and initiating measures to foil illegal cross-border movements, if realized in true spirit, would ensure 'peace, stability and security' across the international border (MEA, 2014). On the other hand, China has to lend a hand with India and Myanmar to curb the influx of drugs and small arms into the region for the eventual success of any regional/sub-regional cooperation. Besides this, the highways/corridors once reopened to regulate the formal border trade in Indo-Myanmar sector would substantially check the illegal exodus of drugs and small arms into the region through various surveillance mechanisms.

A critical study of the subject indicated that the challenges largely outweighed the opportunities. Thus, the need of the hour is to frame action oriented policies along with a fresh vision document in the context of India's Northeast-Act East policy, and then transform them into practical actions at the ground level for the benefit of all the stakeholders in the region. There are enough options within the Indian system for ideas and initiatives from the northeast to take wing. It requires northeast India's political leaders to first agree among themselves on a common vision for the region and to show greater creativity in their dealings with the central government. If the ground is not ready, no trade and commerce can bear fruit. When a region would flourish economically, it could contribute to the growth of country's economy as a whole. Moreover, it will create a viable economic corridor for which the centre will give more attention to the northeast thereby making the centre-state relations stronger in the Indian federal structure.

END NOTES

1. The concept of sixth schedule was coined by Nicholos Roy, a Khasi from undivided Assam to protect the rights of the tribal people within a state geographical area as against the domination or exploitation of dominant non – tribal population (Mukhim, 2013). As per the provisions of sixth schedule, 'There shall be a District Council for each autonomous district Consisting of not more than thirty members, of whom not more than four shall be nominated by the Governor and the rest shall be elected on the basis of adult suffrage.' (ii] 'There shall be a separate Regional Council for each area constituted an autonomous region under sub-paragraph (2) of paragraph 1 of this schedule'(Ministry of Law, Undated)
2. Neoliberal paradigm is a pattern being linked to a minimalist state resorting to market driven liberal economic policies based on liberalization, privatization and deregulation. It is also interpreted as an economic ideology to expand capitalist globalisation (Mc Lean and McMillan, 2003). The neoliberal philosophy draws intellectual inspiration from Francis Fukuyama's work on 'The End of History and the Last Man' where he observed that 'a remarkable consensus concerning the legitimacy of liberal democracy as a system of government had emerged throughout the world over the past few years, as it conquered rival ideologies like hereditary monarchy, fascism, and communism'. He also posited that liberal democracy may form the 'end point of mankind's ideological evolution and the final form of human government' making up 'the end of history'. He further mentioned that 'while earlier forms of governments were characterised by grave defects and irrationalities that led to their eventual collapse, liberal democracy was arguably free from such fundamental internal contradiction' (Fukuyama, 1992:11).
3. The 'vision 2020' mentioned: (i) empowerment of the people by maximizing self-governance and participatory development through grass-roots planning. Such planning will help to evolve development strategy based on the resources, needs and aspirations of the people'; (ii) 'rural development with a focus on improving agricultural productivity and the creation of non-farm avocations

and employment; (iii) 'development of sectors with comparative advantage agro-processing industries, modernization and development of sericulture, investment in manufacturing units based on the resources available in the region, harnessing the large hydroelectric power generation potential and focus on developing services such as tourism that will help to accelerate development and create productive employment opportunities;' (iv) 'maximising self-governance, introduction of participatory planning, rural development and development of sectors with comparative advantage call for significant augmentation of capacity of the people and institutions both in the government and private sectors. Capacity development will have to address the issue of imparting skills among the people to enhance their productivity, generating a class of entrepreneurs within the region willing to take risks. They will also have to be provided with the necessary support through the creation and development of institutions at all levels to undertake planning;' (v) 'augmenting infrastructure, including rail, road, inland water and air transportation to facilitate a two-way movement of people and goods within the region and outside, communication networks including broadband and wireless connectivity, and harnessing of the vast power generation potential, all of which will open up markets for produce from the region, attract private investment, create greater employment opportunities and expand choices for people of the region;' (vi) 'connectivity of NER with ASEAN would require opening up the sea route through the Chittagong port and the land routes through Myanmar and China. In addition, opening up the land route through Bangladesh could enormously benefit both countries and diplomatic efforts should focus on improving relations with the neighbours;' and (vii) 'ensuring adequate flow of resources for public investments in infrastructure, implementing framework for private participation in augmenting infrastructure and creating an enabling environment for the flow of investments to harness the physical resources of the region for the welfare of the people' (MDONER, 2008).

4. Arunachal Pradesh, Assam and Sikkim share 516 km land border with Bhutan. Arunachal Pradesh and Sikkim share 1300.35 land border with the Peoples Republic of China. Arunachal Pradesh, Manipur, Mizoram and Nagaland share 1643 km land border with Myanmar. Assam, Mizoram and Meghalaya share 1880 km land border with Bangladesh (MDONER, 2015).
5. The Association of Southeast Asian Nations (ASEAN) came into existence through ASEAN Declaration (Bangkok Declaration) signed by its original members viz. Indonesia, Malaysia, Philippines, Singapore and Thailand at Bangkok on 8 August 1967. Later, the membership got increased to ten with the entry of Brunei Darussalam in 1984, Viet Nam in 1995, Lao Peoples Democratic republic in 1997, Myanmar in 1997 and Cambodia in 1999. The objective of ASEAN is to augment ' economic growth, social progress and cultural development in the region through joint endeavors', develop 'regional peace and stability through abiding respect for justice and the rule of law', increase 'active collaboration and mutual assistance on matters of common interest in the economic, social, cultural, technical, scientific and administrative fields' and uphold 'close and beneficial cooperation with existing international and regional organizations with similar aims and purposes, and explore all avenues for even closer cooperation among themselves'(ASEAN, Undated).

6. The Mekong–Ganga Cooperation (MGC) was formed between the two civilisational rivers in 2000 at Vientiane, the capital of Lao PDR by India and five ASEAN countries i.e. Cambodia, Lao PDR, Myanmar, Thailand and Vietnam for closer economic cooperation in the field of culture, tourism, education, transport and communications. (Ministry of External Affairs, Undated).
7. BCIM (Bangladesh, China, India and Myanmar) is a regional/ sub-regional grouping between the south-West China, India's northeast, Bangladesh and Myanmar which is intended towards economic integration through trade, transport, industry, tourism, investment and other cooperative ventures in order to bring inclusive development in the region. BCIM initially conceptualized as Kunming Initiative through track II (Civil society level) diplomacy in 1999 became a track I (Governmental Level) regional/sub regional forum during the visit of Chinese Premier Li Keqiang to India in May 2013. The two sides declared to establish a Joint Study Group among the BCIM countries for deeper engagement to flourish connectivity, trade, and people-to-people linkages paving the way for BCIM Economic corridor (Pattnaik, 2016c).
8. The Regulation 1 of 1873 denoted a 'Regulation for the peace and Good Government of certain Districts on the Eastern Frontier" which is described Inner Line Regulation of 1873, empowered the Local government to 'prescribe and from time to time alter, a line, to be called inner Line in each or any of the districts of Assam.' The Regulation states 'The Local government may by notification in Calcutta Gazette, prohibit all British subjects or any class of British subjects, or any persons residing in, or passing through such districts, from going beyond such line without a pass under the hand and seal of the executive officer as he may be authorized to grant such pass; and the local government may from time to time cancel or vary such prohibit. Any British subject or other person to prohibit who goes beyond inner line without a pass shall be liable on conviction before a magistrate to a fine not exceeding Rupees Hundred for the first offence and to a fine of not exceeding Rupees 500 or to simple or rigorous imprisonment for not exceeding three months, or to both for each subsequent offence' (MDONER, 1873).

6

India-Myanmar-Thailand (IMT) Trilateral Highway and its Likely Impact on the Economic Integration Between NER and ASEAN

Gurudas Das and Malabika Das

1. ASEAN in India's Look East/Act East Policy

The centrality of ASEAN in India's Look East/Act East Policy needs no repetition. In fact, India's economic engagement with ASEAN and other East Asian as well as Asia Pacific countries since the adoption LEP in 1992 has caused a tectonic shift in its foreign trade. The direction of the focus of India's foreign trade has shifted from the West to East leading to a fundamental change in the nature of India's economic interdependence (Das, et al: 2016). While much of the boost in two-way trade came from Sino-Indian economic engagements which grew from US$ 0.2 billion in 1990 to US$ 70.7 billion in 2016, the two way India-ASEAN trade has also made significant progress. It went up from US$ 7.06 billion in 2000-01 to US$65.04 billion in 2015-16 thereby registering more than 9 fold increase within 14 years.

India's ASEAN trade is characterized by the dominance of countries like Singapore, Indonesia, Malaysia and Thailand. These four countries together contributed more than 80 per cent of India's ASEAN trade in 2015-16. Among the CLMV countries, India's trade with Vietnam has made spectacular progress. The share of Vietnam in India's

Table 6.1: Share in India's Total Trade with ASEAN (in %)

S.No.	Country	2000-2001	2005-2006	2010-2011	2015-2016
	ASEAN	7.425	8.442	9.076	10.114
1	Brunei	0.049	0.206	0.457	0.895
2	Cambodia	0.130	0.117	0.133	0.303
3	Indonesia	18.552	20.607	27.775	24.517
4	Lao Pd Rp	0.088	0.026	0.024	0.335
5	Malaysia	25.278	16.800	18.484	19.659
6	Myanmar	3.320	2.990	2.380	3.158
7	Philippines	3.762	3.429	2.330	2.945
8	Singapore	33.153	41.226	30.167	23.098
9	Thailand	12.293	10.739	11.641	13.061
10	Vietnam	3.375	3.860	6.608	12.029

Source: Export Import Data Bank.

ASEAN trade has gone up from 3 per cent in 2000-2001 to 12 per cent in 2015-16. What is striking is the fact that in spite of being the next door neighbor, two way trade between India and Myanmar has never been substantial. The share of Myanmar in India's ASEAN trade kept on hovering around 3 per cent during the last 14 years (table 6.1). Trilateral cooperation among India, Myanmar and Thailand has a huge potential to break this Indo-Myanmar trade stagnancy and create an environment of win win situation for all the stakeholders.

2. Continental Route and the Geo-Economics of Trilateral Cooperation

The trilateral highway connecting India's northeast, Myanmar and Thailand has a number of geo-economic implications. We are not entering into the past in order to explain as to why cross-border connectivity remained weak particularly along the 1643 km long Indo-Myanmar border as a lot has already been written on the geo-political importance of Mynamar. The geo-economic spins that will arise once the trilateral highway is opened for traffic and motor vehicle rules across the countries are harmonized are listed below.

(i) The continental route for India to reach ASEAN countries and vice versa will come into existence and provide an alternative to sea route through which two way India-ASEAN trade is currently flowing.

(ii) Currently, a merchant ship takes 12.1 days to reach to the port of Bangkok from Kolkata, a distance of over 5360km that moves through the congested Malacca Strait while a truck will take only 7.30 days to reach Bangkok at 40 kmh or 3.65 days at 80 kmhthrough the Trilateral Highway, covering a distance of 3212 km. The distance differential between the sea route and continental route stands to be 2184 km (table 6.2).

(iii) In fact as far as distance differentials between the sea route and continental route from the major cities in east and northeast India to Bangkok are concerned, the trilateral highway will bring Thailand nearer in terms of both spatial and temporal dimensions. The sea route to Bangkok from the major cities in northeast India is about 3 times lengthier than the Continental Route and it takes about 3 times longer travel time (table 6.2) at 40kmh and 5 times longer at 80 kmh.

(iv) Eventhough the distance of Bangkok from Kolkata, the nearest metropolitan city from north eastern region, is about 1.67 times more along the sea route compared to the Continental Route, it takes about 3.32 times more time to reach.

(v) However, as the land transport is about 7.5 times costlier than sea transport, the spatial and temporal advantages of the Continental Route get offset due to cheaper cost of travel along the sea route.

(vi) Except Manipur, where the trilateral highway begins in Indian side, no other states in north eastern region is having any clear cost advantage if they choose to do business with Thailand using the Continental Route (table 6.3).

(vii) While considered the trade-off between continental route and the maritime route for India's northeast, the former involves a slightly higher transport cost along with significant travel time advantage, however, the cost advantage of the latter appears to be marginal compared to travel time disadvantage (table 6.3).

(viii) It is evident that it would not be cost-effective for mainland India to trade with Thailand using the Continental Route. Except north eastern states, Maritime Route is cheaper for India's business. However, for trade in perishable and semi-perishable goods, where the value loses with time, and when

Table 6.2: Distance between Major cities in eastern and north eastern India and Bangkok along the Continental Route (Trilateral Highway) and Sea Route

		Distance and travel time						
From	*To*	*Continental Route via Trilateral Highway*			*Sea Route via Malacca Straight*			
		Distance (kms)	*Travel Time (days) 40 km/hr for 11 hr*	*Travel Time (days) 80 km/hr for 11 hr*	*R*	*W*	*T*	*Travel Time (days)*
Agartala	Bangkok	2510	5.70	2.85	1680	5360	7040	15.92
Aizwal	Bangkok	2377	5.40	2.70	1657	5360	7007	15.87
Guwahati	Bangkok	2460	5.60	2.80	1081	5360	6441	14.56
Imphal	Bangkok	1971	4.48	2.24	1742	5360	7102	16.06
Itanagar	Bangkok	2521	5.73	2.86	1252	5360	6612	14.95
Kohima	Bangkok	2108	4.79	2.39	1335	5360	6695	15.13
Kolkata	**Bangkok**	**3212**	**7.30**	3.65	—	**5360**	**5360**	**12.10**
Shillong	Bangkok	2441	5.55	2.75	1181	5360	6541	14.78
Silchar	Bangkok	2226	5.05	2.53	1407	5360	6767	15.30

Note: (i) For calculation of travel time on the roadways, average speed of 40 kmh/80kmh and 11hr driving schedule in a day are assumed. (ii) While calculating travel time on the sea, average speed of 10 knots/hr is assumed.

Source: Author's Calculation.

Table 6.3: Distance and Transportation Cost between Major cities in eastern and north eastern India and Bangkok along the Continental Route (Trilateral Highway) and Sea Route

From	*To*	*Continental Route via Trilateral Highway*		*Sea Route via Malacca Straight*			
		Distance (kms)	*Cost per tone (In US$)*	*Distance (kms)*			*Cost per tone (In US$)*
				R	*W*	*T*	
Agartala	Bangkok	2510	75.30	1680	5360	7040	71.84
Aizwal	Bangkok	2377	71.31	1657	5360	7007	71.15
Guwahati	Bangkok	2460	73.80	1081	5360	6441	53.87
Imphal	Bangkok	1971	59.13	1742	5360	7102	73.70
Itanagar	Bangkok	2521	75.63	1252	5360	6612	59.00
Kohima	Bangkok	2108	63.24	1335	5360	6695	61.49
Kolkata	**Bangkok**	**3212**	96.36	—	5360	5360	21.44
Shillong	Bangkok	2441	73.23	1181	5360	6541	56.87
Silchar	Bangkok	2226	66.78	1407	5360	6767	63.65

Note: For calculating cost US$ 0.004 tonne/km along sea route and US$ 0.03 tonne/km along the roadways have been used.

Source: Author's Calculation

businesses take advantage of time utility—the Continental Route might come in handy even for the mainland traders based in Kolkata who would be able to send consignments in 3.65 days instead of 12.10 days to Bangkok.

(ix) It is important to note that while the average cost of carrying per ton of goods from the north eastern states is $69.80 along the continental route, the same amounts to $63.95 along the maritime route. Thus, the continental route costs only $5.85 more per ton. Considering the costs involved in inter-modal transshipment, the cost advantage of maritime route gets wiped up along with huge gain in delivery time while the continental route is used. Thus, in the final analysis, IMT highway will transform the business environment in favour of India's northeast.

(x) By way of connecting Thailand, Myanmar and India's north eastern region (NER), the trilateral highway will kick start sub-regional cooperation for development. As both Myanmar and NER are resource rich underdeveloped regions, Thailand, being industrially advanced, will play the role of engine for

IMT (India, Myanmar and Thailand) cooperation. Technology, capital and expertise of Thailand while combined with the natural resources of otherwise industrially underdeveloped Myanmar and NER will help in forging a strong resource-industry linkages in IMT area which will propel the growth.

(xi) This trilateral cooperation will not only transform NER from land-locked area to land-linked area, the Continental Route will provide the much needed logistical space for which the region could not reap the benefit of India's Look East Policy and has remained as a passive onlooker while the coastal regions flourished.

Figure 6.1: Pineapple Production and Export by Leading Countries

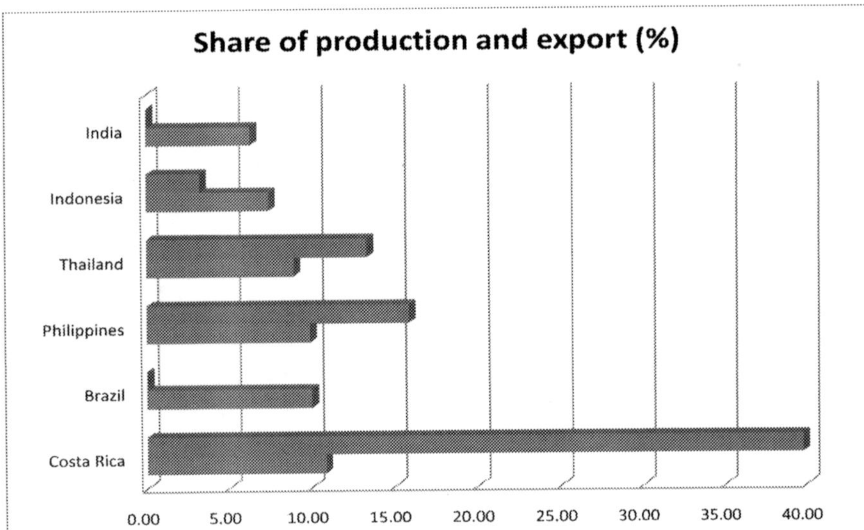

	Costa Rica	Brazil	Philippines	Thailand	Indonesia	India
Export	39.75	0.06	15.89	13.37	3.29	0.06
Production	10.84	10.02	9.92	8.92	7.41	6.34

(xii) How IMT cooperation can set the ball rolling ? We shall cite the examples of two cases: pineapple and ginger that grow in plenty in the hills and plains of NER.

(xiii) While India produces 6.34 per cent of global production of pineapple, she only shares 0.06 per cent of the global exports. Within India, NER contributes 48.33 per cent of the total national production. Thailand produces 8.92 per cent of the global production but shares 13.37 per cent of the global export. As Thailand is one of the leading food processors and world's largest exporter of pineapple juice (17.92 percent global share), pineapple produced in NER if exported to Thailand will be beneficial for both as it faces severe crisis of pineapples in almost three quarters in a year (Q1, Q2 and Q4). Thus, supplying pineapples to Thailand via IMT highway will be a win-win situation for both the countries. This resource (in NER)-industry (in Thailand) linkage will ensure remunerative price for the farmers as well as profit margin for the intermediaries leading to rise in level of their income.Our estimation shows that the traders might reap about 90 percent return on their investment even after paying nearly double farm gate price (Paul and Das, 2017).

Figure 6.2: Pineapple Production in India by States

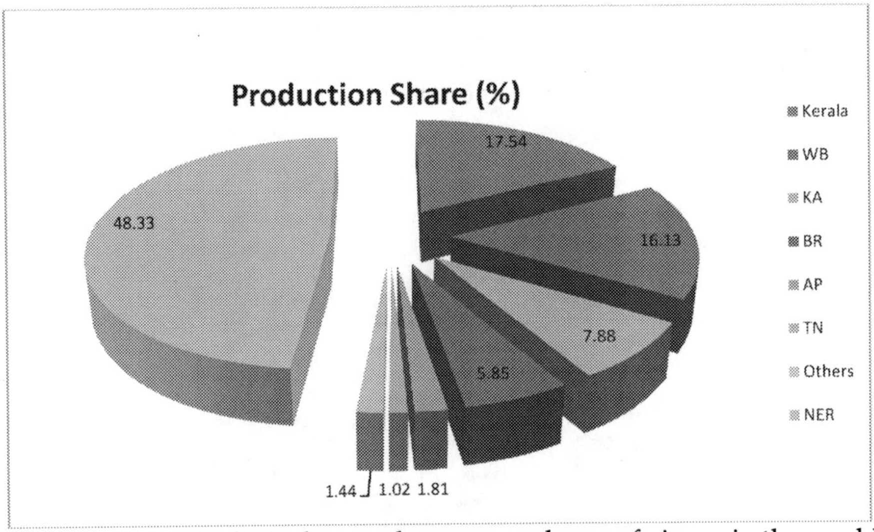

(xiv) While India is the number one producer of ginger in the world which alone produces 26.6 per cent of the global production, it only shares 2.74 per cent of the total global exports of ginger. In contrast, China produces 15.19 per cent of the global production but shares 52.16 per cent of the global exports (Figure 6.3). Within India, 56.52 per cent of the national production comes from the states in north eastern region. Much of this ginger is sold raw at a lesser price without any processing and value addition. A significant part of this raw ginger is exported to Bangladesh across the border in South Assam.

Figure 6.3: Production and Export Share of Ginger by leading Countries (in %)

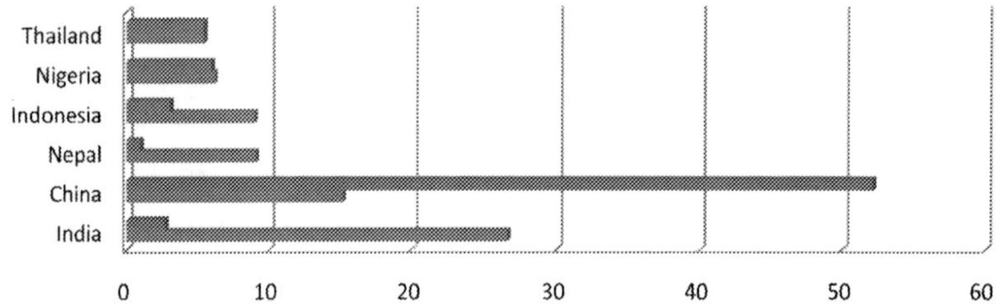

	India	China	Nepal	Indonesia	Nigeria	Thailand
Export	2.74	52.16	1.01	3.08	5.98	5.50
Production	26.6	15.19	9.15	9.06	6.23	5.45

Figure 6.4: Ginger production in India by states

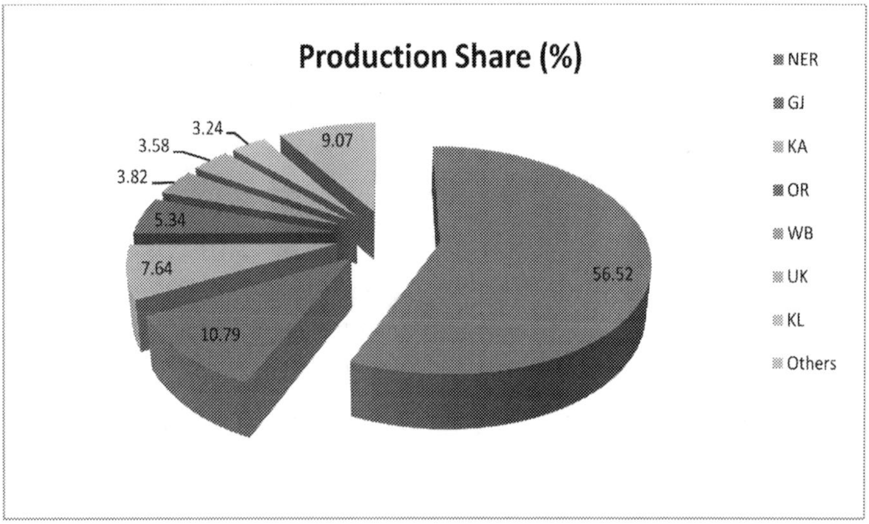

As Thailand is one of the net importers of ginger and offers much higher price compared to Bangladesh, it will be beneficial for both the ginger cultivators in NER and ginger merchants in Thailand to enter into trade. Thailand will have access to raw materials and NER will have access to a lucrative market. The technology, processing efficiency and market penetration skill of the Thai firms while combined with the raw material availability in NER will create a win-win situation for the stakeholders in both the countries. As Japan and Singapore are also net importer of ginger, the ginger traders in Thailand due to their close network in those countries might reap additional benefits by importing surplus available in NER (Paul and Das, 2017).

Apart from pineapple and ginger, north eastern region is also rich in bamboo plants. While India is one of the leading country in the world in bamboo resources, more than 40 per cent of them are grown in the north eastern region. As bamboo shoots are popular in China and other South East Asian countries, there is a huge opportunity for the Thai processing firms to enter into trade with the players in NER.

Besides the opportunities for strengthening resource-industry linkages, there is a huge opportunity for cross-border cultural tourism along the trilateral highway as Buddhist cultural prints bind these three regions: Thailand, Myanmar and NER. More than 300 years old Tawang Monastery, the second largest monastery in the world after Potala Palace in Lhasa, Tibet, is situated in NER. Rumtek Monastery, about 250 years old, is in Sikkim. A sizeable Buddhist population lives in Arunachal Pradesh (11.77 per cent), Mizoram (8.51 per cent), Sikkim (27.39 per cent) and Tripura (3. 41 per cent) (Census of India: 2011). Apart from religion, Thailand, being the second most preferred tourist destination after China in the Asia Pacific region, can incorporate both Myanmar and NER into its circuit of natural and adventure tourism.

Thus, trilateral cooperation along the Continental Route is certain to strengthen the dyadic resource-trade (Das: 2010) linkages as well as triadic resource-industry-trade linkages if Thai entrepreneurship is combined with resource availability in Myanmar and NER.

Conclusion

As geo-political concerns of the states are increasingly giving way to geo-economic advantages, India (NER), Myanmar and Thailand (IMT) cooperation can easily become a reality. Pending the demarcation of long border, Thailand and Myanmar have already embraced each other as their exists some sort of complementarity between the Thai and Myanmar economies. While Thailand imports natural gas, forest products, minerals and horticultural products from Myanmar, it exports processing and manufacturing products to Myanmar (Chirathivat and Cheewatrakoolpong, 2015). As part of its "Look West Policy", Thailand has made considerable investments in a number of infrastructural projects like Dawei Development Project, Dawei Road Links to Thailand and East-West Corridor. Similarly, India has also invested in Kaladan Multi-modal Transit Transport Project, India-Myanmar Friendship Highway, Sittwe port in Rakhine State in Myanmar, on the Bay of Bengal. With Myanmar's transition to democracy and pent up demand for development, it will certainly utilize the geo-economic advantages instead of acting as the geo-political stooge of the neighbouring powers (Das: 2016). Once IMT comes into existence, NER will act as India's continental pivot to ASEAN.

Acknowledgement

The ideas expressed here were earlier presented in a seminar entitled "India-Myanmar-Thailand Trilateral Relationship: Way Towards A Stronger ASEAN-India Partnership", held during September 22-23, 2016, organized by the ASEAN Study Centre, Chulalongkorn University, Bangkok, Thailand.

7

Economic Implication of Kaladan Multi-model Transit Transport Project (KMTTP) for India's NER and ASEAN

Suwa Lal Jangu

From Look East Policy to Act East Policy

Rest of the India looks to and now acts in the NER and ASEAN through the so-called "Look East (Act) Policy". It is a policy of economic and strategic orientation to South East Asia. The heart of this policy is to situate the country's remote northeast in India's engagements with the 'Tiger economies' of south-east Asia. Connectivity holds the key to doing "Act East" through northeast—with physical connectivity linking northeast to Myanmar and the rest of South-east Asia. It is aimed to connectivity, cooperation and extension of India's reachability with immediate eastern neighbours and beyond ASEAN. A land route through the NER to South Asia is an essential component of India's broader "Look East' policy (LEP). Its domestic imperative is aimed to the economic development of the north eastern region. The "Look East is more than a political slogan or a foreign policy orientation," as Natwar Singh, former Foreign Minister, said in the India-ASEAN Business Summit in New Delhi, October 2004 (Kumara, 2005).

In response to India's eastern oriented policy, the ASEAN especially by Thailand and Vietnam, the Look West Policy (LWP) was announced in 1997. The LWP of these two countries was aimed to access to emerging market of South Asia specially India and Bangladesh. Prime

Minister Narendra Modi announced a parallel vision – the Act East Policy (AEP) which is specifically geared to India's northeast. He described the northeast as the "Gateway to India" for two way flow of trade, tourism and investment from and to countries contiguous to its borders (The Frontier Dispatch, 2016:3). The expectation at the minimum from the AEP is that of substantial increase of cross border traffic in people and goods. It is indeed the objective of AEP to gradually transform the NER into a connectivity zone and from there into a development zone. In other words as trade and commerce, tourism and travel improve with better connectivity, the AEP will lead to productive partnerships across the board and transform the NER from a "No Go" area into one which is developed with the people's welfare at its core (The Frontier Dispatch, 2016:4). Under the Act East Policy, the immediate priority is to build the required infrastructure right up to the border areas in the NER. Establishing connectivity and communication links to the cross-border points through which trade and economic exchanges with the countries neighbouring and the NER. It also involves promoting Indian investment in infrastructure in partner countries, especially Myanmar, particularly in respect of Kaladan Transit route and tri-national highways to connect the NER to ASEAN.

The Kaladan project can be a practical way to materialize its "Look (Act) East Policy' for NER. It will also explore many benefits of transit connectivity with ASEAN, Myanmar in particular. The Kaladan project is also projected as a promising way to materialize ASEAN's LWP of connecting and integrating with South Asian economies. As it will enhance the connectivity among the NER, Bangladesh and Myanmar would mitigate geographical disadvantage of, and open new opportunities for the three regions. Therefore, to considering the strategic role of NER and Myanmar, the Kaladan project for Myanmar and NER can be the core of the regional strategy to enhance ASEAN-India connectivity.

Status of ASEAN's Inland Waterway Transport Connectivity

The ASEAN region is generously endowed with some 51,000 km navigable inland waterways playing an active role in transport development, especially in Vietnam, Cambodia, Lao PDR, Myanmar and Thailand. Some are canals and single river, while others form parts of major deltas. The Lancang-Mekong River is famous in the world for its enormous contribution to the national and regional inland waterway transport system (IWT). Others, including the Thanlwin River in Myanmar, the Chao Phraya River in Thailand and the Red River in Vietnam, are also important for inland waterway transportation (ERIA Study Team, 2010:3.1-3.95).

The ASEAN's regional inland waterways play a vital role in the economic development of the region. The inland waterway is a cost-effectiveness, relative fuel efficiency (see to the Figure 7.1) and environment friendly. It has importance for the mobility, welfare and development of remote communities in several countries of the region. River freight also involves much lower external costs associated with noise and air pollution, infrastructure investment, congestion and accidents. Waterway is cheaper than other modes of transportation. Coastal shipping and inland water transport is a fuel efficient, environment friendly and cost effective, especially for bulk goods. While the road transportation cost per km is 1.50 and for the Railways it is Rs.1, for waterways, it would be 25 to 30 paisa (Mishra 2016).

Figure 7.1: Energy efficiency: Distance that one tonne of freight can be moved with one litre of fuel by various mode of transport

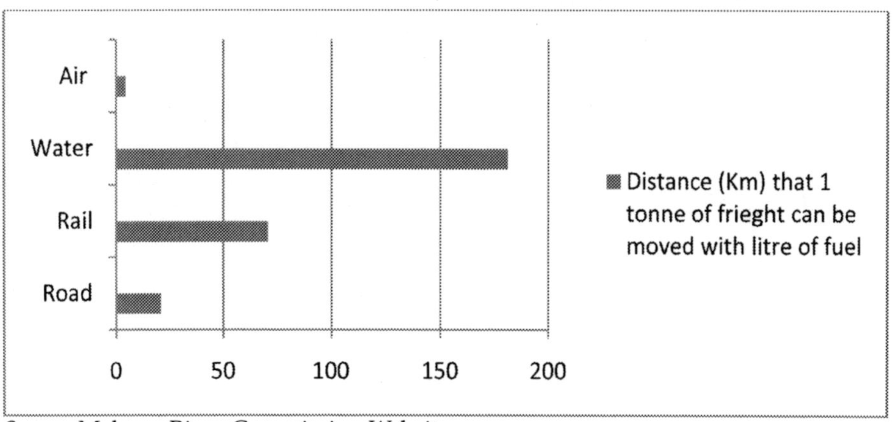

Source: Mekong River Commission Website

The network of main navigable waterways in Myanmar comprises the following river systems: the Ayeyarwady, Chindwin, Sittoung, Kaladan, Leinmyo, Thanlwin, Gyaing and Ataran systems. These rivers, with their numerous tributaries, offer 6,650 km of commercially navigable waterways. There are approximately 400 river stations on the Ayeyarwady and Chindwin systems, of which 16 are larger ports, each with an annual cargo handling capacity of at least 40,000 tons. Owing to the relatively poor coverage of road and rail, large areas along the Ayeyarwady and Chindwin valleys are accessible only by water. Hence IWT has the largest share of the cargo volume transported in Myanmar. It is estimated that nearly five million tons of cargo and 45.8 million passengers are transported by IWT annually (ERIA Study Team 2010:3.1-4.95)

Highest density of the world's inland waterway of transport system is found in ASEAN region. More than 30 per cent of all-kind of transportation is inland waterway among four ASEAN countries – Thailand, Vietnam, Cambodia, and Laos. ASEAN highway transport system is constituted a part of Trans-Asian Highway. It is quite interesting to note the continuation of certain Highway links across the sea/river and their connectivity by 'Ferry Links'. Thailand has 13 highway linkages with four neighbouring States (Cambodia, Lao PDR, Malaysia and Myanmar), which is also the highest among ASEAN members states. This is followed by Lao PDR and Malaysia (ERIA Study Team 2010:3.1-5.95).

In-land water way transportation is only 3.5 percentage of all-kind of transportation in India while in ASEAN region it is 35 percentages. It is noted that despite sharing its border, Lao PDR and Myanmar do not have any direct highway linkages between them. The AH-2 and AH-3 passing through Thailand connects both the nations. To facilitate transportation of goods in transit, support the implementation of the ASEAN Free Trade Area (AFTA), and further integrate the region's economies, priority routes classified as 'Transit Transport Routes (TTR)' were identified. The 35 sections on various ASEAN Highways across ASEAN Member States were designated as TTR. In Myanmar, the inland waterways share is higher than the road in ASEAN countries. This may be due to large navigable river length and existence of poor quality of roads in Myanmar (ERIA Study Team, 2010:3.1-6.95).

Sittwe Port and Kaladan River: Physical Profile

Sittwe, formerly called Akyab is a town on Western Myanmar. Sittwe is the capital city of Rakhine State in Myanmar. It is the chief settlement of the Arakan region. It is situated on the Bay of Bengal (BoB) at the mouth of the Kaladan River on the Paton Penninsula at the confluence of river Kaladan into BoB. Sittwe occupies the eastern side of a hilly ridge of Arakan Hills affording shelter from the southwest monsoon. After the cession of Arakan to the British in 1826, Sittwe replaced Myohaung as the region's seat of government and rapidly grew from a small fishing village into a leading port of Burma. Although heavily damaged during World War II, the port was rebuilt, and it handles both coastal and international trade. Sittwe is the site of a dockyard, diesel electric plant and several rice mills. It has air transportation service and a regular ferry links it with Chittagong in Bangladesh. The town is at the confluence of the Mayu, Kaladan and Lemro rivers—all navigable.

The river Kolodyne—also known as Chhimtuipui in Mizoram—emanates from central Mizoram and ends in Bay of Bengal at Sittwe—a port in Myanmar. The Kaladan river is navigable within Myanmar from its confluence point at Sittwe to Paletwa. Beyond that point, the shallow eaters and sharp curves make navigation infeasible. Lomusau is the India border point in Myanmar is 62km away from Paletwa. The Kolodyne River is also known by name of Kaladan and Sittwe is also called by name of Akyab in Myanmar.

Chhimtuipui and Lungleng rivers as the two tributaries of Kolodyne riverine Mizoram. The Kolodyne river flows from India's Mizoram to Sittwe through Haka, the capital city of Chin state in Myanmar. Kaladan River is the largest inland water way in India's southern Mizoram, Chin and Rakhine states of Myanmar. The coastal region in western Myanmar is separated from the mainland by the Rakhine Yoma mountain range. The Sittwe, at the mouth of the Kaladan River in Rakhine coast is an important harbor, which emerged as a center for rice export after British occupation in 1826. (Rochhamliana, 2008: 248).

Strategic Importance of Sittwe Port

It seems that wrong judgment is being made by the partition-era politicians who agreed to give away non-Muslim majority areas like Chittagong Port and the surrounding areas to Pakistan. It left India's own north eastern region landlocked, resulting in its isolation, the disruption of its traditional trade route and subsequent plunge into insurgency. Moreover, Bangladesh – which owes its very existence and survival to India rather choose to play by allowing its soil to be used as a sanctuary for anti-India terrorists and refusing to give India permission to use its territory to transit to the northeast. Bangladesh has turned down several requests by India to allow river transport transit from the northeast to the sea, compelling India to explore Sittwe in Myanmar, and focus is on developing Kaladan river transit route.

By the time the Sittwe Port is ready, Kaladan will become fully navigable and the connectivity of the rest of India with the north eastern region and ASEAN would improve significantly. Given the 1640-km land border with Myanmar, and the shared maritime space in the Bay of Bengal (BoB), India believes it does not have the luxury of elevating its commitment to democratic values above the immediate economic and strategic interests there. Former Minister for development of north eastern region (DoNER) Mani Shankar Aiyar says, "Bangladesh's refusal to permit transit facilities to India and its turning down repeated requests to use the Chittagong Port for NER will be history" (Rochhamliana, 2007).

The former External Affairs Minister, Pranab Mukherjee also highlights the importance of connectivity and trade between the NER and neighbours. As he says, "Geography is opportunity and the very geographical location of the NER makes it the doorway to ASEAN and *vice versa,*—a doorway for these economies into India" (Sarkar, 2007). India's determination to quicken the pace of implementation of the Kaladan project comes amidst the recent decision in Beijing to build an energy pipeline from the South Western province of Yunnan to the Sittwe Port. Through the Kaladan project, India would be in able to counter Chinese influence and geopolitical strategic position in Myanmar.

The Sittwe port is well connected to the Shwe gas bloc area that had been developed by China. India also has some significant gas stakes in these blocs. Both countries had set up a joint venture to extract gas from here. China had already installed a gas pipeline from the Shwe to Yunnan province. India also has a plan to bring gas from the Shwe gas reserve up to NER through pipeline along with Kaladan trade route. It is noted that officially the construction work of Kaladan project commenced from December 2010. But yet to be it completed, while, China's energy pipeline project had been already completed in 2014 (Jangu, 2016:136).

India's NE-Bangladesh's Chittagong—Myanmar's Sittwe: An Economic Strategic Tri-Juncture

For India and Bangladesh, Myanmar's 'geo-strategic location' at the tri-junction of South Asia, Southeast Asia and India's north eastern region is of critical significance. Four Indian States—Mizoram, Manipur, Nagaland and Arunachal—share borders with Myanmar. Similarly four Myanmar's States—Rakhine, Chin, Kachin and Sagaing—also share border with India and Bangladesh. Moreover, the border between Bangladesh (Chittagong Track) and Rakhine State is also crucial from India's perspective because it provides an alternative and a crucial route to Myanmar and ASEAN. Major factors that draw India's attention to Kaladan project are the problem of the NER's landlocked situation. Bangladesh is reluctant to give India a transit route to connect NER with the mainland.

India wants Myanmar to ensure that the area west of Chindwin River remains free of Chinese influence. It is important to seek stability on the north eastern border by ensuring economic prosperity of the region especially in view of the fact that it is a land-bridge to the south-east Asian region. Indo-Myanmar bilateral relationship is much important to India since India's LEP is destined to shape India's attitude towards the Asia Pacific for the foreseeable future. The President Pranab Mukherjee recently said that India's LEP has been the main driving force for improvement in the bilateral relations. Having understood the geopolitical potential of northeast, the then External Affairs Minister, Pranab Mukherjee, had laid emphasis on the economic significance of the geographical location of the region, through his 'Geography as Opportunity" in Shillong. He says:

> With the paradigm shift from state centralism to interdependence and global and regional cooperation, India is aware of the geo-political potential of the NER as a gateway to East and Southeast Asia. I am convinced that by gradually integrating this region through cross-border market access, the NER can become the bridge between the Indian economy and what is beyond doubt the fastest growing and dynamic region in the world (Pudiate, 2010:137).

Myanmar has realized that it is being stifled by China, must look for an alternative in India—particularly in view of India's rising economic potential and her LEP and mutual strategic and security interests. Myanmar also plays an important role in the economic reinforcement of India's LEP in general and NER in particular. The tri-juncture of Chittagong, NER and Sittwe is an India's gateway to ASEAN as it is the only juncture of India-Bangladesh-Myanmar which shares a land and maritime boundary with South Asia and Southeast Asia. Bangladesh has also shown its interest to join in India's Kaladan project. The project will also open opportunities for Bangladesh specially to access the market of India's NER. With India becoming a summit level partner of ASEAN, democratic reforms in Myanmar, Myanmar joined SAARC as an economic partner, increasing deeper relations between India and Bangladesh, etc. developments compelled India to expand her economic relations with Myanmar and ASEAN.

The dependence on "chicken neck" and the expectation on the Kaladan project in connecting the NER and the mainland India have roots in the strained relationship between India and Bangladesh. The trilateral trade of India, Myanmar and Bangladesh will pass through the Kaladan transit route, the landscape of the three regions would be changed dramatically. As India and Bangladesh have already reached to an agreement to transit trade through inland waterway in Bangladesh, the efficiency and volume of trilateral trade would be increased significantly.

Kaladan Project: Origin and Plan

The Kaladan Project is a flagship project of India in Myanmar. It is conceived and proposed by India's Ministry of External Affairs (MEA) in 2003. The project has already received approval from the Government of Myanmar. Meanwhile, India obtained in-principle approval from former Planning Commission too. Finally in 2004, India and Myanmar signed an agreement on Kaladan project. In April 2006, an inter-ministerial meeting convened by the MEA decided to designate Hmawngbou in Lawngtlai District of Mizoram as the Trade Point on the India side near to Kolodyne River on the India's border with Myanmar. During 19-21 January 2007, in Myanmar, the then Foreign Minister Pranab Mukherjee and Myanmar's Minister for Planning and Economic Development discussed on the Kaladan project in respect of investments (Ministry of External Affiars, Government of India 2007). The project was conceived by New Delhi and formalized under its Look East Policy in 2008. The main goal of the project is to develop trade with Myanmar and other Southeast Asian nations. But between 2004 and 2008, the project could not have commenced due to differences between India and Myanmar. These differences were related to the control rights over the Sittwe port and Paletwa's transshipment station once the project is ready to open. The initial total estimated cost of the project was reported to be US$ 214 million out of which Government of Myanmar was to provide US$ 10 million and the rest by the Government of India (Rochhamliana, 2008:254).

However, exhibiting India's keen interest over the project, on 19 January, 2009, the Government of India superseded the previous decision, and a decision was taken to extend Myanmar a soft loan of US$10 million at an annual interest of 2.5 percent to cover the expenses of its share of the Kaladan project. In 2009, the Inland Waterways Authority of India (IWAI) was appointed the project development consultant by the ministry of external affairs, the nodal agency for India. On the Myanmar side, the ministry of foreign affairs is the nodal agency. One more hurdle the project faced was related to financial sharing between the two countries. This was again delayed the project for two years (between 2008 and 2010), final it was resolved in mid-2010 that India will bear the entire expenditure of the project (Business Standard 2015). But, State Peace and Development Council (SPDC) of Myanmar later conveyed its inability to fulfill its commitment of US$10 million. SPDC has though consented on the proposal, but showed reluctance to invest in the project, and only assured to provide free land and security for the project.

So, the Government of India has agreed to provide the amount in the form of a Line of Credit (LoC) to the Myanmar Government. But India even that could not did because there was the US's pressure on India not giving LoC to an undemocratic government in Myanmar. But later, during the visit of A.P.J. Abdul Kalam to Myanmar, he announced the decision of India agreeing to provide the amount in the form of LoC (Thakuria, 2007 and 2014). In April 2008, 535 crore rupees was approved for the Kaladal project, but it was revised in October 2015 around 3000 crore rupees (Bhushan, 2016).

Kolodyne project is the strategic edifice that India is building with Myanmar over the past seven years of time. It is an important trans-border infrastructure project that will let the land-locked north eastern region gain easy access to the Bay of Bengal through Myanmar. It envisages a Multi-model Transit Transport Corridor and, building of an energy pipeline that will bring natural gas from Myanmar via NER to the whole India. The feasibility study, carried out in 1999-2000, brought out that river Kolodyne is navigable from its confluence point with the Bay of Bengal (BoB), near Sittwe up to Kaletwa on its north. Beyond, Kaletwa, towards India's Mizoram border, the river is not navigable owing to shallow water depth and frequent rapids. The transport by road is, therefore, proposed for this stretched. The proposed road link from Kaletwa in Myanmar on NH54 forms a part of proposed development of the trade route along the river Kolodyne between Mizoram and Chin state in Myanmar. The last village on the Kaladan project is Zochachhuiah in Mizoram state where the Kaladan Highway enters Myanmar (Lalthanfeli, 2010).

The project was finalized when international community's attention remained fixed on pro-democracy movement in Myanmar, India and Myanmar gave final touches to the Kaladan project. It shown India's determination to bring the project on ground, so therefore, India went ahead and did not hesitate on signing the agreement with Myanmar. By that way, India paved the way for development of the Sittwe Port, an important component for the implementing LEP. Out of the three components of the Kaladan project – road, water and port; the source of continuing disagreement was the control of the port. India's desire to control the port is backed by its massive financial commitment. However, when Myanmar expressed its reservations over India's proposal of developing the port on build-operate-transfer mode (Mujtaba 2007), India softened its stand and offered the former right of immediate use of the Sittwe Port once it is ready for navigational purposes and agreed to hand over the port soon after its completion. The new offer made by India to Myanmar is a major shift in India's strategic approach. It also gives an idea of the level it can go to in accommodating Myanmar's sensitivities.

The Kaladan Multi-Model Transit Transportation: A Strategic Route

On 21st April 2016, Chin State Chief Minister PuLianLuai in Myanmar informed that with INR 20 billion funding from Indian government, Myanmar is building an arterial highway to connect Kaletwa in south Chin state to 645km away from Chikha sub-town in northern Chin state. This Kaletwas-Chikha highway will also be connected to the

Map 7.2: A Bird View of Kolkata-Chhattagong-Kaladan Transit-Route-Sittwe Port

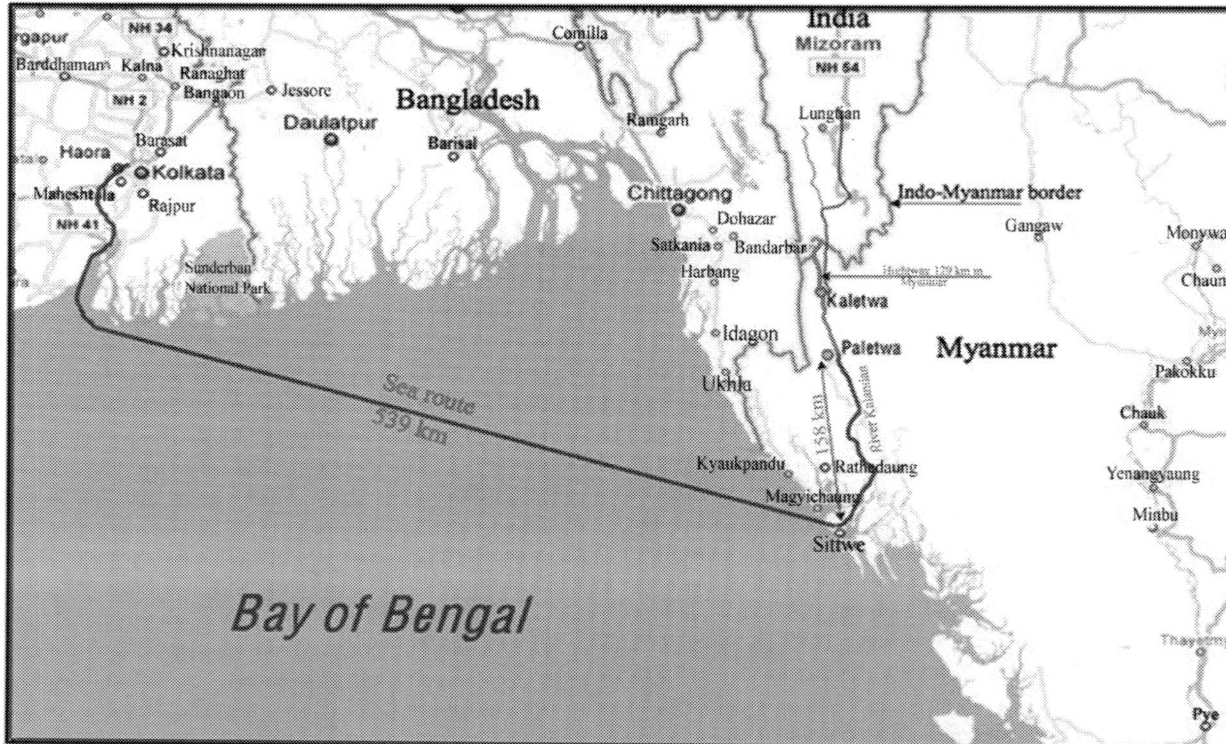

Source: http://www.scribd.com/kaladana-project/

National Highway 502 in India at two places on the Indian border. Paletwa to Zochachhuah on NH502A in south-west Mizoram and at the Khenman in Myanmar to NH502A Behiang in east Mizoram (Mukherjee, 2016). These two National Highway on India-Myanmar border in Mizoram and national highway of Myanmar on India-Myanmar border in Chin State will also be ground for India-Myanmar border train route connecting Moreh in Manipur via Mizoram to Paletwa in Myanmar. There is a possibility of extending rail connectivity from Jawaharnagar in Tripura to Kalay in Myanmar via Mizoram (257km). This train route will also soon be connected with Bangladesh's railway system once the elevated Akhaura-Agartala rail link is completed by end of 2017(Bhomik, 2016).

Technical Feasibility of Kaladan Project

MEA has entrusted Rail India Technical Economic Service (RITES) for presentation of Detailed Project Report (DPR) for the Kaladan project. It has submitted its reports to the MEA in October 2003. Finally, India and Myanmar signed the agreement for the development of the Kaladan project in April 2004. The feasibility study recommended Sittwe to Kaletwa to be waterway and Kaletwa to India-Myanmar Border and from Lomasu to Lawngtlaias roadway. The main components of the project are:

1. Development of Terminal at Sittwe Port
2. Development of Inland Waterway transit route from Sittwe to Kaletwa (160km)
3. Development of Roadway from Kaletwa to Lomasu on India-Myanmar border (62km)
4. Development of Highway from Mizoram-Myanmar border upto Lawngtlaiin Mizoram (109km)

Development of terminal at Sittwe Port basically means development of Port and Inland Water Transport (IWT) facilities at Sittwe including berths for ships and IWT vessels, cargo handling system, covered and open storages and other infrastructure facilities. Planning of facilities proposed at Sittwe Port has been carried out considering the following:

1. Annual volume of cargo: 1,00,000 tons
2. Type of cargo: break-bulk or general cargo

3. Average ship size: 6,000 DWT (initial) 20,000 DWT (ultimate)
4. Berth Occupancy: 50 per cent
5. Draft alongside Jetty: 7.2m (initial) 9.5m (ultimate)
6. Physical dimensions of Port Jetty: 219m × 15.2m
7. Transportation Equipment: 4 tractors, 16 trailers and 4 fork lift trucks
8. Total backup area requirement: 140m × 120

Besides these, handling equipment at port jetty (landing straggle or small pier) is proposed to be one general cargo crane of 10 ton capacity with a maximum outreach of 25.5m with hook attachment suitable for general cargo operations. Two types of vessels – Sea vessel and IWT vessel are proposed for this port.

Proposal for development of inland waterway system includes:

1. A minimum depth of 2m is available from Sittwe to Paletwa
2. Deepening, widening and other river training works are required further upstream up to Paletwa
3. Blasting of rocks, outcrops and removal of landslides and sand shoals at specific locations along river course.
4. Installing six barges of vessels at river bank
5. Transshipment IWT terminal at Kaletwa.

Detail proposal for development of Highway includes the following:

1. Project road length: 68km (Kaletwa to Lomasu at India-Myanmar Border) and 85km (from Lomasu to NH-54 inLungtlai town)
2. Carriageway width: 3.75m (Kaletwa to Lomasu at India-Myanmar Border) and 3.75m (India-Myanmar border to NH-54)
3. Roadway width: 8.8m (Kaletwa to India-Myanmar border) and 8.8m (India-Myanmar border to nh-54)
4. Culverts: 387nos (Kaletwa to India-Myanmar border) and 461nos (India-Myanmar border to NH-54)
5. Bridges: 11nos (Kaletwa to India-Myanmar border) and 2nos (India-Myanmar border to NH-54). (For more details visit http://mdoner.gov.in/print/content/introduction).

Figure 7.3: A Physical and Economical outlines of the KMTTP

Source: http://www.thehindu.com/1232344/03/04/2008/

Economic Implications of Kaladan Project to NER and ASEAN

Although, India-ASEAN trade significantly increased in the recent years, still the progress is slow. In opinion of scholars that one of major obstacles to the expansion of trade between India and ASEAN is that the high cost of moving goods across the borders. It reflects in scholars' works that insufficient infrastructure for physical connectivity in both sides. The share of India in Myanmar's border trade is 1.6 per cent and Myanmar's share in India's border trade is 8.7 per cent. Myanmar's border trade with India has been slow as compared to those with China and Thailand. The border areas are mountainous, and the road infrastructure is generally insufficient to accommodate a large amount of international trade (Umezaki, 2012).

Perhaps, the government of India realized that the future of the NER lays in political integration with the mainland India and economic integration with Southeast Asia. The ongoing construction work of Falam airport in Chin State near to Champai district of Mizoram will provide air connectivity between Aizawl and Imphal in the NER. It will also provide an important connectivity between Sittwe port and north Chin State in Myanmar (Hla 2017). Jairam Ramesh, former

Minister of Commerce, Government of India during his Mizoram visit spoke on the great economic significance of the Kaladan Project. India will invest to develop the Sittwe Port and improve navigability on the Kolodyne River in Myanmar. This would enable the opening of another route for trade between the northeast and the rest of India with southern Mizoram as the hub (Ramesh, 2005).

The Kaladan project is considered as a cornerstone of India-Myanmar economic ties. People are anxious to see the project materialize. It is observed that the project would make economic ties between the two regions (India's NER and Myanmar) "meaningful' (Win, 2017). It will make an alternative route for trade between the NER and rest of the world. The existing border trade between the NER and Myanmar is limited because of certain infrastructural constraints. There would be need of massive transport related facilities to meet the needs after the opening of Kaladan project. Storehouses, godowns, cargo-platforms, fueling stations, truck parking spaces and other lodging and transport facilities are to be constructed at Lawngtlai, Aizawl and other pickup and drop points in Mizoram.

For the wider road transport connectivity from Lawngtlai Kaladan Project highway to the rest of NER, two more road routes would be required. One road route may be from Lawngtlai to Tripura passing through Mamit district, and second, may be from Lawngtlai to Manipur passing through Champai district in Mizroam. One more road route as the existing highway between Aizawl to Lawngtlai would be required to upgrade to connect Silchar in Assam. A Food Park was recently set up on the outskirts of Imphal marks a good beginning that can be further expanded and specialized. It could also become a processing center for fruits, pulses and other agricultural products that can be imported from Myanmar. Similar Parks could be set up elsewhere in the NER including for spices and medicinal herbs. As two more such Parks have been set up in Tripura and Nagaland each. Economic implication of Kaladan Project in the NER would be followings:

1. Economic exchange between the NER and ASEAN will increase
2. Physical connectivity between the two regions will improve
3. Economic and development activities will increase within the NER

The region's specialty in creating bamboo and wood based handcrafted items and uniquely designed hand woven textile items are popular among Myanmar customers. Small scale industries such as those making farm implements and tools, stationery, plastic extrusion items, carpentry units, could also develop markets beyond the border. There is need of setting up at least one multi-product Special Economic Zone (SEZ) on the connecting border points in four states as Tripura, Mizoram, Manipur and Nagaland. Myanmar has the lowest rail connectivity in ASEAN countries; it wants to develop its railway system, for this, it is looking towards India.

Map 7.4: Kaladan Multi-model Transit Transport Project: A projected outline of the route

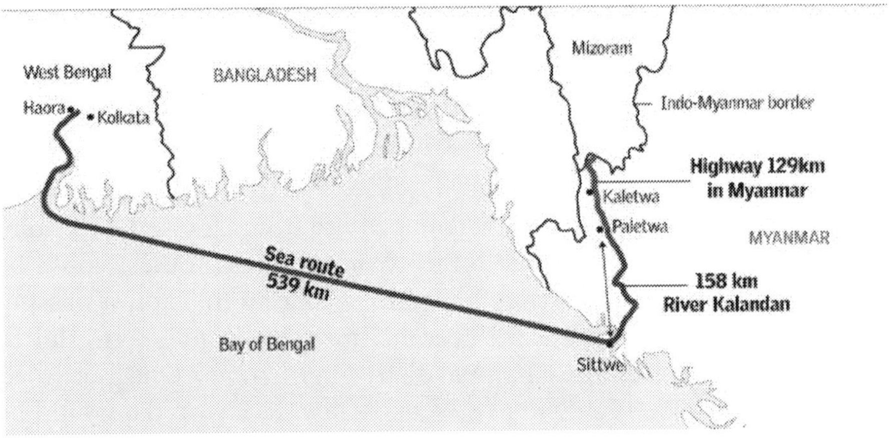

Source: http://en.m.wikipedia.org/wiki/Kaladan_Multi_Modal_Transit_Transport_Project

There can be collaboration in the modernization of Myanmar's Railway Locomotive factory in Sagaing region and the Coaches factory in Mandalay region. India can invest to taking over and revamping existing textile mills in Myanmar. India can establish garments making units in Mizoram and Manipur that can be exported to Myanmar through inland waterway. The present commodity-basket between NER and ASEAN being fast-moving consumption goods (FMCG) and flexi-volume are suitable for transportation by KMTT-way. The Kaladan transport corridor again throws up many opportunities. The NER states, particularly those which are closest to the Kaladan corridor, viz. Mizoram, Tripura and Silchar (Assam) would find added markets in the Rakhine and Chin States of Myanmar. The Kaladan project will also provide one more model of transport as 'gas pipeline' between the NER and Myanmar. To bolster ties with Myanmar, the Inland Waterways Authority of India (IWAI) has entered into an agreement with India Ports Global Private (IPGP) to facilitate inland waterways and ports. This agreement is aimed to explore and facilitate more inland waterways and ports between India and Myanmar (*Economic Times*, June 20, 2016).

Economic implication of Kaladan Project on India and Myanmar relations would be followings:

1. India will success to counter Chinese influence in Myanmar
2. It will make trade in favour to India and increase to trade diversity and basket
3. Myanmar will access the northeast region's market

Business community of both side, can set up joint or single ventures of manufacturing and processing units in their respective states close to Kaladan transport route. Such manufacturing set ups can access markets of NER and ASEAN through Kaladan transport route. Mizoram itself has a rich variety of horticulture and floricultural production, medicinal and spice products. The state boosts of over 12 per cent of India's bamboo production that can be used further development of bamboo based products and for setting up paper industry. The state's high literacy rate could be strength in attracting IT industry. A parallel gas pipeline from Shwe point in Myanmar to Lawngtlai in India's Mizoram state also has a possibility. Once the Kaladan project is executed, the private sector of India will invest in the NER and as well as in Myanmar. Indian investors have in recent years spent approximately 80 per cent of their FDI on mergers and acquisitions, which are rare in Myanmar (Bissinger, 2012:17).

The Rakhine and Chin states of Myanmar have several agricultural resources that could allow promote contract farming. Bamboo and fisheries offer significant scope for development. There are four newly established industrial zones viz. SEZ at PonnarKyun, Dawei, Thilawa and Kyaukphyu in Myanmar. These four SEZs offer opportunities of investment for Indian companies. Possibilities could also be explored for a large pulp and paper mill that can source bamboo from both Rakhine and Mizoram States.

Map 7.5: Inland waterway in north eastern India

Source: Lambert Conformal Conical Projection is prepared by Cartography and Reproduction at Cartographic Lab, IWAI, Noida, India.

Map 7.6: ASEAN-India vision of trade and investment

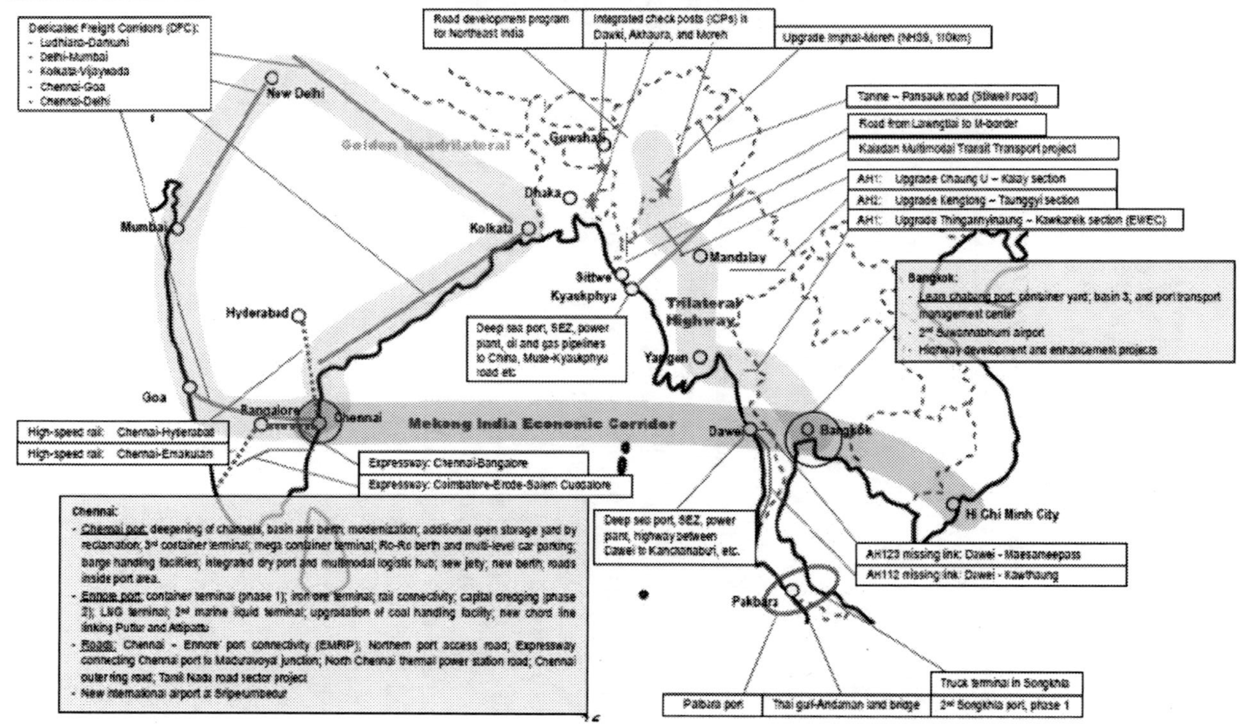

Source: http://aic.ris.org.in

Economic Implication of Kaladan Project in ASEAN would be followings:

1. ASEAN will access nearest market of India and South Asia
2. Look West Policy of ASEAN will come in action
3. It will work as a bridge between South East Asia and South Asia

As far as the NER's economic interaction with Myanmar is concerned, except low key trading activities, there is not much happening at the moment. NER's trade with Myanmar for the last 15 years (1998-2013) constitutes only 3.2 per cent of the NER's total trade with the neighbouring countries. Moreover, whatever legal trade takes place across India-Myanmar border mainly characterized by transit trade through border trade centers – buying and selling of third country/beyond the region originated goods (Das et al,. 2017). Major exports by the NER to Myanmar include cotton yarn, auto parts, soyabean meal, and pharmaceuticals products while major imports by India from Myanmar are betel-nut, dried ginger, green mung beans, black matpe, matpe, turmetric roots, resin and medicinal herbs. The current trade items between NER and Myanmar are mainly non-manufactured, unpolished, rough and raw material and rough packaging. There is not a single manufacturing hub cross the border in either side (Choudhary, 2016). Unlike NER-Bangladesh trade, sizeable linkages between trade and local resource base have not been developed in the case of NER-Myanmar trade. One of the reasons for weak cross-border economic linkages appears due to the similarity of resource based and competitive trading interests between NER and Myanmar.

The Kaladan project, once completed, will address the much needed access to the seas for the landlocked northeast India. It will provide an access route to NER to reach out ASEAN market for the exportable products from the region. Ultimately, it will help fulfilling India's Act East Policy. Myanmar will benefit from additional revenue collected through goods going to India. It will also have a 225km long navigable waterway for development of transportation based economic infrastructural facilities (Dikshit, 2008).

The Kaladan Project: Problems and Progress

The speed of work progress of the Kaladan project is very slow. Its annual growth rate is between 7-10 per cent; till May month of 2016, as before the beginning of monsoon season, the work progress was 66 per cent and it made progress only four percent during June 2016 to March 2017 and next monsoon as on its schedule on first June 2017. Actually progress used to make during six months of time in 12 months; the work progress in eight months is to be almost 1-2 per cent due to monsoon. The construction works of these two links between Kaletwa and Lawngtlai are going slow that is reason of being delay in the completion of the project. This delay was due to problem in land acquisition process, environmental clearance and weather conditions (Lalthanfeli, 2010). There has been some opposition to the Kaladan project in Rakhine and Chin states of Myanmar and Mizoram in India.

The ongoing Anti-Kaladan movement is taking place under the banners of Arakan Rivers Network, Chin People Human Rights Organisation and Zo Indigenous Forum. The major reasons for opposition are: first, environment assessment is not done at any stage of the project, and second, consultation to local people those live on river bank is not taken for this project. Environment assessment for the dredging the river and setting up barges on the river for ship cargo was required (Bhushan, 2016).The following weak points are made on the basis of the author's field study, observation and collection of information from the various officials that involve in the Kaladana project.

1. Progress rate of this project is very slow as 7-10 per cent per year largely due to bad monsoon
2. Delay in the process of land accusation and obtaining environmental clearance to the project from the affected people especially in Sixth schedule area in Mizoram.
3. Environment movements under the banner Arakan River Network sometime halted the process of dredging in Kaladan river in Myanmar.
4. People's protest against the shifting the land-port point after the terminating river route from Paletwa to Kaletwa in Myanmar.
5. The dispute regarding control over Cargo point at Sittwe port

and Kaletwa point by Indian or Myanmarese authority after completing the project.

6. The National Highway—NH54 passes through the Sixth Scheduled Areas in Lawngtlai district of South Mizoram, getting public consent is very difficult and time taking process because local residents use to migrate during off season and return one month before monsoon.
7. Logistic and material supply for the construction is also slow and not timely.

Even as the two countries have given the final touch to the Kaladan project, the project was stagnated due to an issue of disagreement regarding the control over Sittwe Port between the two countries. Till now not a single connectivity project between the NER and Myanmar is completed. The Kaladan project is running delay more than four years than its scheduled time of completion. Now it will be completed by April 2019, almost five years later than its earlier schedule in 2014. On 19thApril 2016 Minister of State in the Ministry of External Affairs, Government of India, General V K Singh informed that 66 per cent of the new two-lane-per-direction 12-meter-wide 99.83km National Highway 502A (NH502) starting from NH-54 at Lawngtlai to Zorinpui in Mizoram on Indian side will be completed by June 2018. Other aspects of the project including the port, waterways and 109km Lomasu on the India-Myanmar border to Kaletwa will be completed by April 2018.

Conclusion

This project will provide an alternative access route to NER of India and contribute towards the region's economic development. Being a key connectivity project, it will promote economic, commercial and strategic linkages between India and Myanmar. Completion of the Kaladan project assumes feat urgency as it will provide a vital component to the economic growth of the whole India's NER, offering a trade route—an outlet to tap the economic potential of India's immediate eastern neighbours. The Kaladan project gives an alternative key to unlock to landlocked NER with the rest of world especially immediate eastern neighbours after Siliguri's chicken neck corridor. It will give the most strategic interface link to Myanmar and Bangladesh through the NER's transit land route.

Its economic implication would be multiple and multi-model of connectivity to the ASEAN countries to access India's market through the NER. Kaladan project is going to be a trade route between India and Myanmar. It will also be the first trade route between South Asia and South East Asia regions. It will be a unique route of trade through water and land between two neighbours. The project is likely to be accomplished by the end of 2019. This multi-model transit links between the NER of India and Myanmar will pave the way for enhanced trade and commerce across the border and enable cultural and social integration at the regional level.

The trade route should also bolster India's economic ties with other Southeast Asian countries, while benefiting the 60 million people of the land-locked NER of India. Besides trade, the project seeks to expand Indian economic and political influence in ASEAN region. The Kaladan project will be an interface link between South East Asia and South Asia regions. It will also reduce the Chinese economic and strategic influence in this sub-region. The geo-strategic location of the region is pregnant with potential for the development of transit corridor with the ASEAN region. Therefore, we expect that the Act East phase of the LEP needs to factor into this dimension of the NER-ASEAN sub-regional development cooperation as a strategy for the promotion of development interests of the NER. This project will also be a ground for trans-regional railway connectivity among Bangladesh, India's NER and Myanmar.

INITIATIVES FOR COOPERATION

8

Liberalization and States' Quest for External Trade and Foreign Investment: Status of North Eastern States

H. Srikanth

Introduction

Federal states came into existence to protect the unity of the country and at the same to accommodate regional and cultural diversities (Elazar, 1987; Norman and Karmis, 2005; Benz and Broschek, 2013; Ward and Ward, 2009). Federal set ups have two or more levels of government, each deriving its powers from division of powers enshrined in the countries' Constitution. The history and compulsions of forming federal governments vary. In the classical case of the USA, Canada and Australia, independent states came together to form federal structure by delegating some of their powers to federal government, but without sacrificing their autonomy. In other cases, federal states came into existence as the countries out of their own necessity chose to institute two or three tiers of government and made constitutional division of powers between them. In classical federal set ups, the states are as powerful as federal governments. But in case of countries like India, Pakistan, Spain, etc., the central governments have an edge over provincial governments. Earlier some scholars working on federalism observed that in the post-Second World War, with the emergence of welfare and developmental states, federal governments started becoming more powerful in all federations. This line of thinking is however contested in recent years with the onset of liberalization and globalization. With federal governments choosing to take the back seats, leaving economic development to market forces, the constituent governments at regional levels began taking their own initiatives to negotiate agreements with foreign countries for economic development of their own regions and play bigger roles in shaping the foreign policies of the governments. To explain these changes in the powers, mode of operations and relations between federal and constituent governments, the scholars have come out with new concepts or ideas, such as para-diplomacy, constituent diplomacy, localization of foreign policy, multi-layered diplomacy, etc.(Hazarika, 2014; Sinha, 2017; Tewari and Pant, 2016; Jenkins, 2003).

In case of India, which is officially referred to as the Union of States, the central government always had an advantage over state governments in terms of powers, resources and jurisdiction. The central government has control over major sources of revenue and the states depended on central government for additional resources. The Constitution of India assigned the responsibility of defence and foreign affairs exclusively to central government. State governments had little say in national foreign policy, except in matters relating to border policy making. All major decisions regarding foreign policy making and issues such as foreign investments and trade were decided by central governments, without involving the state governments (Heierstad, 2016).The states had to depend on central government for grants and loans to run the governments. In 1980s, protesting the marginalization of the states, different regional and national parties in power at the state level demanded greater share and greater autonomy to the states. However, it is only after the collapse of the Soviet Union, with India giving up its socialist garb and consciously opting for liberalization, one could notice changes in the working of Indian federation. In the last two decades, taking advantage of the changed national and international situation, some states like Gujarat, Maharashtra, Karnataka, Andhra Pradesh, etc., have begun taking pro-active roles in external affairs and foreign policy making.

Analysing the changing roles of central and state governments in India, the paper seeks to understand whether India's north eastern region which has international border with five neighbouring countries, would be able to explore trade and investment opportunities and replicate the success stories of the mainland states which pursued and promoted their own economic interests.

Changing Role of States in External Affairs

More than the constitutional division of powers, it was the working of the one-party dominance system in India during the first three decades after independence that led to centralization of powers in the hands of central government. As long as the Congress Party dominance continued, many decisions affecting the state interests were taken without the consent of the state governments (Suryanarayan, 2014). During this period, non-Congress governments in power in different states fought for respectable treatment and greater access to resources. The situation, however, changed in 1990s with the onset of the era of coalition politics on the one hand and the beginning of the process of liberalization of economy on the other (Singh, 2011; Sinha, 2004, Baru, 2010, Bagchi, 2008, Jacob, 2016; MEA, 16). Lack of required majority to form governments at the centre compelled the leading national parties to make coalitions with regional parties. This change increased the bargaining power of the state governments. State leaders like Chandrababu Naidu during the first NDA regime and Karunanidhi during the UPA regimes bargained for economic and political concessions. In 2013 on the issue of human rights violations, Tamilnadu threatened to leave the UPA government if India does not vote against Sri Lanka in UNHRC (Jacob, 2016). More recently, Mamata Banerjee refused to toe the central government's line on Teesta River water dispute and took on the BJP leadership even though it was not a partner in the NDA government (Tewari and Pant, 2016).

However, more than the coalition governments, liberalisation of economy has empowered the states by creating new options for development (Ray, 1992). Removal of restrictions on market forces and withdrawal of the central government from active interventionist and welfare role, have compelled and at the same time facilitated the states' increasing economic role abroad. The state governments began to scout for external agencies/institutions to provide loans or aid to their economic programs and development projects in their states. To attract external foreign investments and promote trade and facilitate technological transfers, the state governments have started vying with one another liberalizing their economies and offering incentives of different kinds to attract foreign investments. To attract foreign investments, almost all states came out with what they christened as New Economic or Industrial Policy, promising easy clearances, less bureaucratic procedures, offer of land, electricity, water and other infrastructure, tax incentives, and assured profits. States like Gujarat, Andhra Pradesh, Karnataka and Telangana have set up separate cells/ forums to attract NRI investments into the states invoking linguistic and regional loyalties (Tewari and Pant, 2016). Some states like Kerala, Punjab, Telangana, etc., established Foreign Ministries of their own to promote foreign investments with the help of NRIs belonging to the respective communities/states. It has now become very common to see Chief Ministers of different states visiting different foreign countries along with their state ministers and businessmen from their states to promote trade, investment, technology transfers, promotion of tourism, expansion of infrastructure, etc., in their respective states. States like Gujarat, Maharashtra, Karnataka and Andhra Pradesh have proved successful in receiving major chunk of foreign investments into their states and creating jobs in certain sectors of economy.

Role of Central Government in Emerging Federal Relations

The pro-active role of some of the states in foreign policy making should not mislead one to the view that central government has become less important in the changed circumstances. Still the central government continues to play important roles to facilitate the states' initiatives in external affairs. Centre is still the final authority in foreign affairs, having the responsibility of regulating commercial activities and protecting the 'national interests' (Hazarika, 2014).No states can take up any initiatives with foreign countries that are perceived as inimical to the security and integrity of the Indian state. Central guarantee is still crucial for any state initiatives with foreign countries. On their part, most foreign agencies also do not enter agreements with state governments without sovereign guarantee from Government of India. By pursuing liberalization policies, the centre has provided a window of opportunities for states to pursue their economic diplomacy (USITC, 2015).

Central government provides institutional framework to link the states and the foreign diplomats. Recently the Ministry of External Affairs (MEA) has created States Division in Ministry of External

Affairs to facilitate interactions between state governments and foreign diplomats/investors. Every Indian ambassador is asked to specialize in two states, so that they could help liaison between state governments and foreign governments/potential foreign investors (MEA 2016). MEA has also started setting up Videsh Bhavans in different state capitals to house its branch secretariats, passport offices and emigration aid offices. Every year central government organize *Pravasi Divas*, 'Make in India' campaigns, etc., in different capitals to attract NRI investments into the states. Centre facilitates development of states by expanding infrastructural facilities, like expansion of telecommunication, information technologies, transport networks, etc.

Essential Conditions for Success of Constituent Diplomacy

The liberalization policies pursued by central governments from the time of P.V. Narasimha Rao to Narendra Modi have created certain conditions that enabled some states to take pro-active role in pursuit of their regional economic interests abroad. But here it needs to be noted that not all states in mainland India have not succeeded in their external missions (USITC, 2015). The study of the modus operandi of the states that successfully negotiated with foreign countries, attracted foreign investments, technological transfers and ensured job creation in certain sectors of economy would give us some idea of the essential conditions required for the states' success. The first and foremost is the existence of pro-active political leadership with neo-liberal orientation that can project the states as destinations for foreign investments. Narendra Modi in Gujarat, Chandrababu Naidu in Andhra Pradesh and more recently K. Chandrasekhar Rao in Telangana have emerged as icons who have sought to attract the attention of foreign investors with their pro-business initiatives. However, no amount of publicity will help in attracting foreign investment, if the states do not have the necessary infrastructure, technological base and human resources. The states should have effective roadways, railway network, air and sea connectivity, hospitality industry, etc., to be able to attract the investors' attention. Further, the investors expect the state governments to demonstrate that they assure good governance, free of corruption and red tape and ensure business environment that guarantee returns for their investments. The experience shows that the states which have witnessed the growth of regional bourgeoisie, conscious of its political and economic interests are likely to be more successful in their external missions. The NRIs that maintain close familial, cultural and economic relations with the states of their origin play a very important role in facilitating foreign investments. The existence of considerable number of resourceful NRIs in rich countries is proved a blessing to the states like Gujarat, Punjab, Karnataka, Andhra Pradesh, Telangana and Kerala. The states which have their own resources and are less dependent on the central governments for funds enjoy better chances of success in its external policies. Finally, the state governments' equations with central government also play a significant role in the states' capacities to explore and attract foreign investment. Good relations or effective bargaining power with central government helps. The success of some of the states mentioned above should not lead to the conclusion that all the states in the mainland India have benefitted from the liberalization process. In fact, the post-liberalization phase witnessed increased regional inequalities and differences in the levels of economic development of the states and their ability to attract foreign investments and markets (Ghosh, 2013; Das and Barua, 1996).

What North Eastern States Possess and What It Lacks

The discussion on the dynamics of successful states helps us to assess what north eastern states can or cannot do. True, the geographical location of the region and historical, cultural and linguistic affinities with countries they border provide certain opportunities to north eastern states to take advantage of the Look/Act East policy for economic development. In line with central government initiatives, the state governments in the north eastern region are also coming out with what they project as New Economic or New Industrial Policies, guaranteeing incentives for investment and trade (Government of Assam, 2014; Government of Manipur, 2011). However, whether the opportunities become actualities or not depend on several factors. Still there are many obstacles that need to be overcome, before the north eastern states take advantage of changing political economy of Indian federalism. As long as the governments and the peoples are obsessed with security concerns and suffer from xenophobia, there is little possibility of building friendly business relations with the neighbours. In the region, still historical and ethnic animosities overpower cultural and linguistic similarities between the people and the territories. Existence of same ethnic, cultural and linguistic groups on either side of the border could be an advantage, provided the communities are numerically more in number, economically strong and politically powerful. Unfortunately, the ethnic communities like the Khasis, Garos, Kukis, Nagas, even Bengali Hindus living on the other side of the borders are ethnic minorities who have limited powers in the countries of their habitation. They cannot be of much help in building strong bonds between the countries. Barring in Assam to some extent, other states do not have a strong indigenous/regional bourgeoisie that has base in industry, business and trade. Although some highly educated and successful individuals from the region are settled abroad, a number of such NRIs from the north eastern states are insignificant and they are of little help in mediating with foreign companies and attracting foreign investments into the region. The political parties in the region are led by middle classes who are ethno-centric in character.

Barring a couple of exceptions, the region lacks visionary political leadership that can plan and execute long term external linkages with neighbouring countries. Comparatively, a tiny state of Tripura under Manik Sarkar could take more initiatives to create environment for developing trade and business links with Bangladesh, compared to its counterpart Assam, wherein the leaders as well as the masses seem to be more concerned about foreign immigrants and border fencing than border connectivity. Political leadership in Manipur and Nagaland, mired in their own internal political and ethnic problems, is not in position to take full benefit of the states' connectivity with Myanmar. Not much progress is done in case of improving border trade with China, partly because of continuing animosities between India and China on the one hand and partly due to lack of inertia on the part of central government and state leadership in Sikkim and Arunachal Pradesh. Probably poor road conditions and lack of other infrastructural facilities leave little opportunities to Mizoram to take advantage of its borders with Bangladesh and Myanmar. Further, almost all states in the northeast are predominantly dependent on central funds for running administration and for undertaking developmental activities. Inadequate infrastructure, weak industrial and technological base, prevalence of corruption, absence of work culture, social unrest and feeble administration stand in the way of the states taking advantage of the process of liberalization. Finally, the weak bargaining power of the north eastern states at all India level and the inability of the state representatives to make their voices and concern heard in Delhi also affect the states' performance. In view of these ground realities, the north eastern states will not be able to take advantage of opportunities thrown open by changing nature of federal relations in the country, beyond a point.

Conclusion

The study proves that as on now the process of liberalization and the subsequent developments in federal relations have little significance to north eastern states. The states in the region are not in position to reap benefits out of liberalization process because of absence of basic conditions required for the states to 'take off'. The studies show that northern states together could not attract even one percent of the foreign investments flowing into the region. Between 2001-11 Assam and the northeast states together have attracted only 0.01% the total FDI inflow to India (Siddhanta, 2014; Neog, 2014).With unfavourable business environment, absence of regional bourgeoisie and insignificant NRIs from the region abroad, in the near future one cannot expect the north eastern states to secure foreign investments from the leading institutional agencies in a big way. Given the situation, for the success of its Look/Act East Policy, the central government should continue to play an important role for development of physical infrastructure and human resources in the region.

It is unfortunate that despite historical, cultural, linguistic and ethnic similarities, the north eastern states have not succeeded in developing better relations with the neighbours because of the security concerns and xenophobia. The state of Assam is economically more developed than rest of the states and had trade and cultural relations with Bangladesh. Yet their real or imaginary fear of Bangladeshis influx and their obsession with border fencing did not allow Assam to take advantage of their proximity to Bangladesh. Tripura was one of the states that was most affected because of the immigration from East Pakistan/Pakistan. However, by normalizing its relations with Bangladesh, the state government in Tripura under the leadership of Manik Sarkar was also successful in controlling illegal immigration, neutralizing tribal insurgencies and improving trade relations with

Bangladesh (Bhaumik, 2009; Dey, 2009). Contrasting experiences of Assam and Tripura show that effective governance, trust and confidence building measures should precede trade and business relations between the north eastern states and their neighbours. Physical connectivity makes little sense in the absence of trust and friendship. Gradual and small initiatives by state governments do help in strengthening the relations with neighbouring countries. Thailand and Bangladesh are more reliable trade partners and sources of investment (RIS, 2011; Balaji, 2016). In fact, much of the foreign investment into the northeast has come from Thailand and Bangladesh. Investments from China are still elusive (Neog, 2014; Goswamia and Saikiab, 2012). As is said, bird at hand is worth two in the bush. It therefore makes better sense for north eastern states focus more on their immediate neighbours than wait for big foreign investments to flow from the West or from China. However, such external initiatives should be accompanied by measures that strengthen physical, economic and emotional connectivity among the north eastern states. Producing only for external markets is risky. The northeast should concentrate on the areas in which it has comparative advantage and develop necessary industries, infrastructure and technical skill to produce those commodities which are sought both in the region and abroad (Goswamia and Saikiab, 2012). As most north eastern states are small, economically underdeveloped and politically weak, it is essential that the states in the region pool their resources and come together as one unit to negotiate with the central government and the neighbouring countries. Without conscious and concerted efforts of the states and peoples of the northeast, the initiatives such as Look/Act East policy are unlikely to have positive impact on the development of the region.

9

Initiatives of the State Governments in Forging Economic Ties Across the Border of Northeast India

Bidhan Barman and S. Basumatary

Introduction

India's relationship with Association of South-East Asian Nations (ASEAN) is a key pillar of our foreign policy and the foundation of our Act East Policy. ASEAN comprises of Indonesia, Singapore, Philippines, Malaysia, Brunei, Thailand, Cambodia, Lao PDR, Myanmar and Vietnam. India's focus on a strong and multi-faceted relationship with ASEAN is an outcome of the significant changes in the world's political and economic scenario since the early 1990s and India's own march towards economic liberalization. India's search for economic space resulted in the 'Look East Policy'. The Look East Policy has today matured into a dynamic and action oriented 'Act East Policy'. Prime Minister Sri Narendra Modi at the 12th ASEAN-India Summit and the 9th East Asia Summit held in Nay Pyi Taw, Myanmar, in November, 2014, formally enunciated the 'Act East Policy'. The upgraded look east policy to act east policy continues to be driven by economic and security interests. It is extended beyond Southeast Asia underlining the importance of the geopolitics of the region. It is therefore about renewed attempt at bolstering ties with the region, taking part in the emerging strategic discourse, etc. The north eastern states have to play vital role for the success of Act East Policy.

Statement of the Problem

The legal and formal arrangements for trade through northeast to southeast Asia are now more or less complete. But is north eastern region ready for it? This region is not yet economically as developed as the rest of India. After partition of India in 1947 northeast lost its natural trade routes through what is now Bangladesh. Its land connectivity with the rest of India remained limited to the 26 kms 'Chicken's neck' in northern West Bengal.

As far as trade itself is concerned many countries and regions in the world have become prosperous through trade. In fact, countries like Taiwan, South Korea, Hong Kong, Singapore and Malaysia have achieved their present status and level of development through trade. But what has northeast to offer to, say, China in exchange for the plethora of goods which that country is already exporting to this region. Industrial products are very limited. Agricultural products will need proper processing and packaging before the same can be exported. The service sector in northeast is not doing badly. But the quality is low. Tourism has not been so attractive because facilities are not up to the mark (Das 2011) and also because of media's projection of northeast security environment in very bad light.

There is no doubt that insurgency and illegal migration in northeastern states are big issues. The north eastern states have been affected badly by insurgency involving number of insurgent groups (Bhagawati, 2007). Even as a conducive socio-cultural atmosphere is a pre-requisite for economic development, the same has been violated due to insurgency in the region. Insurgency problem of north eastern states is a treat to social stability and stands as a barrier to economic development. Insurgency creates so many socio-economic, political problems to the society, which pull back the process of economic development of this region. There is historical evidence that the insurgency prone countries are economically and socially backward and their rate of economic development is very slow. The north eastern region has been suffering from this problem for a long period. The adverse effect of this problem is reflected in overall economic backwardness of this region.

An extremely concentrated endeavour will be required to achieve economic development of northeast and its principal state of Assam before northeast can be ready for participation in Look East Policy.

When the Thai trade delegation visited Assam in June, 2007, the Union Minister for Development of North Eastern Region (DONER) said that Rs.15,000 crores would be spent on infrastructure development in north eastern region in the Eleventh Five Year Plan. Unfortunately, nothing much has happened during the past 7 years. Another problem is the quality of the leadership in the northeast. It has not been visionary and has failed to tackle terrorism, militancy, insurgency and migration issue, which have further vitiated the climate for trade and investment.

It is illogical to talk about extending the linkages with Southeast Asia if there are no potential markets on the Indian in general and particularly in north eastern side of the border. The economic reforms, policies initiated by both Central and State governments do not complement the existing infrastructure in these states. The trade between India and ASEAN countries is mostly manufacturing products and is restrictive towards the agricultural products. Therefore, the north eastern states do not have the comparative advantage in India's export to ASEAN. In order to take the advantages of the growing trade alliances, effort should be on improving inter-state connectivity and market integration.

Method of Enquiry

The methodology of this paper is descriptive and the required information are collected from different secondary sources like books, memoranda, pamphlets, research articles, news paper, and government records.

Presentation of Data

The north eastern states account for only 8 per cent of India's geographical spread and a mere 4 percent of its 1.25 billion populations. The importance of the region obviously lies in its strategic location—surrounded by Bangladesh, Myanmar, China and Bhutan. In fact, 98 percent of northeast share borders with these neighbouring countries. Owing to historical, political and social reasons, the northeast has been in the backwaters of India when it comes to economic development. It is an admitted fact that due to inadequate attention from the Government of India coupled with lack of initiative of the States, the region finds itself at the lower rungs of development ladder. Let's look at some of the comparative basic indicators:

Table 9.1: Indicators of development

Particulars	*Per Capita Income (2013-14)*	*Road Density per 1000 sq km*	*Road Density per 1000 population*
All India average	33731	965.73	2.77
North Eastern Region	77949	1154.60	7.61
Arunachal Pradesh	76370	196.96	13.77
Assam	44263	2936.51	7.38
Manipur	77529	1345.32	10.27
Meghalaya	41573	739.11	6.98
Mizoram	61458	292.11	6.35
Nagaland	76210	436.67	3.89
Sikkim	176491	263.95	3.17
Tripura	69705	3026.23	9.09

Source: Lok Sabha, *Ministry of Road Transport & Highways, 2008.* Note: Road length per unit area is higher than National average in Nagaland, Assam and Tripura. Road density per 1000 population in all the NE States is higher than the national average. Given the low density of population and hilly terrain of the Region, this is an expected outcome.

The income figures in table 9.1 might look flattering for the north eastern states but the reality is that low population density has made it considerably bloated. For instance, the share of below the poverty population in the total population is 26.1 percent in India while the same is more than 34 percent in northeast.

Export Hotspot and Potentiality of Northeast India

By no means, northeast can be termed as hotspot for export of her produce to the neighbouring countries. The current export value from India is $ 254.4 billion and the northeast contributes a negligible $0.01 billion. Nearly 94 percent of exports from the NER comprises tea and coal. Remaining 6 percent is accounted for by boulder stones, limestone and fruits.

The north eastern region which is regarded as a biodiversity hotspot of the world is endowed with huge natural resource wealth. Aside from coal, oil and natural gas, the region has immense potentiality to economically prosper through planned cultivation of Bamboo, Rubber, agri-horticulture and Hydel Power. These four categories should be the bedrock of export from the region.

According to a study conducted by Indian Chamber of Commerce, northeast has 65 percent of the national bamboo production value and 20 percent of the world. Mizoram alone accounts for 40 percent of the country's bamboo production value. UN's Industrial Development estimates that bamboo production in the northeast will grow to $ 5.5. billion. Regrettably, bamboo cultivation and its export still remain as an idea. According to Rubber Board, India ranks third in rubber cultivation globally, but stands 19th when it comes to exporting rubber with a meager 1.48 percent share of the world market. China tops the list with 11 per cent share globally. In the northeast, rubber is cultivated in Tripura, Assam, Mizoram and Meghalaya. Tripura steals the show. With 35,760 ha of rubber plantation area, Tripura is regarded as "second Rubber Capital of India", after Kerala. Although, rubber has a huge market in the western countries, including USA, northeast is yet to reap the bonanza. At present agricultural production of the region is insufficient to meet its domestic consumption and a fair bit is being imported from the national pool. Vegetable production of north eastern region is only 4.5 percent of the total national yield, according a study undertaken in 2005 by Agricultural and Processed Food Products Exports Development Authority (APEDA). The study revealed that fruits production in the northeast is 23.35 lakh tones which are only 5.1 percent of the national production. Mizoram accounts for 12 per cent of the fruits produced in northeast. The region has excellent quality of turmeric, ginger, chilly, orange, pineapple, mushroom, bamboo shoot, areca nut etc which have a huge export potential. The Region has an identified potential for hydro power to the tune of 63,247 MW out of which only a small percent has been utilised till recently (table 9.2).

Table 9.2: Hydropower potential in NER

Particular	*Identified Potential (MW)*	*Hydro Power Utilized (percentage)*
Arunachal Pradesh	2384	9.77
Meghalaya	50328	13.45
Sikkim	4286	60.85
Others	6249	9.84
Total	63247	

With a view to harnessing the hydro power of the region, in 2008 the Government of India announced "Hydro Policy 2008 with a mission which was termed as 50,000 MW hydro initiative". Several incentives were added to a package for attracting private invests in this sector. Till recently, projects of only 14,000 MW were allotted to private players. The status of these projects is not available. The combined installed capacity of the NER is 3513.08 MW. As on August 2015, the per capita consumption of power in NER was 249.65 KW per hour as against national average of 1010 KW per hour. The gap is yawning.

Tourism can only develop in an atmosphere of peace and the north eastern region of this country has not known peace for many years. Very often, peace is broken by guns, bomb blast, strike/bandh etc. There are many good spots in the region which may attract tourists. Tawang in Arunachal Pradesh has a Buddhist monastery which is visited by many people. Parasuram Kund in Lohit district of Arunachal Pradesh also attracts many people. In Assam, national parks at Karziranga and Manas are two such attractions. Shillong in Meghalaya with its salubrious climate attracts many people. Jatinga in Dima Hasao (erstwhile North Cachar hills) where birds allegedly commit suicide is also another destination. Large number of people outside has special fascination for the Vaishnavite culture of Manipur, specially the Manipuri dace. The state of Manipur, Mizoram, Tripura and Nagaland may easily attract visitors. It is seen that the region is not organizing its tourism in the viable manner. But it is admitted by everybody that it has got great opportunity. The Centre may facilitate the expansion of tourism by developing road and air communications.

Initiatives of Government of India

The important philosophy behind the Look East Policy is to forge closer and deeper economic integration with its eastern neighbours. It is rather a late recognition of the strategic and economic importance of the region to India's national interests. The Look East Policy is the product of various compulsions in the post-Cold War era. The focus on economic content of international relations, emergence of regional economic groupings, forces of globalization, and slow process of economic integration within South Asia and China's growing assertiveness in the Asia Pacific region compelled India to rethink the basic parameters of its foreign policy. The growing trends toward regionalism and India's apprehension of being marginalized and isolated in the post-Cold War international system are the main reasons for paying more attention to the rapidly growing economies of East and Southeast Asia (Gordon 1995). The geographical proximity of northeast with East and Southeast Asia compelled India to focus on the north eastern region.

In the beginning, the focus of India's Look East Policy was to forge closer economic ties with ASEAN member states. Consequently, India became a Sectoral Dialogue Partner in March 1993, a full Dialogue Partner in 1995, and a member of the ASEAN Regional Forum in July 1996 and finally to a Summit Level Partner in 2002. The second phase, which began in 2003, is more comprehensive in its coverage, extending from Australia to East Asia; with ASEAN as its core (Sinha 2003). The new phase marks a shift in focus from trade to wider economic and security cooperation, political partnerships, physical connectivity through road and railway links. Thus, India-ASEAN cooperation now covers broader fields including trade and investment, science and technology, tourism and human resource development, transportation and infrastructure, and health and pharmaceuticals. India signed "Long Term Cooperative Partnership for Peace and Prosperity" with ASEAN, which is the corner stone of India's Look East Policy (Haokip 2010). India finally signed the ASEAN-India Free Trade Agreement (FTA) with the ten members of ASEAN in August 2009. This agreement was hailed as the world's largest FTA—a market of 1.8 billion people and combined GDP of $ 2.7 trillion.

A number of schemes were introduced for the development of communication links. To name a few:

i) East-West Corridor connecting Silchar to Porbandar (Gujarat).
ii) India-Myanmar-Thailand Trilateral Highway.
iii) Mekong-India Economic Corridor.
iv) Moreh-New Delhi-Hanai rail link.
v) Kaladam Transport Corridor connecting NE with Sitwee port in Myanmar.

Over and above, under a Sub-Regional Group called Bangladesh, China, India and Myanmar Economic Corridor (BCIM-EC) which envisages harnessing economic complementary in trade and infrastructure, a road link was proposed connecting Northeast-Sylhet-Dhaka-Chittagong-Mandalay-Yangaon-Kunming. These initiatives have been taken for the benefit of India in general and particularly for the north eastern States. But the connectivity within the north eastern states is very poor. The presence of national highway is also not good in most of the north eastern areas. The Central Government has envisaged connecting the north eastern state capitals to the East West highway through the Seven Sister's Corridor project. This will link the capitals of the seven states and the border points of Bhutan, Bangladesh and Myanmar. Many Thai companies have shown interest in investing in this project. From East West Corridor, the road will extend to the Golden Jubliee Rail link border point which will further connect Assam (Kokrajar) with Bhutan. This road will extend through Akhaura in Tripura to Ashuganj Port border pint with Bangladesh. It will also link up with the existing Moreh-Myanmar Friendship road will pass through the Dima Hasao (erstwhile North Cachar Hills) in Assam and constructing a four-lane highway in such difficult terrain is a major hindrance. Precious little has happened on the ground so far.

Initiatives of State Governments in Forging Economic Ties across the Border of Northeast India

Most of the north eastern states suffer from militancy and demand of statehood by different ethnic groups of the states. Due to insurgency, tourism industry is badly affected. Infrastructural facilities say for example-power, roads, bridges housing, water supply etc. are urgently necessary to gear up this sector. But since a huge amount of state fund is to be spent annually for maintenance of law and order, and the funds provided by the central government in different heads are diverted, it is not possible on the part of the state governments of NER to provide funds for infrastructural development. From last a few years, to settle the problem of insurgency or militancy the government of India and state governments of northeast both welcome the militant groups for dialogue to solve the problem insurgency. Accordingly, many insurgent groups of northeast have responded the call of State governments. Like NDFB, DHD (N), DHD (Garlosa group), UPDS, MNF, ULFA, BLT, NSCN (IM) etc. From last a few years the north eastern states have adopted the active role for the development of infrastructure, political stability and for good governance. In tourism sector north eastern governments are working for better felicities for the visitors. The Assam government to showcase the tourist sector of Assam at the global arena Miss Priyanka Chopra Indian and Hollywood actor has been appointed as a brand ambassador. North eastern states celebrates different festival, like hornbill festival in Nagaland, and recent Namami Brahmaputra river festival are the great initiative by the State government to encourage the foreign investors in India. President of India Sri Pranab Mukherjee said, inaugurating the five-day Namai Brahmputra festival in the banks of the river at Kachmarighat (on 31st March to 4th April 2017), Assam have diverse and distinctive culture, the strength as its ability to manage diversity and forge unity in divergence. The President of India also said that Assam's immense potential is emerging as an economic hub of East India and Southeast Asia and is the gateway and most effective location to put into effect the Prime Minister's Act East Policy. He also mentioned that Southeast Asia is emerging as an important destination for India's investment and trade. Signing of historic Tripartite Agreement for the dredging the Brahmaputra (NW-2) and other National Waterways in Assam and for using dredged materials for construction of Highways and development of inland waterways infrastructure. The dredging of Brahmaputra shall be completed with the dredging in Bangladesh to provide a sustainable trade route to Chittagong port. More importantly, north eastern states government has been trying to maintain peace in the state, which is very important for the development of trade.

Suggestions

Northeast India houses of many important Buddhist sites and important monasteries. Once the path of the Buddha can be traced from Arunachal Pradesh to Myanmar and beyond, India could then utilize the Buddhist heritage circuits, so that there is an increase in the Asian pilgrims annually. This in turn will encourage greater interaction leading to an increase trade, commerce and tourism in the entire region. While leading the Buddha Purnima prayers in May 2015, Prime Minister Sri Narendra Modi had said that "the 21st Century will be Asia's century and without Buddha, this cannot be Asia's century." Clearly Prime Minister Modi's placing of Buddhism at the centre of India's diplomatic initiatives is a creative idea (Majumdar 2016). A high profile Chinese Ambassador, Hu Shich, echoes the image of India as a cradle of wisdom that has given it an unique identity when he had said "India conquered and dominated China culturally for 20 centuries without ever having to send a single soldier across her border." China has already started deriving geopolitical benefits from its Buddhist links. It is not necessary for India to undertake counter measures simply to checkmate Chinese Buddhist influence in India's neighborhood. More importantly, it is a high time for India to think of the ways in which it can win the hearts of the Buddhist population of Southeast Asia that will entail for enduring relations between the two regions.

The service sector will have to be upgraded keeping in mind the fact that north eastern region India is a seismic zone and therefore any construction will have to be friendly to the environmental needs. Simple cottages with clean essential facilities for a comfort break internet access and connectivity are the basic requirements that need to fulfill which would attract visitors from not just Southeast Asia but from different parts of the world. Needless to say the least for this to happen, air connectivity, roads will have to sufficiently improve. For example state capitals should be connected by direct flight to the capitals of the ASEAN countries together with simplifying travel formalities.

North eastern farmers should be encouraged to adopt crop diversification for absorbing the modern youth in agricultural sector for employment. For this purpose, the lead farms under the able leadership of educated farmers or organizations like NGOs in almost all the block level administrative units should be set up to initiate the process. This would create an atmosphere of confidence in other farmers to go for diversification which promises more income and assured employment in the region. A sense of inclusion and participation of local communities is crucial in making programmes work successful. Locals need to be given effective control over resources and development schemes must have their participation and not to be devised and dictated by central authorities. At last, the north eastern people should come forward with some innovative ideas for the development of this region.

Conclusion

The 'Act East Policy' is expected to usher in a new era of development for the northeast through network of pipelines, road, rail and air connectivity, communication and trade. However, many challenges need to be overcome of which the region is embroiled for the past several years before any meaningful activity can take place. Starting from various forms of insurgent activities to the problem of illegal migration and drug trafficking which are all transnational in character, the Central government of India need to forge cooperation from the neighbouring countries. Such cooperation with the neighbouring countries should not antagonize the people of northeast. The trans-border communities can be restored through border trade and inter-country trade which the border region should not act merely as a transit corridor but as a source of local manufacture and enhancing people-to-people contact. The emphasis should be on industrialization and growth. The Indian government and the north eastern states government jointly must adopt proactive role and provide not only infrastructures but also political stability, peace and good governance. More participation of the north eastern people in production and distribution activities and raising agricultural productivity should be given prime importance. Trade alone will not be sufficient to transform the region into a sustained development path. In addition, growth in trading activities will only benefit those people who possibly are from outside the north eastern region and who are economically more powerful to exploit the resources of the north eastern region. As far as my study is concerned, the success of the policy depends on the commitment of the Central government to implement the policy and to give role for the Northeastern states in 'Act East Policy'.

TRADE AND INVESTMENT

10

NER-ASEAN: Resources and Trade Potential

Ujjwal Kanti Paul

Introduction

Over the last two and half decade, the Look East Policy (LEP) of India has helped the country to reorient its trade and investment strategies from *West to East*. During 2011-14, the Association of South East Asian Nation (ASEAN) and its three member countries (China, Japan and South Korea) have emerged as the top trading partner of India occupying a share of nearly 23 percent in the total trade. During the same period, these countries were also the second largest investor in India with 23.23 percent share in the total investment (Das et al. 2016). However, almost the entire trade and investment growth bypassed the peripheral north eastern region (NER) of the country that shares a contiguous land border of over 1700 km with Myanmar—considered as India's gateway to Southeast Asia. As a result, in spite of having a rich reserve of natural resources and a talented pool of human capital, the economic growth of the region lagged behind the rest of the country. Out of the eight states here, the per capita income of four states—Assam, Manipur, Meghalaya and Tripura—comprising nearly 90 percent of region's total population, is lesser than country's average income. While there is no unanimous opinion among the scholars that provides an exhaustive explanation for the failure of LEP in India's NER, geographical isolation coupled with the poor state of infrastructure are identified as the major factors that thwarted the competitive advantage of the region. Several cross-border connectivity projects such as India-Myanmar-Thailand highway, Trans-Asian railway network, Kaladan Multimodal Transport Project etc. have been envisaged to overcome these challenges. These logistical initiatives are likely to turn NER from an isolated landlocked peripheral territory to a land-linked territory integrated with the rapidly growing economies of the Southeast Asian region.

NER occupies 7.8 percent of country's total land space and has a share of 3.8 percent of country's total population. Out of the total geographical area nearly 65 percent is under undulating tracks and hills and remaining 35 percent is plain. Blessed with rich biodiversity and conducive agro-climatic conditions, NER produces a wide variety of fruits, vegetables, rare and rich flora and fauna, flowers, herbs and aromatic plants etc. Agriculture constitutes 26 percent of the total GDP of NER and engages about one-third of the total work force. However, the productivity of most of the crops (food grains, vegetables and fruits) is very low in the region compared to other part of the country. According to Rios et al. (2008), policies aiming at increasing agricultural productivity should also consider complementary investments in marketing infrastructure as improved market access can drive productivity by providing incentives, information and cash flow for working capital. However, connectivity is a necessary but not a sufficient condition for development. The economic progress of NER would depend not only on the redefined physical and institutional linkages with the neighboring nations, but also on how efficiently the resources of the region are utilized and marketed leveraging the revamped connectivity. The current literature does not satisfactorily answer as to how will dyadic and triadic value chain linkages between NER and East and South East Asian countries be established? Which resources in NER can profitably be marketed to the ASEAN and its member countries? The present paper intends to fill this void by way of presenting a detail description of some of the major resources in NER that can be profitably traded across the border.

NER is a vibrant source of horticultural crops that can be marketed to distant markets within the country as well as exported to other countries. Major horticultural crops grown in the NE region include citrus, pineapple, kiwi, mango, guava, litchi, banana among fruits, potato, onion, tomato, cauliflower, cabbage, brinjal, beans among vegetables, chrysanthemum, rose, orchids etc. in flowers, ginger, turmeric large cardamom, coriander, cumin among spices and cashew nut, arecanut and tea among plantation crops.

Pineapple

India is the sixth largest producer of pineapple in the world. During 2012-13, India produced 6.69 percent (1570 thousand MT) of world's total pineapple from over 10 percent (105 thousand ha) of total land under pineapple cultivation. NER produces more than 48 percent of India's total pineapple, albeit using nearly 70 percent of the total area under cultivation. The non-use of any chemical inputs is cited as one of the major factors behind low productivity of crops like pineapple in the region. Nevertheless, it brings a wonderful opportunity to market this perennial crop at a premium price to the increasingly growing health conscious customer segment that demands chemical-free food. However, in the absence of access to the developed market, currently, a large part of produce is either wasted at the orchard or sold in the local market at a very low price. As a result, growers have almost no incentive to invest in productivity enhancing resources.

India's share in the global pineapple export market is less than 1 percent (Figure 10.1). This sharply contrasts the performance of other major pineapple producers in the world such as Costa Rica, Thailand and Philippines. For instance, Costa Rica – the largest pineapple producer in the world – enjoys nearly 40 percent share in the global pineapple export market from just 11 percent share in production.

Figure 10.1: Share of production and export of pineapple

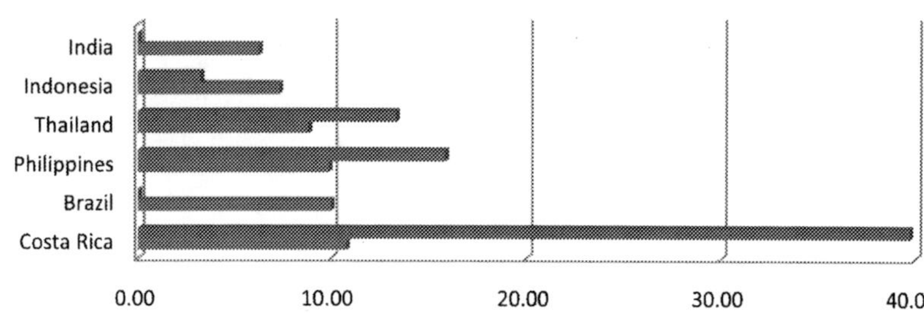

	Costa Rica	Brazil	Philippines	Thailand	Indonesia	India
Export	39.75	0.06	15.89	13.37	3.29	0.06
Production	10.84	10.02	9.92	8.92	7.41	6.34

Source: FAOstat (http://www.fao.org/faostat/en/#data), Comtrade (http://comtrade.un.org/db/dqBasicQueryResults.aspx?px=H1&cc=091010&r=699&y=2015)

While pineapple is grown in almost all the ASEAN countries, Thailand, Philippines and Indonesia are the leading producers. Table 10.1 provides a comparison of the trend of area, production and yield of pineapple between India and ASEAN countries. It can be seen that the yield per hectare of pineapple in India is less than half of that of Philippines, Malaysia and Indonesia. This suggests that a bilateral trade relation between ASEAN and India will not only boost the trade, but will also contribute towards transfer of productive technology and know-how.

Table 10.1: Area, production and yield of pineapple in India and ASEAN countries

Country	*Area (ha)*			*Production (tonnes)*			*Yield (tonnes/ha)*		
	2005	*2010*	*2014*	*2005*	*2010*	*2014*	*2005*	*2010*	*2014*
Brunei Darussalam	111	122	130	992	1078	1155	8.94	8.84	8.88
Cambodia	1841	2134	2267	19292	22426	23689	10.48	10.51	10.45
Indonesia	9962	12141	16000	925082	1406445	1835491	92.86	115.84	114.72
LAO PDR	4200	3150	5160	41000	42310	61695	9.76	13.43	11.96
Malaysia	10300	10567	9456	340000	331081	335725	33.01	31.33	35.50
Philippines	49215	58547	61643	1788218	2169233	2507098	36.33	37.05	40.67
Thailand	98208	93312	72376	2183280	1966000	1914830	22.23	21.07	26.46
Vietnam	36200	34953	35724	470000	514742	591456	12.98	14.73	16.56
India	82800	91900	109880	1278900	1386800	1736740	15.45	15.09	15.81

Source: http://www.fao.org/faostat/en/#data/QC

Table 10.2: Export and import scenarios of pineapple in India and ASEAN countries

Country	*Export Value ('000USD)*			*Import Value ('000USD)*		
	2001	*2007*	*2013*	*2001*	*2007*	*2013*
Brunei Darussalam	0	0	0	330	302	925
Cambodia	0	0	0	8	46	136
Indonesia	76729	71627	157444	194	297	330
Malaysia	11179	18321	13891	233	842	2716
Philippines	161698	247799	422401	156	1041	631
Thailand	275310	549788	662750	247	483	3601
Vietnam	9865	20183	13494	70	0	83
Singapore	21061	21572	18894	7072	18165	18340
India	1105	1110	2176	1089	832	2341

Source: http://www.fao.org/faostat/en/#data/TP

From table 10.2 it is clear that ASEAN nations are not only the leading producers of pineapple, but exporters and importers as well.

Between 2001 and 2013, the export of pineapple in ASEAN countries has more than doubled. Thailand is the largest exporter of pineapple with an export growth rate of over 140 percent. Despite insignificant production, Singapore is the fourth largest pineapple exporting player in ASEAN. However, the import growth rate of pineapple among ASEAN players has outpaced that of export growth. Between 2001 and 2013, the import of pineapple among ASEAN countries has grown over three times.

The proposed IMT highway can be used to market these pineapples to Thailand which inadvertently suffers due to the shortage of raw material in almost nine months in a year (Eapsirimetee 2013). Securing access to a steady source of chemical-free pineapple will be a win-win proposition for both the countries. While the growers in the region will fetch higher price, the Thai marketers will be able to meet their production target. Small scale fruit processing units can be set up in major production regions through public-private partnership. These units can process the pineapples before exporting them to the Thai market. Obtaining organic certification will make the produce even more valuable. Table 10.3 highlights shows that pineapple traders in Cachar district of Assam can reap over 125 percent return on investment by exporting pineapples to the Thai market.

Table 10.3: Approximate cost and profitability of selling pineapple at the Thai market (via IMT highway)

Sl. No.	*Particulars*	*Amount*
1	Current farm gate price (Rs/ton)	6035
2	Proposed price at the secondary market (Rs/ton)	10000
3	Distance (km)	1400
4	Transportation cost (Rs 6/km/ton)	8400
5	Transit fee (Rs.5/ton/km)	7000
6	Wastage (20 percent)	2000
7	Miscellaneous (Rs/ton)	200
8	Total Cost (Rs/ton)	29000
9	Avg. wholesale price (Rs/ton)	60000
10	Margin (%)	106.89
11	Price after adjusting premium for organic production (20% of avg. wholesale price)	72000
12	Cost incurred for certification (10% of total cost)	2900
13	Margin after adjusting for premium and certification cost (%)	125.7

Source: Author's estimation.

Ginger

With 26.6 percent share in the total production, India is the largest ginger producer in the world followed by China (15.19 percent). Table 10.4 highlights the trends in area, production and yield of ginger in ASEAN and India over 2001 to 2013. It is clear that ASEAN countries are lagging significantly behind than India in terms of area harvested and ginger production. Between 2001 and 2013, the production of ginger among ASEAN players has grown by just 6 percent Vis-a Vis almost 200 percent in case of India. However, in terms of yield, India is significantly trailing behind the ASEAN nations.

Table 10.4: Area, production and yield of ginger in India and ASEAN countries

Country	*Area (ha)*			*Production (tonnes)*			*Yield (tonnes/ha)*		
	2001	*2007*	*2013*	*2001*	*2007*	*2013*	*2001*	*2007*	*2013*
Brunei Darussalam	0	0	0	0	0	0	0	0	0
Cambodia	0	0	0	0	0	0	0	0	0
Indonesia	21000	51000	7445	128437	178502	155286	61160	35000	208582
LAO PDR	0	0	0	0	0	0	0	0	0
Malaysia	992	880	893	4366	10150	8831	43991	115341	98891
Philippines	3681	3974	3963	23424	27946	28216	63635	70322	71203
Thailand	9927	9048	9730	177389	153284	161157	178693	169412	165629
Vietnam	0	0	0	0	0	0	0	0	0
India	70081	106100	136000	230000	393400	683000	32819	37078	50221

Source: http://www.fao.org/faostat/en/#data/QC

From table 10.5, it can be seen that Thailand and Indonesia are the two leading exporters of ginger whereas Malaysia is the leading ginger importing nation. India is also a significant importer of ginger. Between 2001 and 2013, the export and import of ginger in ASEAN grew by 1.2 times and 3 times respectively. During the same period, the corresponding growth in India's export and import of ginger was nearly 7.5 times and 6 times respectively.

However, India's share in the global ginger export market is just 2.74 percent (Figure 10.2). China, on the other hand, has more than 52 percent share in the global ginger export market. A close observation of India's ginger trade discerns some peculiar trend. The largest proportion of India's ginger (35.61) goes to Bangladesh. However, Bangladesh pays the least price per kilogram. Whereas, Singapore, Thailand and Japan jointly receive less than 10 percent of India's total ginger despite paying the highest price per kilogram. This highlights

Table 10.5: Export and import scenarios of ginger in India and ASEAN countries

Country	*Export Value ('000USD)*			*Import Value ('000USD)*		
	2001	*2007*	*2013*	*2001*	*2007*	*2013*
Brunei Darussalam	0	0	2	280	170	1207
Cambodia	4	0	0	1	2	0
Indonesia	3511	1635	14909	22	297	5927
Malaysia	282	1261	382	4289	11408	34251
Myanmar	312	460	600	0	0	0
Philippines	62	5	108	123	1179	246
Thailand	11174	14891	33383	165	409	3970
Vietnam	300	1611	3935	57	1039	5459
Singapore	1233	944	1473	3642	8293	11088
India	4496	7986	34226	3416	15258	20130

Source: http://www.fao.org/faostat/en/#data/TP

the need for reorientation of India's ginger trade. Nearly 57 percent of India's ginger is produced in NER. With 45 percent of region's total production, Assam is the largest ginger producing state in the region followed by Meghalaya (18 percent), Arunachal Pradesh (16 percent) and Nagaland (10 percent).

Figure 10.2: Share of production and export of ginger

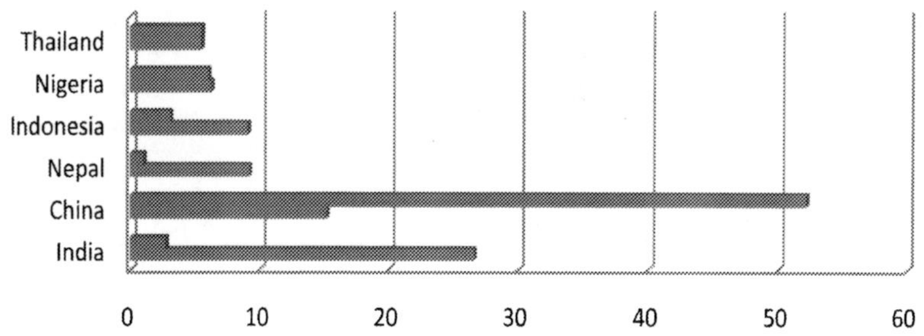

	India	China	Nepal	Indonesia	Nigeria	Thailand
Export	2.74	52.16	1.01	3.08	5.98	5.50
Production	26.6	15.19	9.15	9.06	6.23	5.45

Source: FAOstat (http://www.fao.org/faostat/en/#data), Comtrade (http://comtrade.un.org/db/dqBasicQueryResults.aspx?px=H1&cc=091010&r=699&y=2015)

NER can export the locally produced ginger either as fresh or after processing them as biscuits, candy, juice, beer etc. to the leading importing nations like Japan, Singapore, Thailand, etc. Moreover, like pineapple, most of the ginger in the region is produced without applying any synthetic input. As a result, various ginger products can be sold at a premium price after using necessary organic certification.

Bamboo

With 25 percent of country's total forest cover, NER has gained worldwide attention for its diverse and extensive forest resources. Nearly 64 percent of the total area in the region is covered by forests (CFI 2006). Bamboo is one of the most significant constituent of forest. Nearly 65 percent of global bamboo resources are available in the Asian province and with 30 percent of the global total; India has the largest bamboo resources in the world (Figure 10.3).

Figure 10.3: Countries with the largest bamboo resources

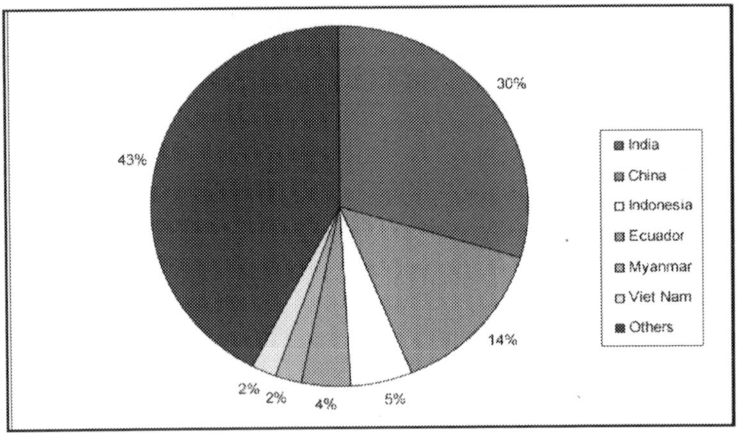

Source: FAO (2007).

Within the country, NER (40.11 percent) has the maximum bamboo resources followed by Madhya Pradesh (9.36 percent), Chhattisgarh (8.14 percent), and Maharashtra (8.21 percent). Despite having significant bamboo reserve, India's share in the global bamboo market is almost negligible. Table 10.6 shows that China which has just 14 percent share in the global production enjoys more than 65 percent share in the global bamboo export market. India, on the other hand, has less than 1 percent share. Surprisingly, despite having enormous bamboo reserves, India is the third largest importer of bamboo products in the world with a share of 1.51 percent of the global import. In the year 2012, China exported nearly 1238 USD million worth bamboo and rattan products like bamboo shoots (241 USD million), bamboo woven products (375 USD million), industrialized bamboo products (413 USD million), furniture (54 USD million). Its leading trade partners were USA (25 percent), EU (20 percent), Japan (20 percent), Australia (4 percent) and Malaysia (3 percent).

Table 10.6: Highlight of global bamboo trade in 2012

Country	*Export share*	*Country*	*Import share*
China	65.81	Canada	2.85
Indonesia	9.34	China	1.70
Viet Nam	4.55	India	1.51
Philippines	1.91	Malaysia	0.54
India	0.11	Viet Nam	0.21
Others	18.27	Others	93.19

Source: INBAR 2012

Likewise China, NER can also become a major bamboo exporter in the world with the help of proper strategies and practices. Small scale bamboo processing units could be established in the region using PPP framework and products like boiled bamboo shoots, furniture, handicrafts etc. can be exported to neighboring ASEAN and its member countries like Thailand, Japan, Malaysia, etc.

Energy

Being the third fastest growing region in the world, the demand for power in Southeast Asia is projected to grow at an increasing rate over the next few decades. By 2040, ASEAN needs to produce 354 GW more power (more than double of its existing capacity) to sustain the economic progress (IEA 2015). Though ASEAN countries are rich in energy resources, meeting this high demand will be challenging. It is estimated that NER has a total reserve of about 2225 GW of energy comprising of coal, natural gas, crude oil and hydropower (table 10.7).

With 148 GW, India ranks fifth in the world in terms of usable hydropower potential and NER has nearly 42.54 percent share in country's total potential. However, nearly 93 percent hydropower potential in NER is yet to be harnessed. This sharply contrasts the

Table 10.7: Energy potential of NER

Country	*Coal (GW)*	*Natural Gas (GW)*	*Crude Oil (GW)*	*Hydropower (GW)*	*Total (GW)*
India (NER)	1484.15	227.02	464.66	50	2225.83

Source: World energy council 2013 accessed from https://www.worldenergy.org/wp-content/uploads/2013/09/Complete_WER_2013_Survey.pdf. Alam and Islam (2015), World Energy Council, Zhenming (2011), Hennig et al. (2013), Ministry of coal, Govt. of India, FICCI, ADB (2014), OXFAM (2015). Note: 1 tonne of coal equivalent = 0.0081 gigawatt hours (GWh) and then further dividing GWh by 8760 (24*365) to obtain Giga watt (GW). On the other hand Mtoe has been converted to GW by using the formula 1 Mtoe=11630 Gwh

scenarios in south and western region where more than 65 percent of the total potential has already been harnessed. Central Electric Authority (CEA) has identified 168 large dams in the Brahmaputra basin. By exploiting the potential hydropower opportunities, NER can not only satisfy the domestic demand but also supply to the ASEAN and other East Asian countries. However, this requires investment, technical know-how, consensus building with the locals, obtaining necessary approvals from the statutory bodies etc. By leveraging the AEP, NER can integrate itself with the ASEAN regional power system and help meeting the rising power demand in the region.

Figure 10.4: Status of hydropower potential development in India

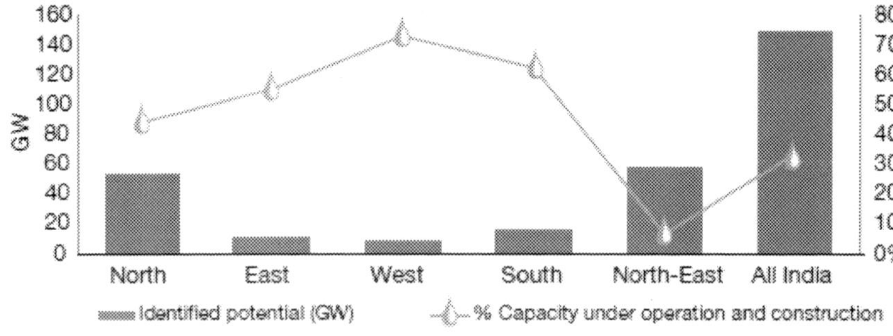

Source: https://www.pwc.in/assets/pdfs/publications/2014/hydropower-in-india-key-enablers-for-better-tomorrow.pdf

Conclusion

Act East Policy is pregnant with all the potentials to escort NER out of underdevelopment and poverty. It is important that we recognise the centrality of NER in AEP. For this purpose, statutory provisions are required to empower these bordering states in the region to enter into cross-border business deals. However, centrality of NER itself will not guarantee the development of NER, unless the foot-soldiers of development of the region (politicians, bureaucrats, entrepreneurs, academicians, activists) do not deliver at the ground, the fruits of AEP will also remain elusive in NER.

11

India-ASEAN Trade Relations: With Special Reference to North Eastern Region (NER) of India

A. Pushpalata Singh and Monalisa Das

Introduction

The Association of Southeast Asian Nations (ASEAN) is a regional organisation comprising ten Southeast Asian nations, which promotes inter-governmental cooperation and facilitates economic integration amongst its members. ASEAN is a vital global hub of manufacturing and trade, as well as one of the fastest-growing consumer markets in the world. Its principal aims include accelerating economic growth, social progress and socio cultural evolution among its members, alongside the protection of regional stability and the provision of a mechanism for member countries to resolve differences peacefully. ASEAN share land borders with India, China, Bangladesh, East Timor and Papua New Guinea and Australia.

Over the past decade, trade and investment relations between India and ASEAN have continued to improve. Total bilateral trade increased more than threefold from US$21 billion in 2005-06 to US$65 billion in 2015-16. Research and Information System for Developing Countries/ (RIS) has been deeply involved in the process of strengthening ASEAN-India cooperation since 1992 when India was admitted by ASEAN as a Sectoral Dialogue Partner. The India-ASEAN Eminent Persons

Lecture Series was launched in December 1996 to facilitate people-to-people interactions to complement the evolving partnership between the two regions. The ASEAN-India Centre (AIC) has been established at the RIS for undertaking research and fostering policy dialogue for continued interaction for strengthening ASEAN-India Partnership. It has also brought out a number of publications and organised important events on various aspects related to the process of ASEAN-India cooperation. The first Roundtable on ASEAN-India Network of Think-Tanks (AINTT) was held in 2012 at New Delhi. The second Roundtable was organised in 2013 at Vientiane, Lao PDR and the third Roundtable took place in 2014 at Hanoi, Vietnam.

Since Independence, India has made great strides in many areas of human endeavour and is today on its path of becoming one of the leading nations of the 21st century. Though there has been substantial economic progress in the last two decades, the fruits of development are not being equally distributed to all parts of the country and some areas like the north eastern states have lagged behind. Given its geographic position, long international borders, nearness with the ASEAN countries and its rich resources, the north eastern region (NER) has great potential to become the centre of economic activity and trade for India and the ASEAN. But despite being blessed with a fairly wide resource base, the region remains among the most under-developed areas in the country. Thus, it is in this connection that the present study aims to study the trade relation between ASEAN and India with special reference to north eastern region.

Review of Related Literatures

A considerable number of literatures have examined India-ASEAN trade relation from different point of view, while some of these are mentioned as follows. Bhaumik (2014) seeks to focus on the considerable obstacles encountered in carrying forward India's 'Look East' through northeast, specially the problems caused by the nature of physical terrain, the history of violent conflicts in the region and its immediate neighbourhood which remains volatile, and the poor state of transport infrastructure and local industries in northeast India and Myanmar, through which India has to access other ASEAN countries by land. The study reveals that there is a possibility to save cost through bulk handling but causes long time lags in delivery. Further suggested the to use a land route to a country like Laos or northern Burma, though not until we have connectivity through the Trilateral Highway and the Asian Railway is successfully established and running efficiently. Singh (2010) examines initiatives for economic integration of the NER with ASEAN and suggests removal of the northeast population's general sentiment that they are alienated from the rest of India, the creation of adequate infrastructure and favourable environment for free movement of economic and non-economic resources, besides others. Appropriate economic policy for the region as a whole and creation of support infrastructure only could help the region realise its economic growth and trade potential especially in the context of newly signed India-ASEAN free trade areas (FTA). Chutia (2015) makes an attempt to assess the prospects of border trade for northeast India with the South Asian countries. He explains the potential goods of the region and reported obvious gap between policy and implementation. The study suggested proper implementation of the policies for betterment of border trade with north eastern region. Haokip (2015) has examined prospects and challenges for northeast India from the perspective of India's Look East Policy, and also explores the possible community–geography trade-offs in such borderlands. The study recognizes 'borders' as crucial in attempting to address the problems of the northeast, assesses the prospects of 'Looking East' through this region and the challenges posed to it by post-colonial territoriality and other domestic problems.

Objectives of the Study

The study aims to achieve the following specified objectives:

i) To analyse the trend and pattern of India's trade with ASEAN and

ii) To examine the prospects and challenges of NER in expanding India's trade with the ASEAN.

Methodology

The present study is based on secondary data retrieved from Export Import Data Bank, Government of India, Department of Commerce. Considering the export and import the status of a country's foreign trade can be best measured. Hence in order to investigate the trend and pattern of India's foreign trade with ASEAN, time series data related to exports and imports are used in this study. Further to analyze prospects and challenges of NER in expanding India's trade with the ASEAN secondary data obtained from North Eastern Development Finance Corporation Ltd. (NEDFI) and Import Export Data Bank, Government of India, Department of Commerce are used.

To analyze the pattern of India ASEAN trade simple statistical like percentage tabulation and compound annual growth rate is used in this study. The formula for compound annual growth rate between two time periods is given as

$$CAGR_{(t_0,t_n)} = \left\{ \left({}^{Y_{t_n}}\!/_{Y_{t_0}} \right)^{\frac{1}{t_n - t_0}} - 1 \right\} X\ 100$$

Here t_n and t_0 denote last or final period and base or first time period respectively. For analyzing the trend of trade over the period growth rates are calculated by using both annual growth rate formula and least square growth. Rates of change from one period to the next are calculated as proportional changes from the earlier period by using the following formula:

$$Gr_t = \frac{Y_t - Y_{t-1}}{Y_{t-1}} \times 100$$

Growth rates are calculated as annual averages and represented as percentages except where noted, growth rates of values are computed from constant price series. Least-squares growth rate method allows calculation of growth over long period of time by considering all the observations and provides statistical significance of the estimated growth rate. This method is suitable and significant wherever there is a sufficiently long time series to permit a reliable calculation. The least-squares growth rate is estimated by fitting a linear regression trend line to the logarithmic annual values of the variable in the relevant period. The regression equation takes the following form which is equivalent to the logarithmic transformation of the compound growth equation:

$$ln\, X_t = \alpha + \beta t + e_t,$$

where $t = 1, 2, 3, ..., 21$.

In this equation X is the variable growth which is to be estimated, t is time, α and β are parameters to be estimated. e_t indicates an error term which $e \sim N(0, \sigma^2)$. β is the average annual growth rate, and it multiplied by 100 for obtaining the rate into percentage. In order to examine the prospects and challenges of NER in expanding India's trade with the ASEAN simple tabular presentation is done in this study.

Trend and Pattern of India's Trade with ASEAN

ASEAN is a fast expanding trade community in Asia with a growing economic clout. With a combine population of more than 620 million, ASEAN's aggregate economic size surpasses US$2578 billion. Though India's population is double of that of ASEAN but its Gross National Income is less than that of the latter (Table 11.1).

Table 11.1: Basic profile of India and ASEAN

	Population 2014 (in millions)	*Area (in sq km)*	*Gross National Income 2014 (in $ billions)*	
			CER	*PPP*
ASEAN	623.2	4486.7	2578.8	6416.4
India	1295.3	3287.3	2028	7292.8

Source: World Bank

ASEAN lies at the heart of many important global industrial production chains in manufacturing and services trade. These allow countries to specialize in different parts of the production process, tapping the competitive advantages of each location. ASEAN is the fourth-largest exporting region in the world, trailing only the European Union, North America, and China/Hong Kong. ASEAN export to the world in 2014 stood at US$1.3 trillion, with intra-ASEAN exports making up 26 per cent of those exports.

India's exports to ASEAN increased from US$ 2.91 billion in 2000-01 to US$ 25.20 billion in 2015-16 and imports over the same period have grown from US$ 4.15 billion in 2000-01 to US$ 39.84 billion. In terms of market share, the share of imports in India from ASEAN went up from 8.20 percent in 2000-01 to 10.5 percent in 2015-16, over the same period share of exports to ASEAN in India's total exports increased from 6.50 percent to its maximum of 12.00 percent in 2011-12 but after that decreased gradually to 9.60 percent in 2015-16. The current trends of ASEAN-India trade suggest that India could become an increasingly important market for ASEAN's exports and vice versa (Table 11.2).

Table 11.2: India's trade with ASEAN during 2005-06 to 2015-16

Year	*India's Export to ASEAN (in billion US$)*	*Share in India's Total Exports (in percentage)*	*India's Imports from ASEAN (in billion US$)*	*Share in India's Total Imports (in percentage)*
2000-01	2.91	6.5	4.15	8.20
2005-06	10.41	10.10	10.88	7.30
2006-07	12.61	10.0	18.11	9.70
2007-08	16.41	10.10	22.67	9.00
2008-09	19.41	10.30	26.20	8.60
2009-10	18.11	10.10	25.80	8.90
2010-11	25.63	10.3	30.61	8.30
2011-12	36.74	12.00	42.16	8.60
2012-13	33.00	11.00	42.87	8.70
2013-14	33.13	10.50	42.28	9.20
2014-15	31.81	10.20	44.71	10.00
2015-16	25.20	9.6	39.84	10.50

Source: Import Export Data Bank, Government of India, Department of Commerce

On the basis of Table 11.2, the trade balance and trade volume of India with ASEAN is depicted in Figure 11.1. From which it is clear that the total volume of trade has increased immensely over last ten years. During 2009-10 there is decline of total trade by approximately 1.7 billion US$. Since then there is a steep rise trade volume up to 2011-12 and 2011-12 recorded highest trade volume, but afterwards a relatively declining trend is witnessed. Considering the trade balance of India with ASEAN during 2005-06 to 2015-16, no single year has been traced with positive trade balance. Rather there is a decreasing trend over the time; however 2010-11 has evidenced the minimum trade deficit after 2005-06. On this note India's gains from trade in terms of net export is not accumulation to its economic growth.

Considering the annual growth of India's export to ASEAN highest increase s observed in the year 2011-12, followed by 2010-11, 2007-08, 2006-07 and 2008-09, while four financial years have recorded negative growth out of which 2015-16 has shown highest decline in export to ASEAN. However the overall average growth is positive and stood at 11.32 percent, but negative in case of share of India's total exports to ASEAN. The share of India's total exports to ASEAN has shown

Figure 11.1: India's trade balance and volume of trade with ASEAN

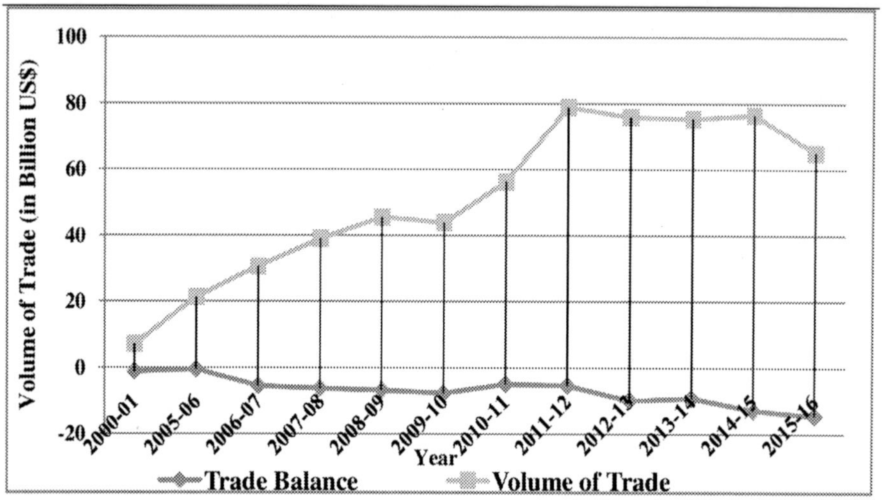

Source: Compiled from Table 11.2 (Trade Balance=1-3, and Volume of Trade=1+3)

highest increase in 2011-12, followed by negligible increase at 1.98 and 1 percent during 2008-09 and 2007-08 respectively, all other years have shown a declining trend. Further the growth of India's imports from ASEAN and share in India's total imports are positive for most of the financial years are found positive with overall positive average growth rate 15.75 percent and 4.22 percent respectively.

Table 11.3: Annual growth rates of India-ASEAN trade from 2006-07 to 2015-16

Year	*India's Export to ASEAN*	*Share in India's Total Exports*	*India's Imports from ASEAN*	*Share in India's Total Imports*
2006-07	21.13%	-0.99%	66.45%	32.88%
2007-08	30.13%	1.00%	25.18%	-7.22%
2008-09	18.28%	1.98%	15.57%	-4.44%
2009-10	-6.70%	-1.94%	-1.53%	3.49%
2010-11	41.52%	1.98%	18.64%	-6.74%
2011-12	43.35%	16.50%	37.73%	3.61%
2012-13	-10.18%	-8.33%	1.68%	1.16%
2013-14	0.39%	-4.55%	-1.38%	5.75%
2014-15	-3.98%	-2.86%	5.75%	8.70%
2015-16	-20.78%	-5.88%	-10.89%	5.00%
Average	11.32%	-0.31%	15.72%	4.22%

Source: Authors' Compilation from Import Export Data Bank, Government of India, Department of Commerce

In order to validate the growth rates over the study period and to check the statistical significance of the estimates least square growth rate is estimated and shown in Table 11.4. The results reveal that all the estimated models for measuring growth ate statistically significant except share of India's export to ASEAN on time. India's export to ASEAN has grown significantly at approximately 11 percent, while the share of India's exports' growth is insignificant during the study period. Volume of import from ASEAN has shown significant rise of 12.23 percent and 1.81 percent increase in share of India's import to ASEAN. This implies ASEAN is occupying a substantial place in India's import bundle but the converse is not pertinent.

Table 11.4: Least square growth rates of India-ASEAN trade from 2005-06 to 2015-16

Coefficients	*TIME*	*Constant*	R^2	*F*	*Growth Rates*
India's Export to ASEAN	0.109*** (4.99)	2.442 (16.48)	0.734	24.91***	**10.91%**
Share in India's Total Exports	0.002 (0.38)	2.325*** (58.39)	0.015	0.14	**0.22%**
India's Imports from ASEAN	0.122*** (6.51)	2.636*** (20.71)	0.825	42.44***	**12.23%**
Share in India's Total Imports	0.018** (2.33)	2.082*** (39.38)	0.375	5.41**	**1.81%**

Source: OLS Estimates from Import Export Data Bank, Government of India, Department of Commerce Note: 1. Figures in the brackets denote t statistics of the estimated coefficients. 2. ***, ** and * denote coefficients are significant at one, five and ten percent level of significance respectively

In 2005-06, among the ten ASEAN nations Singapore alone accounted for more than 50 percent share in India's total exports to ASEAN. This is followed by Indonesia, Malaysia and Thailand with a market share of 13 percent, 11percent and 10 percent respectively. On the import side, Singapore again stands at the top accounting 33 percent share in India's total imports from ASEAN which is again followed by Indonesia, Malaysia and Thailand with a market share of 30 percent, 24 percent and 10 percent respectively.

In 2015-16, export and import shares in the ASEAN market have undergone a major change. Singapore accounted for 31 percent in India's total exports to the ASEAN followed by Vietnam, Malaysia, Thailand and Indonesia accounting for a share of 21 percent, 15 percent, 12 percent and 11 percent respectively. At an aggregate level, the share of ASEAN in India's total exports fell from more than 10 percent in 2005-06 to 9.6 percent in 2015-16. On the import side, Indonesia has replaced Singapore by becoming the largest source of imports from the ASEAN with a share of 33 percent in total imports from the ASEAN. This is followed by Malaysia, Singapore and Thailand with a share of respectively.

The combined share of 4 countries viz. Singapore, Indonesia, Malaysia and Thailand in the total imports from the ASEAN continues to be high though it has fallen from 91 percent in 2005-06 to 88 per cent in 2015-16 (Table 11.5).

Table 11.5: Country-wise trading pattern over years

Country	*2005-06($ Million)*			*2015-16($ Million)*			*CAGR2015-16/2005-06*	
	Exports	*Imports*	*TB*	*Exports*	*Imports*	*TB*	*Exports*	*Imports*
Brunei	43	1	42	28	554	-526	-4.10	90.50
Cambodia	24	1	23	143	54	89	19.40	52.90
Indonesia	1380	3008	-1628	2841	13068	-10227	7.50	15.80
Lao	5	0	5	38	180	-142	21.40	111.60
Malaysia	1162	2416	-1254	3707	9084	-5377	12.30	14.20
Myanmar	111	526	-415	1068	984	84	25.40	6.50
Philippines	495	235	259	1369	542	826	10.70	8.70
Singapore	5425	3354	2072	7722	7306	416	3.60	8.10
Thailand	1075	1212	-136	3009	5510	-2501	10.80	16.40
Vietnam	691	131	559	5270	2560	2710	22.50	34.60
ASEAN	10411	10884	-472	25195	39843	-14648	9.20	13.60
Global	103091	149166	-46075	262031	380665	-118634	9.80	9.80

Source: Department of Commerce, Government of India; http://commerce.nic.in/MOC/index.asp

India's trade with ASEAN countries has been witnessing a compositional shift. In 2005-06, India's export with ASEAN countries were mainly driven by petroleum oils, precious stones and jewellery and chemicals which accounted for a share of about 23.7, 15.3 and 10.3 percent of India's total exports to ASEAN respectively. However, in 2015-16, meat products have emerged as one of the top export items to ASEAN with a percent share of 10.5 percent whose share was only 1.9 percent in 2005-06. Though petroleum products, chemicals and precious stones and jewellery have increased in absolute number but its percent share in total exports have gone down. It is also found that there has been an increase in share of certain high end manufactured exports in India's total exports over the decade despite intense competition. These include pharmaceuticals, transport equipment, non-ferrous metals (Table 11.6).

Table 11.6: India's exports to ASEAN

Items	*2005-06*		*2015-16*		*CAGR*
	U.S.$ Million	*Share in Total*	*U.S.$ Million*	*Share in Total*	*2015-16/ 2005-06*
1. Fresh Vegetables & fruits	76	0.7	216	0.9	11
2. Meat products	193	1.9	2649	10.5	29.9
3. Fish products	97	0.9	1089	4.3	27.4
4. Spices	46	0.4	499	2/0	26.9
5. Sugar	22	0.2	488	1.9	36.3
6. Oil cakes & fodder	527	5.1	225	0.9	-8.2
6. Petroleum products	2463	23.7	3766	14.9	4.3
5. Chemicals	1071	10.3	1698	6.7	4.7
a. Inorganic	84	0.8	130	0.5	4.5
b. Organic	834	8	1234	4.9	4
c. Special chemicals	153	1.5	334	1.3	8
7. Pharmaceuticals	163	1.6	717	2.8	16
8. Plastic & raw materials	148	1.4	348	1.4	8.9
9. Rubber & products	88	0.8	226	0.9	9.9
10. Precious stones & Jewellery	1590	15.3	1106	4.4	-3.6
11. Paper & pulp	25	0.2	131	0.5	18
12. Cotton	165	1.6	602	2.4	13.8
13. MM filaments/fibre	108	1	273	1.1	9.7
14. Iron & steel & articles	675	6.5	723	2.9	0.7
15. Non ferrous metals	469	4.5	1322	5.2	10.9
16. Mechanical appliances	348	3.3	1617	6.4	16.6
17. Electrical &electronics	280	2.7	798	3.2	11
18. Transport equipment	698	6.7	2150	8.5	11.9
19. Optical/photo instruments	78	0.7	356	1.4	16.4
Sub-total	9330	89.6	20999	83.3	8.5

Source: Department of Commerce, Government of India; http://commerce.nic.in/MOC/index.asp

Considering the growth of export over last ten years, it has been observed that demand for sugar, meat products, fish products and spices in ASEAN market are considerably high. This indicates that the trading volume between India and ASEAN can be enlarged by these products' export to ASEAN from India. Further exports of pharmaceuticals, mechanical appliances, optical/photo instruments and cottons are increasing over the years, denoting hope for greater trade receipts from ASEAN.

Table 11.7: India's imports from ASEAN

Items	*2005-06*		*2015-16*		*CAGR*
	U.S.$ Million	*Share in total*	*U.S.$ Million*	*Share in total*	*2015-16/ 2005-06*
1. Pulses	254	2.3	**835**	2.1	12.6
2. Palm oil	1025	9.4	5782	14.5	18.9
3. Petroleum products	9		2806	7	77.6
4. Coal	843	7.7	**4842**	12.2	19.1
5. Chemicals	1062	9.8	**3053**	7.7	11.1
a. Inorganic	85	0.8	329	0.8	14.5
b. Organic	802	7.4	2075	5.2	10
c. Special chemicals	175	1.6	649	1.6	14
6. Pharmaceuticals	5		136	0.3	39.1
7. Plastic & raw materials	369	3.4	**1759**	4.4	16.9
8. Rubber & products	123	1.1	995	2.5	23.3
7. Precious stones & Jewellery	69	0.6	**817**	2.1	28
8. Wood & products	571	5.2	**973**	2.4	5.4
9. Paper & pulp	163	1.5	**358**	0.9	8.2
10. MM filaments &fibres	137	1.3	321	0.8	8.9
11. Iron & steel & articles	353	3.2	**1272**	3.2	13.7
12. Non-ferrous metals	202	1.9	**1602**	4	23
13. Mechanical appliances	1989	18.3	3741	9.4	6.5
14. Electrical &electronics	1298	11.9	4142	10.4	12.3
15. Transport equipment	502	4.6	1908	4.8	14.3
a. Rail equipment	0.3		1		
b. Autos & component	70	0.6	598	1.5	23.9
c. Aircraft & parts	139	1.3	209	0.5	4.2
d. Ships	293	2.7	1100	2.8	14.1
16. Optical/photo instruments	200	1.8	617	1.5	11.9
Total 1 to 16	9174	84.3	35959	90.3	14.6
Total ASEAN	10884	10.6*	**39843**	15.2*	13.9
Total Global	103091		262031		9.8

Source: Department of Commerce, Government of India; http://commerce.nic.in/MOC/index.asp

In contrast, India's imports from ASEAN in 2015-16 are concentrated and dominated by palm oil, coal, electrical and electronic equipment and mechanical appliances, chemicals and petroleum products. These five items accounted for more than 50 percent share in India's total imports from the ASEAN (Table 11.7)

Prospects and Challenges of NER in Expanding India's Trade with the ASEAN

Northeast India is mostly hilly; it has plains on both sides of the river Brahmaputra and the Himalayan range around it. The flora and fauna of this region is numerous and varied. The region accounts for 7.9 percent of the total land space of the country. The region is of strategic importance for the country on account of the fact that nearly 90 percent of its borders form India's international boundaries. This region is connected with the rest of India only through a narrow corridor in North Bengal, having an approximate width of 33 km on the eastern side and 21 km on the western side. This narrow corridor is popularly known as the "Siliguri neck" or the "Chicken's neck".

Table 11.8: State-wise gross state domestic product at constant (2011-12) prices

State	*GSDP - Constant Prices (Rs. in Crore)*					*(% Growth over previous year)*			
	2011-12	*2012-13*	*2013-14*	*2014-15*	*2015-16*	*2012-13*	*2013-14*	*2014-15*	*2015-16*
Arunachal Pradesh	11063	11288	12338	13110	14401	2.03	9.31	6.26	9.84
Assam	143175	147342	154525	166709	NA	2.91	4.88	7.88	NA
Manipur	12915	12985	14116	15030	NA	0.54	8.71	6.48	NA
Meghalaya	19918	20354	20726	21002	22704	2.19	1.83	1.33	8.1
Mizoram	7259	7778	9038	9634	NA	7.15	16.21	6.59	NA
Nagaland	11839	12442	13826	14115	NA	5.09	11.13	2.09	NA
Sikkim	11165	11421	12114	12882	13722	2.29	6.07	6.34	6.51
Tripura	19208	20873	22819	25086	NA	8.67	9.32	9.94	NA
NER	236542	244483	259502	277568	50827	30.87	67.46	46.91	24.45
All-India GDP	8736039	9226879	9839434	10552151	11350249				
% share of NER in All-India GDP	2.71%	2.65%	2.64%	2.63%	0.45%				

Source: Data Bank North Eastern Development Finance Corporation Ltd. http://databank.nedfi.com

From table , it is seen that at constant (2011-12) prices, the GSDP of the region in 2011-12 was Rs 236542 crore which increased to Rs 10552151 crore in 2014-15.The growth rate of the region is also on its rising trend recording 9.94 percent in 2014-15. But it reflects a poor share of NER in all-India GDP and this share is also gradually declining.

Potential Sectors for Development

The NER is quite rich in respect of its deposit of mineral resources. Available mineral resources in this region include coal, petroleum crude, natural gas, lime stone, siliminite, dolomite, uranium, china clay, kaolin, fuller's earth, feldspar etc. (Table 11.9).

Table 11.9: Mineral resources of different states of NE region

States	*Minerals*
Arunachal Pradesh	Coal, Limestone, Petroleum, Dolomite
Assam	Coal, Limestone, Petroleum, Granite, Silimanite, Iron ore, Quartzite, Feldsper, Clay, Natural Gas, Oil
Manipur	Chromite, limestone
Meghalaya	Coal, Limestone, Granite, Sillimanite, Iron ore, Quartzite, Felsper, Clay
Mizoram	Coal, Limestone, Oil, Natural Gas
Nagaland	Coal, Limestone, Petroleum, Slate, Marble
Sikkim	Zinc, Lead, Copper, Dolomite, Coal, Quartzite, Graphics, Talc
Tripura	Kaolin, Iron Ore, Limestone, Coal, Natural Gas

Source: Data Bank North Eastern Development Finance Corporation Ltd. http://databank.nedfi.com

The limited industrialisation that the region has so far seen has been centred around a few resource-based industries such as petroleum and natural gas, tea, coal, jute, forest products, some mineral based industries and some micro household industries such as handloom and handicrafts. The organised sector includes tea, petroleum, paper, cement, plywood, coal, jute, sugar and a few others while the unorganised sector represents a majority of enterprises in the region and includes the handloom and handicrafts, small food processing units, etc. Thus, most important industries in the region are the tea and petroleum industries. The flow of trade in the NE region has therefore been witnessed around these commodities. With rich mineral bases, the region's exports have primarily been raw materials such as coal, limestone, bamboo, fruits and vegetables while it has been importing mostly finished products from neighbouring countries, especially Bangladesh.

The overall trade involving NE India has grown from ~1,628 crore INR in 2009-10 to ~2,615 crore INR in 2013-14 at a CAGR of 13 per cent. However the share of the region in trade between India and its eastern neighbour is only 1 percent (FICCI, 2014). In spite of having enormous potential, the share of GDP of NER in all India GDP is very low.

Table 11.10: State-wise value of production of khadi and village industries in north eastern region of India 2009-10 to 2015-16
(in INR Lakh)

States	*2009-10*	*2010-11*	*2011-12*	*2012-13*	*2013-14*	*2014-15*	*2015-16* (P)*
Arunachal Pradesh	3902.68	4283.26	4714.43	5188.6	5642.5	5956.62	4765.29
Assam	48505.2	53146.74	58500.34	64350.74	69940.57	73780.33	59024.26
Manipur	8401.77	9211.1	10135.33	11152.66	12121.76	12784.37	10227.49
Meghalaya	9928.76	10887.69	11987.66	13194.08	14352.91	15142.58	12114.06
Mizoram	18957.27	20787.89	22884.2	25187.43	27391.38	28898.2	23118.56
Nagaland	10428.15	11428.85	12577.19	13761.33	15043.2	15871.77	12697.41
Sikkim	3413.07	3742.69	4120.14	4534.83	4931.67	5202.91	4162.32
Tripura	8961.42	9826.82	10818.93	11907.82	12949.94	13662.25	10929.8
India	**112498.32**	**123315.04**	**135738.22**	**149277.49**	**162373.93**	**171299.03**	**137039.19**

Source: Data Bank North Eastern Development Finance Corporation Ltd. http://databank.nedfi.com

India's economic growth could benefit from developing NER and exploring areas of potential in the region. Socio-economic indicators show a high level of regional imbalance and socio economic backwardness among north eastern states. The region is lagging behind other states in terms of per capita income, industrial growth, foreign investment and infrastructure. Even after 60 years of planned economic strategy the country has not succeeded in providing basic infrastructure and resource base to this geographically isolated and ethnically sensitive region. India's approach towards a balanced and sustainable economic growth under globalisation and liberalisation is not expected to achieve its targeted objective unless the compelling issues of regional imbalances are tackled with effective policy framework. The first step to attract industries to the region is to improve the industrial, transportation and support infrastructure. Currently, the region suffers from issues like poor roads and connectivity, inadequate power and storage facilities, insufficient number of custom clearance facilities, inefficiency in handling, etc. These issues are hindering the prospects of serious investments by industrial players in the region. To take advantage of the region's geographic location and speed up the evolving connectivity with Southeast Asia and the ASEAN, it is proposed that a northeast frontier economic corridor should be developed. Economic corridors that connect economic agents along a defined geography could provide a vital boost to the pace of development in resource-rich regions such as the northeast, where economic development has been slow (FICCI, 2014). There should be government programmes focused on export promotion from the NER. The identified products should be directly or indirectly available in the region. Further these identified products should have adequate infrastructure for sustained production/ processing. There must be sufficient demand for the identified products in the ASEAN market.

Conclusions

Economic growth and international trade are closely related to each other. Growth like changes in factor endowments, technology, tastes over time has an impact on the international trade. Growth in the factor endowment may affect terms of trade of a country. In case of India-ASEAN trade the present study reveals that over the last 11 years India's gain from trade is not positive where import growth and volume is much higher than that of the exports. However insertion foreign capital into the study may bring some different picture. Further considering production of importable commodities with high cost of production in a nation might not be good for optimal resource utilisation. Hence production of these importable goods and the related inputs associated with are needed to be considering further for measuring gains from trade. The study reveals that the growth of export over last ten years demand for sugar, meat products, fish products and spices in ASEAN market are considerably high. This indicates that the trading volume between India and ASEAN can be enlarged by these products' export to ASEAN from India. Further exports of pharmaceuticals, mechanical appliances, optical/photo instruments and cottons are increasing over the years, denoting hope for greater trade receipts from ASEAN. In contrast, India's imports from ASEAN in 2015-16 are concentrated and dominated by palm oil, coal, electrical and electronic equipment and mechanical appliances, chemicals and petroleum products. India's gain from trade with ASEAN can be judged by considering production costs of these importable goods and availability of related inputs associated with these commodities. Further encouraging production of these exportable goods may help to reduce trade deficit of India with ASEAN. Considering the potentials of north eastern region of India and its topography the government programmes are needed to be introduced with special focus on export promotion from the NER. The identified products should be directly or indirectly available in the region. Further these identified products should have adequate infrastructure for sustained production/processing. There must be sufficient demand for the identified products in the ASEAN market.

12

Indo-Myanmar Border Trade at Moreh-Tamu Sector: Retrospect and Prospect

Thangjam Chandra Devi and N.B. Singh

Introduction

The introduction of the 'Look East Policy' by the Government of India in 1991 and its subsequent Indo-Myanmar Border Trade agreement which became operational from 12 April, 1995 under the barter trade mechanism was considered as an opportunity for economic development for the north eastern region in general and Manipur in particular. Moreover as all goods from and to India have to pass through the state, the region has the possibility of developing commercially. The agreement is also highly significant as Myanmar is the land bridge that connects India to the ASEAN markets. With Myanmar becoming an ASEAN member, common markets of as many as 500 million consumers will be the entry point to South East Asian market (Singh, 2012).

With the trade opening, the gains from it to the economy would be enormous. And the positive benefits would be reflected through an increase in economic activities, employment, and high growth trajectories. It has also opened up the state to the vast opportunities for private sector investments in the field of manufacturing and industries that are export oriented. Since the state has vast untapped natural resources, the trade opening has provided an opportunity to harness it and create the vent for surplus. Further if an economy specialize in the production of one or two commodities and efforts are made to export them, it not only widens the market but also helps in employing the already existing resources more productively and efficiently. As a result, unemployment and underemployment can be reduced; domestic saving and investment increase; there is a larger inflow of factor inputs into the expanding export sector and forward linkages with other sectors of the economy. Initiation of international trade also provides the market, one of the most important factors for commercializing the agricultural sector. It would thus help in raising the income and the standards of living of the people. The expansion of the market leads to a number of internal and external economies, and hence leads to reduction in cost of production. As growth and exports have a dual causality and choosing the right strategy between export-led growth and growth-led export for development is insignificant and in the case of India and Myanmar border trade both the strategies would have to be adopted simultaneously (Das, 2016).

The main objective of the paper is to review the performance of the border trade since its beginning and to look into the prospects of optimising the gain from trade opening. The study is an explorative work primarily based on secondary data. The study has been organized into four sections including introduction. Section II discusses the performances of the Indo-Myanmar border trade in relation with Manipur. It will be followed by the prospects of the state vis-a-vis Indo Myanmar border Trade in section III. Section IV consists of the conclusion drawn from the analysis which is also the last section of the paper.

Performances of the Moreh-Tamu Border Trade

The amount of India's trade with Myanmar increases gradually from US$ 5662 million to US$ 135794 million showing the existence of a large trade potential between the two countries (appendix 1). Even though imports exceed the exports of India, the volume of the trade is expanding. Since the opening of the bilateral trade, India's export to Myanmar has increased from US$ 33469.95 million to US$ 314405.30 million during 2013-14 with the major item being pharmaceutical products. During the corresponding period India's import also grew from US$ 39132.41 million to US$ 450199.79 million with the major importing item being a bean species, vignamungo, hepper or vigna radiate and wilczek.

Comparing to other trading partners of Myanmar like China (87 percent) and Thailand (12 percent), the volume of India's border trade is also very less (0.8 percent) (Das, 2016). Moreover both the exports and imports in border trade show an erratic trend. During 1996-97 the volume of exports at Moreh-Tamu border trade stood at US$ 31.71 million and further decreased to US$ 14.52 million in 2013-14. In the corresponding period the imports increased from US$ 15.14 million to US$ 48.47 million. However, the formal trade volume (Moreh-Tamu) does not represent the actual volume of trade that is being carried out. It only represents the barter trade that is taking place through the Land Custom Station (LCS) with GR formalities (Priyoranjan, n.d). If we consider the informal trade that is taking place at Gate No. 2, then the figures would be very high. Since there are no explicit checks on the trade being carried out at the Gate No. 2 from both the governments, trade seems to be prospered there. And there are no official accounts kept the volume of trade taking place at Gate No. 2. The Government of Manipur has estimated the value of informal trade to be Rs. 2000 crore per year.

Though the LCS at Moreh is the busiest, handling 99 percent of the border trade with Myanmar, the formal trade at Moreh-Tamu is highly unstable and only contributes a very small amount (less than 1 percent of the total Indo-Myanmar trade). Another feature of the border trade is the absence of any product originating from the region. Out of the 62 tradable items none from the state is in the export basket. Among others this might also be another reason of the poor performance of border trade. The increase of the number of tradable items from 22 to 62 shows that there has been a huge prospect for optimising the gains from trade by inclusion of the products originating from the state.

The opening of the trade is expected to affect the economic indicators of the state like higher employment, higher income, better economic performances etc. It should have a direct impact on the sectors like transport, storage and communication, trade, hotels and restaurants, banking and insurance, construction, manufacturing, NSDP and lastly the PCI of the state. The annual compound growth rates of the different sectors during the period 1996-2013 are shown in table 12.1 below.

Table 12.1: Sectoral compound growth rate during 1996-2013

Sectors	*Estimates of b*	R^2	*Growth rate*
Primary	0.030740 (7.336182)*	0.756515	3.1217
Manufacturing	0.061907 (20.51539)*	0.961088	6.3863
Transport, Storage and Communication	0.066248 (12.39653)*	0.899808	6.8492
Trade, Hotels and Restaurants	0.046149 (20.43607)*	0.960796	4.7230
Banking and Insurance	0.111048 (26.71466)*	0.976702	11.7449
Real Estate	0.016117 (10.00048)*	0.853460	1.6248
Public Administration	0.066508 (6.935402)*	0.734789	6.8770
Other Services	0.052741 (7.204064)*	0.749626	5.4157
NSDP	0.052128 (8.767976)*	0.816963	5.3511
PCI	0.030440 (5.168846)*	0.602032	3.0908

Note: * implies significance at 1%.

The sectoral growth rates after the opening of the trade shows a mix result. Sectors like banking and insurance, public administration, manufacturing, transport, storage and communication, other services and NSDP grows at a rate higher than 5 percent. Out of these banking and insurance has the highest growth rate of 11.74 percent while the real estate has the least growth rate of 1.62 percent. The primary sector also grows at a rate of 3.12 percent. Another indication of the positive impact of trade can be examined from the structural change in the employment scenario. Agriculture continues to dominate the picture though its share has reduced slightly.

Table 12.2: Percentage distribution of usually working persons by PS+SS by broad industry division: Rural

NSS round	*Agri.*		*Mining & quarrying*		*Manufac turing*		*Construction*		*Trade*		*Transport*		*Services*	
	M	*F*	*M*	*F*	*M*	*F*	*M*	*F*	*M*	*F*	*M*	*F*	*M*	*F*
50	66.0	60.3	0.1		3.7	26.2	4.1	0.6	3.8	5.6	2.4		19.6	7.0
55	78.0	69.6	0.1	1.8	2.2	18.6	1.3		2.7	5.8	2.0		13.7	4.2
61	69.4	69.1	0.5	0.6	3.1	17.2	5.0	0.1	5.3	8.7	3.4		13.2	4.4
66	60.7	35.0	0.4	0	4.9	18.4	9.5	24.3	8.1	18.5	2.7	0	13.7	3.8
68	55.9	24.1	0.2	0.5	3.1	17.4	13.8	40.5	6.9	9.7	4.2	0.4	15.2	5.6

Source: Various reports of NSSO

The percentage sector-wise distribution of workers by PS+SS is shown in table 12.2 and 12.3. Post trade opening the percentage of population employed in agriculture has declined over the years for both rural and urban areas. Whereas manufacturing, construction and trade in both rural and urban category show an increasing trend except in rural female manufacturing category. Another feature is that manufacturing and trade sub-sector has remained predominantly a female industry. It may be due to the fact that traditionally small business and unregistered household manufacturing are carried out mostly by female. Construction also shows a dramatic rise in the proportion of male workers for both categories. While, construction, transport and service sector are mainly dominated by males. In rural area the proportion of female workers show a rapid rise in construction sub-sector indicating that the workers who quit from agriculture are being absorbed into this sub-sector. And that the trade opening has failed to provide employment in the related sectors. The reason for low employment generation may be due to the predominance of informal trade where people take these occupations as part time job. Another reason might be the heavy taxation from traders by insurgency groups which made the profit margin very less.

Thus despite all the expected positive benefits of trade opening, the effect of the actual trade in the state is nowhere to be seen. One of the reasons may be the absence of items manufactured or produced in the state in the export basket. The benefits that will get from trading of home produced product will be much greater than trading of the products that are not produced in the home state. Thus, in order to optimise the benefits from border trade, we need to develop the resource based industries.

Table 12.3: Percentage distribution of usually working persons by PS+SS by broad industry division: Urban

NSS round	*Agri.*		*Mining & quarrying*		*Manufac turing*		*Construction*		*Trade*		*Transport*		*Services*	
	M	*F*	*M*	*F*	*M*	*F*	*M*	*F*	*M*	*F*	*M*	*F*	*M*	*F*
50	30.9	26.1			4.4	34.2	3.8	0.3	10.8	19.5	4.6	0.2	43.7	19.6
55	29.3	26.3	1.3		5.5	21.5	6.0	0.3	16.4	27.4	4.4	1.9	37.1	22.5
61	31.3	21.5			7.8	29.0	6.5		17.0	26.1	6.0		31.0	23.4
66	24.3	7.1	0	0	5.8	32.8	9.2	0.3	25.6	35.9	4.4	0	29.7	23.8
68	23.1	11.6	0	0	8.2	44.2	13.2	0.3	17.4	24.8	9.3	0	26.0	15.1

Source: Same as table 2

Prospects

With the formal opening of Indo-Myanmar border trade, the region has been showered with many opportunities. Due to its ecological diversity and fertility of soil which are essential components of successful organic farming, the state can undertake it in a large scale. A certified organic product fetch good price in international market and its demand is increasing over the year. Organic farming envisages a comprehensive management approach to conserve soil health, ecosystem and over all environment of the region vis-à-vis improving the quality of produce. And this requires diversification towards organic farming.

The objectives of diversification of agriculture vary from country to country. The green revolution technologies have provided large amount of marketable surplus of dominant rice in the East and Southeast countries leading to the fall in the price of rice both in international and domestic market and farmers are exposed to secular declined in their income. In these countries income stabilization becomes the main objective for diversification of agriculture through direct public policy in the 80s. In India, crops diversification towards high value crops started during 1990s, coincidental with the liberalization of the economy.

In Manipur, the diversification of agriculture towards high value organic products can help in stimulating the economy and also provide employment opportunities. As high value crops can also generates additional employment through creation of associated activities like processing, packaging, marketing etc. Since many of the high value crops are highly perishable the knowledge of the educated youths which constitute sizable proportion of the rural labour force can also be utilized in the development of agro processing industries. Various institutions like North Eastern Industrial Consultants (NECON) and CMI Social Research Centre have also identified the feasible processing Industry that can be set up in the state (Table 12.4, only horticulture crops). Thus, the region can take the advantage of trade opening and export its products to the ASEAN markets.

Table 12.4: Surplus quantities available and type products that can be produced

Sl.No.	Name of Crop	Surplus (in MT)	Types of products
1	Fruit		
	a) Pineapple	24000	Squash, Juice, Canned, Jam, Jelly, candy etc
	b) Orange	1962	Squash, Juice
	c) Papaya	5320	Canned, extraction of papain
	d) Passion fruit	5300	Squash, Juice
2	Spices		
	a) Ginger	7045	Oil extraction, paste, candy, RTS drinks
	b) Chillies	22200	Pickles, Powder, dried, paste

Source: Modified from CMI Social Research Centre, "Export potential of Horticultural Products from north eastern states".

Indo-Myanmar border trade provides an ample scope for the marketing of farm sector. The trade can be optimised only when the export basket is filled with products from the resource based industry of the state. The development of major industrial units is not likely to be in the near future at the present geo-political environment, organic products give a viable option to fill the export basket. However, all these requires good infrastructure, favourable business environment and well designed public policy to steer the diversification of agriculture. Given the necessary steps from the relevant government authority the state can really become the hub of organic farming since the state has already an abundant supply of natural resources like horticulture crops. Another added benefit about diversification towards organic farming is that it also helps in the conservation and enhancement of the environment. By adopting organic farming the costs of agriculture to the environment in terms of natural resource degradation are reduced. This way the twin objectives of maximizing the benefits of trade opening as well as conservation of environment can be achieved.

Conclusion

The common belief of the opening of border trade is that it would help the region in accessing the booming markets of the south east, which in turn would provide the opportunity for industrialisation and growth. However, the reality has been far from the belief. The agreement have a limited impact on the development of the region due to several reasons like lack of connectivity within and outside the state, lack of specialisation in exportable products, low level of industrialisation, underdeveloped infrastructure, existence of underdeveloped market, institutional problems and lastly insurgency problems. If the concerning authority do not take necessary steps to stimulate the trade then the fear of the people that the state will reduce to a mere transit station will come true. However, given these constraints are removed the state has the potential to develop. Along with the positive effects, there is also a huge negative effect of border trade in the region. Since the opening of border trade the transactions of negative items like drugs, smuggling, human trafficking and the activities of criminals have also increased tremendously. The presence of large informal trade also assists to the problems. It is time for the policy makers to make a fresh and comprehensive review of the policies and programmes.

APPENDIX 1

Trends of Indo-Myanmar trade

(in US$ million)

Year	Indo-Myanmar trade		Balance of Trade	Moreh-Tamu border trade		Balance of Trade
	Export	Import		Export	Import	
1996-97	33469.95	39132.41	-5662.46	31.71 (0.10)	15.18 (0.04)	16.53
1997-98	34784.98	41484.49	-6699.51	22.45 (0.07)	35.08 (0.09)	-12.63
1998-99	33218.72	42388.71	-9169.99	05.06 (0.02)	03.74 (0.01)	01.32
1999-00	36822.49	49738.06	-12915.57	03.26 (0.01)	03.68 (0.01)	-04.42
2000-01	44560.29	50536.45	-5976.16	05.26 (0.01)	00.19 (0.0004)	05.10
2001-02	43826.72	51413.28	-7586.56	01.25 (0.003)	08.30 (0.02)	07.05
2002-03	52719.43	61412.14	-8692.71	03.66 (0.007)	12.15 (0.02)	08.49
2003-04	63842.55	78149.11	-14306.56	08.74 (0.01)	08.30 (0.01)	00.68
2004-05	83535.94	111517.43	-27981.49	05.64 (0.007)	05.01 (0.004)	00.63
2005-06	103090.53	149165.73	-46075.2	04.09 (0.004)	03.30 (0.002)	7.39
2006-07	126414.05	185735.24	-59321.19	62.13* (0.05)	01.78 (0.001)	60.35
2007-08	163132.18	251654.01	-88521.83	06.01 (0.004)	16.29 (0.001)	-10.28
2008-09	185295.36	303696.31	-118400.95	01.60 (0.001)	00.76 (0.0003)	00.84
2009-10	178751.43	288372.88	-109621.45	21.50 (0.012)	08.31 (0.003)	13.19
2010-11	249815.55	369769.13	-119953.58	00.26 (0.0001)	03.80 (0.001)	-03.54
2011-12	305963.92	489314.49	-183350.57	01.49 (0.0005)	01.36 (0.0003)	0.13
2012-13	300400.58	490736.65	-190336.07	27.24 (0.009)	20.55 (0.004)	6.69
2013-14	314405.30	450199.79	-135794.49	14.52 (0.005)	48.47 (0.012)	-33.95

Notes: 1. Figure in the parentheses shows the percentage of border trade to Indo-Myanmar trade.
2. * Including defence items.

Sources: 1. Department of Commerce, GOI
2. Das. Ram Upendra. (2016): Enhancing India-Myanmar Border Trade: Policy and Implementation Measures, Department of Commerce, GOI

APPENDIX 2

Tradable items at Moreh-Tamu border trade

List of tradable items	*Items actually traded*	*Items that can be exported from Manipur*
Bamboo, Betel Nuts and Leaves, Chilies, Coriander Seeds, Food Items for Local consumption, Fresh Vegetables, Fruits, Garlic, Ginger, Katha, Minor forest products (excluding Teak), Mustard/Rape seed, Onion, Pulses and Beans, Reed Broom, Resin, Roasted Sunflower Seeds Sesame, Soya bean, Spices (excluding Nut Meg, Mace, Cloves, Cassia & Cinnamon), Edible Oil, Tobacco, Tomato, Sugar & Salt, Milk powder, Rice, Wheat, Maize, Millets& Oats, Scented tobacco, tea, beverages. Bicycle's spare parts, Blades, Bulbs, Fertilizers, Imitation jewellery, Insecticides Coils, Paints & Varnishes, Stainless steel utensils, X Ray paper& Photo paper, Leather footwear, Menthol, Mosquito coils Agricultural machinery/equipments/tools, Bicycle, Bleaching powder, Coal, Electrical & Electric Appliances, Fabricated steel products, Garments/readymade garments/cloths, Handlooms and handicrafts items, Hardware/minor construction materials and electrical fittings, Lime, Medicines, Motor Cycles& Motor Cycle Spare Parts, Other items such as electronic/musical instruments, s tationary item, torch light, Plastic items: water tank, buckets, chairs, plastic pipes and briefcase, Semi precious stone, Sewing machines, Textile fabrics, Three wheelers/cars below 1000 CC. Cosmetics, Life saving drugs, Agarbatti, Cotton fabrics.	Betel nut (whole and split), ginger (dry and fresh), wheat flour, Tata Sumo vehicle, dry grapes, masoorie pulse, Peas, Solar plates and batteries	Bamboo, Chilies, Food Items for Local consumption, Fresh Vegetables, Fruits, Onion, Edible Oil, Tomato, Sugar & Salt, Milk powder, Handlooms and handicrafts items,

Sources: 1. Das. Ram Upendra. (2016): Enhancing India-Myanmar Border Trade: Policy and Implementation Measures, Department of Commerce, GOI.
2. Department of commerce and Industry, Government of Manipur.

13

Export Potential of North Eastern Region of India: An Application of Log-Loss Model

Subroto Chowdhury

Introduction

In the aspiration to find new areas of collaboration and avenues for possible consolidation, global integration in the areas of trade and business has evolved over the years. Strategic collaboration might have been conceived as an idea to boost presence in the emerging markets, but, global economic integration has added a new dimension to the milieu of economic dynamism. Market forces tend to normalize things in its own perspective, however, economic decision making both at the micro and macro level have its own bearing in shaping the market forces. Trade integration plays in integral part in the process of economic integration and is often alternatively used to represent the extent of economic integration. Balassa (1961) defines economic integration as *"the abolition of discrimination within an area"*. And according to Kahnert et. al (1969) economic integration is *"the process of removing progressively those discriminations which occur at national borders"*. Thus forms of cooperation is distinct from the fact that the measures adopted for minimizing discriminating factors amongst countries cannot be termed as integration. Economic integration in its terminological aspect may take up different usage as pointed out by Allen (1963, p.450), but, work of Balassa (1961) in his book has been successful to define integration to a much greater extent. Additionally, Lipsey (1960, p.496) came up with the definition of the customs union theory (economic integration theory) as follows: *"The theory of customs unions may be defined as that branch of tariff theory which deals with the effects of geographically discriminatory changes in trade barriers [among countries]"* Authors like Machlup (1977) identifies integration as the process of combining two separate economies into a larger economic region. Moreover, Machlup (1977) and Staley (1977, p.243) puts integration as *the "utilization of all potential opportunities of efficient division of labor"*.

Forms of Economic Integration

There are mainly four stages of economic integration as proposed by Balasaa (1962). The first is a Free Trade Area (FTA), then a Customs Union (CU), then a Common Market (CM), and finally an Economic Union. Based on the terminological variants of PTA, which may assume the names of *Preferential Trade Area*, *Preferential Trade Agreement* or *Preferential Trade Arrangement*, deemed to have acquired an advantage which helps it to be described as FTAs, CUs and arrangements involving partial trade preferences, in line with the arguments put forward by Panagariya (1998, p.2; and 2000, p.288).

Preferential Trade Arrangements (PTAs) aims at lowering the tariff barriers amongst the participating nations in comparison with that of non participating nations. PTAs has been also defined as an arrangement between two or more countries in which goods produced within the union are subject to lower trade barriers than the goods produced outside the union (Panagariya, 1998, p.2; and 2000, p.288). PTAs *often* take the shape of a *Free Trade Agreement (FTA)* wherein imposing of zero tariffs seems to be prevalent between the member countries and tailored tariff with the non members. The tariff barriers to trade with non-members often results in "trade integration". North American Free Trade Agreement (NAFTA) formed by the United States of America (USA), Canada, and Mexico in 1993 can be cited to be a good example. When the member countries apply a common external tariff on a good imported from outside countries, it results in a FTA known as *Customs Union (CU)*. The most famous example is the European Community (EC), formed in 1957 by West Germany, France, Italy, Belgium, the Netherlands, and Luxembourg can be cited as a best example for CU.

The form of Customs union allowing free movement of labor and capital among member nations is termed as a *Common Market (CM)* and is usually referred to as "factor integration". At the beginning of 1993, the EU achieved the status of a CM. The most advanced type of economic integration results in E*conomic Union,* it aims at integrating the fiscal and monetary policies of the nations thereby forming a unified harmonized policy. This is usually referred to as "policy integration". The extreme case of an Economic Union could be a *Monetary Union (MU).* A good example for the former is the countries of the EU who use a single currency, the Euro.

The Gains from Economic Integration

According to the arguments put forth by Bhagwati and Panagariya (1996, p.82), it is understood that the theory of preferential trade agreements (theory of economic integration) has been evolving over time. The shape and the purpose of economic integrations distinctively reflect the need of the hour, as evident from the contrasting policies. The purpose of integration, often results in factor integration, resources integrating and finally culminating into policy integration at the highest level. Traditional theories that aim at understanding the gains from economic integration often results into static analysis. However, changing economic scenario resulted in dynamic analysis for understanding the gains from economic integration.

Dynamic vs. Static analysis of integration

Economic integration and its dynamic effects were perhaps first highlighted by Balassa (1962), and Cooper and Massell (1965a, p.743). According to Allen (1963. p.451), Balassa (1962) in his work explained on the dynamic effects of integration and listed them as the impact on large-scale economies, technological change, as well as the impact of integration on market structure and competition, productivity growth, risk and uncertainty, and investment activity. Kreinin (1963, p.193) echoed with the view of Balssa (1962). In line with the understanding of Brada and Mendez (1988, p.163-164), it may be subsumed that economic integration plays a pivotal role in reducing risk and raising investments. The idea of risk reduction and increased investments is based on the understanding that integration often results in larger markets thereby ensuring large poll of customers, larger resource availability and more induced return on investment and increased economies of scale. Schiff and winters (1998, p.179) defines the dynamic effects of economic integration as the developments affecting country's economic growth rate over the medium term.

ASEAN and Northeast India (Prologue on the Model)

The case of economic integration amongst the ASEAN countries and that of northeast India (herein after NER) is expected to play a pivotal role in shaping up the policies of respective Governments to promote the dynamics of the trading block. The role of NER and its utmost importance in shaping India's economic integration initiative with that of ASEAN countries is well documented in almost all the documents putting commentary on this issue albeit any exception. The motivation of this study revolves around in finding out the possible areas of integration. The study designs quantitative modeling of the possible extent of integration (extent of export potentiality used as a proxy) of the horticultural resources and Micro Small and Medium Enterprise (herein after MSME) in the states of NER.

The Model

Ceteris Paribus the extent of export potentiality of the horticulture resources and the extent of export potentiality of the MSME in the NER is expected to boost the potentiality of resource integration amongst the NER and ASEAN countries.

Assumptions

1. Extent of export potentiality is expected to be the correct proxy for extent of economic integration of the resources
2. Intra state disparity of the use of resources are kept to be constant
3. Resources availability is assumed to be at constant prices
4. Intra state factor endowments and comparative advantage are held to be constant

Log-loss function is used to derive the coefficients of the constant and beta of the log linear function and the respective probabilities associated with the log linear functional value while minimizing the log loss function (as represented by error of the logit function).

$$\mathcal{L}(q()) = \frac{1}{N}\sum_{n=1}^{N} [-y_n \log(q_n) - (1-y_n)\log(1-q_n)] \ ,$$

$$L_1(1-q) = -\log(q) \ , \quad L_0(q) = -\log(1-q) \ ,$$

$$\mathbf{R}(\eta|q) = -\eta\log(q) - (1-\eta)\log(1-q) \ ,$$

Log-loss is sometimes called Kullback-Leibler loss or cross—entropy term of the Kullback-Leibler divergence.

The Logit Model

For the assessment of export potential of Fruits, Vegetables, Flowers and Spices

$$\text{Log } (p/1\text{-}p) = \alpha + \beta X_i$$

Or

$$Y^* = \alpha + \beta X_i$$

Where,

Y^* = Log (p/1-p)
P = probability of export potential
α = Constant
β = slope coefficient
X_i = Value of production

The probability of export potential is expressed with the help of the following transformation

$$P = \text{Exp } (\alpha + \beta X_i)/1 + \text{Exp } (\alpha + \beta X_i)$$

For the assessment of export potential of MSME

$$\text{Log } (q/1\text{–}q) = \lambda + \delta X_i$$

Or

$$X^* = \lambda + \delta X_i$$

Where,

X^* = Log (q/1–q)
q = probability of export potential
λ = Constant
δ = slope coefficient
X_i = Value of Gross Value Added

The probability of export potential is expressed with the help of the following transformation

$$q = \text{Exp } (\lambda + \delta X_i)/1 + \text{Exp } (\lambda + \delta X_i)$$

Findings

The north eastern states of Arunachal Pradesh, Assam, Manipur, Meghalaya, Mizoram, Nagaland, Sikkim and Tripura are highly conducive for the growth of various horticulture crops. These states have been producing many such crops, which have a very high potential for supplying to the export markets in fresh and processed forms. The geo-climatic situation in the region offers excellent scope for growing different horticultural crops including fruits, vegetables, spices, flowers, plantation crops, medicinal and aromatic plants. A wide range of tropical, subtropical and temperate fruits such as banana, Mandarine orange, pineapple, jackfruit, papaya, hatkora (Citrus microphylla) etc. and vegetables, both indigenous and exotic, are grown in the region. The high altitudinal places in the region provide good opportunities to grow offseason vegetables, including potato etc during the rainy season.

Table 13.1: NER fruit production (2011-12)

States	*Production (000'MT)*
Arunachal Pradesh	107.9
Assam	1763.5
Manipur	286.3
Meghalaya	241.9
Mizoram	211.5
Nagaland	151.3
Sikkim	25.8
Tripura	643.9
NER Total	3432.1
All India	71515.5

Source: Basic Statistics of north eastern region 2015, Government of India, North Eastern Council Secretariat (Evaluation and Monitoring Sector), Nongrim hills, shillong-793003, Issue no. 14, Year of publication: 2015.

As evident from table 13.1, Assam leads amongst the states in NER in the production of fruits.

It can be inferred from table 13.2 through 13.4 that the total log-loss value is minimized at 0.262192, thereby yielding the model parameters to be 1.946 (constant) and 0.654 (production), with the maximum increase in probability (about 4.205 percent) of export of fruits from NER when the production on an average increases by 10,000,000 MT for NER as a whole.

Table 13.2: Log-loss Model (export potential of Fruits in NER) Data

States	*Production*	*exp_pot*	*Y**	*p*	*logloss*
Arunachal Pradesh	0.031438478	1	1.966561	0.877241	(2.10)
Assam	0.513825355	1	2.209737	0.901121	(2.31)
Manipur	0.083418315	1	1.970297	0.877643	(2.10)
Meghalaya	0.070481629	1	2.021411	0.883027	(2.15)
Mizoram	0.061624079	1	2.06194	0.887148	(2.18)
Nagaland	0.044083797	1	1.98552	0.879268	(2.11)
Sikkim	0.007517263	0	2.000844	0.880886	(2.13)
Tripura	0.187611084	1	1.964147	0.876981	(2.10)

Source: Author's Calculation

Table 13.3: Model Coefficients for Log-loss Model (export potential of Fruits in NER)

Model	*coefficients*
Intercept	1.946
Production	0.654
Total Log-loss	0.262192

Source: Author's Calculation

Table 13.4: Simulation data for export potential of Fruits in NER

		Simulation			
Increments	Base	1	100	1000	10000
Intercept	1	1	1	1	1
production	0.125	0.125255	0.149773	0.322423	0.776425
Y*	2.02775	2.027916686	2.043951	2.156865	2.453782
probability	0.88368	0.883697133	0.885335	0.896309	0.920838
change		0.002%	0.187%	1.429%	4.205%

Source: Author's Calculation

As evident from table 13.5, Assam leads amongst the states in NER in the production of vegetables. It can be inferred from table 13.6 through 13.8 that the total log-loss value is minimized at 0.0590 thereby yielding the model parameters to be -0.511 (constant) and 0.433 (production), with the maximum increase in probability (about 16.003 percent) of export of vegetables from NER when the production on an average increases by 10,000,000 MT for NER as a whole.

Table 13.5: NER Region Vegetable Production (2011-12)

	Production (000'MT)
Arunachal Pradesh	84
Assam	3046
Manipur	200
Meghalaya	385
Mizoram	221
Nagaland	223
Sikkim	128
Tripura	553
NER Total	4838
All India	156326

Source: Basic Statistics of north eastern region 2015, Government of India, North Eastern Council Secretariat (Evaluation and Monitoring Sector), Nongrim hills, shillong-793003, Issue no. 14, Year of publication: 2015.

Table 13.6: Log-loss Model (export potential of Vegetables in NER) Data

States	*Production*	*exp_pot*	*Z*	*p*	*logloss*
Arunachal Pradesh	0.017355372	0	-0.50349	0.376722	-0.47276
Assam	0.629338843	0	-0.2385	0.440657	-0.58099
Manipur	0.041322314	1	-0.49311	0.379162	-0.47668
Meghalaya	0.079545455	0	-0.47656	0.383066	-0.48299
Mizoram	0.045661157	1	-0.49123	0.379604	-0.4774
Nagaland	0.04607438	0	-0.49105	0.379646	-0.47747
Sikkim	0.026446281	0	-0.49955	0.377647	-0.47425
Tripura	0.114256198	1	-0.46153	0.386624	-0.48878

Source: Author's Calculation

Table 13.7: Model Coefficients for Log-loss Model (export potential of Vegetables in NER)

Model	*coefficients*
Intercept	-0.511
Surplus	0.433
Total Log-loss	0.05909533

Source: Author's Calculation

Table 13.8: Simulation data for export potential of Vegetables in NER

		Simulation			
	Base	1	100	1000	10000
Intercept	1	1	1	1	1
production	0.125	0.125181	0.142713	0.274829	0.714623
Y*	-0.45688	-0.4568	-0.44921	-0.392	-0.20157
probability	0.387727	0.387746	0.38955	0.403236	0.449778
change		0.0048%	0.4700%	3.9999%	16.0036%

Source: Author's Calculation

As evident from table 13.9, Arunachal Pradesh leads amongst the states in NER in the production of flowers.

Table 13.9: NER Region Flower Production (2011-12)

State	*Production (000'MT)*
Arunachal Pradesh	2860
Assam	0
Manipur	0
Meghalaya	0
Mizoram	349
Nagaland	15
Sikkim	209
Tripura	0
NER Total	3434
All India	75066

Source: Basic Statistics of north eastern region 2015, Government of India, North Eastern Council Secretariat (Evaluation and Monitoring Sector), Nongrim hills, shillong-793003, Issue no. 14, Year of publication: 2015.

It can be inferred from table 13.10 through 13.12 that the total log-loss value is minimized at 0.2054 thereby yielding the model parameters to be 0.000 (constant) and 1.715 (production), with the maximum increase in probability (about 42.953 percent) of export of flowers from NER when the production on an average increases by 10,000,000 MT for NER as a whole.

Table 13.10: Log-loss Model (export potential of Flowers in NER) Data

States	*Production*	*exp_pot*	*Y**	*p*	*logloss*
Arunachal Pradesh	0.83309059	1	1.42875	0.806707	-1.64355
Assam	0	0	0	0.5	-0.69315
Manipur	0	0	0	0.5	-0.69315
Meghalaya	0	0	0	0.5	-0.69315
Mizoram	0.10166036	1	0.174348	0.543477	-0.78412
Nagaland	0.00436936	1	0.007493	0.501873	-0.6969
Sikkim	0.0608797	1	0.104409	0.526078	-0.74671
Tripura	0	0	0	0.5	-0.69315

Source: Author's Calculation

Table 13.11: Model Coefficients for Log-loss Model (export potential of Flowers in NER)

Model	*Coefficients*
Intercept	0
Surplus	1.715
Total Log-loss	0.20544321

Source: Author's Calculation

Table 13.12: Simulation data for export potential of Flowers in NER

		Simulation			
	Base	1	100	1000	10000
	1	1	1	1	1
production	0.125	0.125255	0.149766	0.322383	0.776381
Y*	0.214375	0.214812	0.25685	0.552887	1.331493
probability	0.553389	0.553497	0.563862	0.634805	0.791088
change		0.020%	1.892%	14.712%	42.953%

Source: Author's Calculation

As evident from table 13.13 Assam leads amongst the states in NER in the production of spices.

Table 13.13: NER Region Spices Production (2011-12)

States	*Production (000'MT)*
Arunachal Pradesh	61.6
Assam	261.6
Manipur	24.1
Meghalaya	74.8
Mizoram	115
Nagaland	39.2
Sikkim	54.4
Tripura	18
NER Total	648.7
All India	5951.5

Source: Basic Statistics of north eastern region 2015, Government of India, North Eastern Council Secretariat (Evaluation and Monitoring Sector), Nongrim hills, shillong-793003, Issue no. 14, Year of publication: 2015.

Table 13.14: Log-loss Model (export potential of Spices in NER) Data

States	*Production*	*exp_pot*	*Y**	*p*	*logloss*
Arunachal Pradesh	0.094959	1	1.980755	0.878762	-2.11
Assam	0.403268	1	2.093596	0.890279	-2.20982
Manipur	0.037151	1	1.959597	0.876489	-2.09143
Meghalaya	0.115308	1	1.988203	0.879553	-2.11654
Mizoram	0.177278	1	2.010884	0.881935	-2.13652
Nagaland	0.060429	0	1.968117	0.877409	-2.0989
Sikkim	0.08386	1	1.976693	0.878328	-2.10643
Tripura	0.027748	1	1.956156	0.876116	-2.08841

Source: Author's Calculation

It can be inferred from table 13.14 through 13.16 that the total log-loss value is minimized at 0.2637 thereby yielding the model parameters to be 1.946 (constant) and 0.366 (production), with the maximum increase in probability (about 3.219 percent) of export of spices from NER when the production on an average increases by 10,000,000 MT for NER as a whole.

Table 13.15: Model Coefficients for Log-loss Model (export potential of Spices in NER)

Model	*Coefficients*
Intercept	1.946
Surplus	0.366
Total Log-loss	0.26375

Source: Author's Calculation

Table 13.16: Simulation data for export potential of Spices in NER

		Simulation			
	Base	1	100	1000	10000
	1	1	1	1	1
	0.125	0.126347	0.241869	0.655721	0.946697
Y*	1.99175	1.992243	2.034524	2.185994	2.292491
probability	0.879928	0.87998	0.884375	0.898985	0.908253
change		0.006%	0.505%	2.166%	3.219%

Source: Author's Calculation

As evident from table 13.17 Assam leads amongst the states in NER in GVA in the MSME sector.

Table 13.17: NER Region Micro, Small and Medium Enterprise (Registered Sector) GVA (Rs crore) (2011-12)

States	*GVA (Rs crore)*
Arunachal Pradesh	99
Assam	4643
Manipur	94
Meghalaya	152
Mizoram	182
Nagaland	618
Sikkim	16
Tripura	219

Source: Basic Statistics of north eastern region 2015, Government of India, North Eastern Council Secretariat (Evaluation and Monitoring Sector), Nongrim hills, shillong-793003, Issue no. 14, Year of publication: 2015.

It can be inferred from table 13.18 through 13.20 that the total log-loss value is minimized at 0.088 thereby yielding the model parameters to be 0.000 (constant) and 1.409 (production), with the maximum increase in probability (about 32.414 percent) of export potentiality of MSME from NER when the GVA (gross value added) on an average increases by 10,000,000 Rs Crore for NER as a whole.

Table 13.18: Log-loss Model (export potential of Micro, Small and Medium Enterprise (Registered Sector) in NER) Data

States	*GVA (Rs crore)*	*exp_pot*	*X**	*p*	*Log-loss*
Arunachal Pradesh	0.016437	0	0.02316	0.50579	-0.70479
Assam	0.770878	1	1.086168	0.747659	-1.37698
Manipur	0.015607	0	0.02199	0.505497	-0.7042
Meghalaya	0.025237	0	0.035558	0.508889	-0.71108
Mizoram	0.030217	0	0.042576	0.510643	-0.71466
Nagaland	0.102607	1	0.144573	0.53608	-0.76804
Sikkim	0.002656	1	0.003743	0.500936	-0.69502
Tripura	0.036361	1	0.051232	0.512805	-0.71909

Source: Author's Calculation

Table 13.19: Model Coefficients for Log-loss Model (export potential of Micro, Small and Medium Enterprise (Registered Sector) in NER)

Model	*Coefficients*
Intercept	0
Surplus	1.409
Total Log-loss	0.088099

Source: Author's Calculation

Table 13.20: Simulation data for export potential of Micro, Small and Medium Enterprise (Registered Sector) in NER

		Simulation			
	Base	1	100	1000	10000
	1	1	1	1	1
	0.125	0.125145	0.13929	0.249591	0.67109
X*	0.176125	0.17633	0.19626	0.351673	0.945566
Probability	0.543918	0.543969	0.548908	0.587023	0.720223
change		0.009%	0.917%	7.925%	32.414%

Source: Author's Calculation

Overall simulation data reveals that states in the NER reflects different probabilities of economic integration as reflected in the potential for export as depicted in table 13.21. Simulation study reveals that the increase in 10,000 units ('000 MT) in production of fruits, vegetables, flowers and spices may lead to highest economic integration as depicted by the probabilities. In case of MSME, simulation studies reveals that the increase in 10,000 (Rs Cr) in GVA may lead to highest economic integration in MSME as depicted by the probabilities. Table 13.22 highlights the position of the states in the NER region. Assam shows highest possibility of integration in MSME, fruit, vegetables and spices. Arunachal Pradesh shows highest possibility of integration in flower. The analysis points to an important finding. It reveals that on a whole, NER exhibits excellent opportunity in the possibility of integration in the MSME, fruit, vegetables, flowers and spices.

Table 13.21: Comparison of Simulation data for export potential of Micro, Small and Medium Enterprise, Fruits, Vegetables and Spices in NER

			Simulations All			
Type		Base	1	100	1000	10000
MSME	change		0.009%	0.917%	7.925%	32.414%
Fruit	change		0.023%	2.211%	18.395%	65.885%
Flower	change		0.020%	1.892%	14.712%	42.953%
Spices	change		0.006%	0.505%	2.166%	3.219%
Vegetables	change		0.0048%	0.4700%	3.9999%	16.0036%

Source: Author's Calculation

Table 13.22: Comparison of probability for export potential of Micro, Small and Medium Enterprise, Fruits, Vegetables and Spices in NER (state-wise)

Type *States*	*MSME* *Probability*	*Fruit* *Probability*	*Flower* *Probability*	*Spices* *Probability*	*Vegetables* *Probability*
Arunachal Pradesh	50.58%	25.73%	**80.67%**	87.88%	37.67%
Assam	**74.77%**	**38.54%**	50.00%	**89.03%**	**44.07%**
Manipur	50.55%	***26.97%***	50.00%	87.65%	37.92%
Meghalaya	50.89%	26.65%	50.00%	***87.96%***	***38.31%***
Mizoram	51.06%	26.44%	54.35%	88.19%	37.96%
Nagaland	53.61%	26.02%	50.19%	87.74%	37.96%
Sikkim	50.09%	25.17%	***52.61%***	87.83%	37.76%
Tripura	***51.28%***	29.57%	50.00%	87.61%	38.66%

Legends: **First**—Bold letters; Second—Underline letters; ***Third***—Bold Italics letters
Source: Author's Calculation

Conclusion

Policy initiatives focusing on the developmental paradigms of northeast India have undergone a shift in its focus and milieu. Neighborhood policy has also been reinstated with a better understanding of its importance in regional development. Policy dynamics from Look East to Act East exerts itself to be proactive in nature aiming at trade related governance rather than security related governance. In this backdrop the potential of natural collaboration in the resources availability, financial penetration, inputs usage and trade dynamics between regions may help us to better understand the dynamics of economic resource integration. The present study focuses on investigating the patterns of export potentiality in the areas of horticultural resources and MSME sectors so as to get an understanding of the trade dynamics between regions (case of regions of northeast India and ASEAN. Overall Simulation data reveals that states in the NER reflects different probabilities of economic integration as reflected in the potential for export as depicted in table 13.21. Simulation study reveals that the increase in 10,000 units ('000 MT) in production of fruits, vegetables, flowers and spices may lead to highest economic integration as depicted by the probabilities. In case of MSME, simulation studies reveals that the increase in 10,000 (Rs Cr) in GVA may lead to highest economic integration in MSME as depicted by the probabilities. The study reveals that on a whole, NER exhibits excellent opportunity in the possibility of integration in the MSME, fruit, vegetables, flowers and spices.

LOCAL INITIATIVES

14

ASEAN, NER and Barak Valley

Dipon Ghosh

Introduction

The academic writing on Barak Valley is itself a challenge and herculean task because there are few footprints of works in this area. Any plan or strategy for Barak Valley looks like an imaginary exercise because all these seem to remain folded in papers only. The skepticism can be naturally experienced from the present precarious scenario of this valley especially in economic front. But this does not mean that we should stop our endeavor for the better future. Whatever has been achieved so far is the result of constant effort and relentless exercise of the people of this valley. So, here is an effort to re-explore the potentials of Barak Valley so that it can find its market in ASEAN economies by recognizing and utilizing its resources. And this is not a dream.

The time is changing fast and no country can afford to stay isolated in this era of change. This is also applicable for any region of a country. The Barak Valley which is part of South Assam consisting of three districts (Cachar, Karimganj and Hailakandi) must strive for the socio-economic upliftment by unfolding its hidden potentials. An opportunity is provided by the ASEAN economies which have already deepened its economic ties with India during the last two and half decades. The question arises: why the ASEAN economies? The first reason is the geographical location of Barak valley. Second, the ray of hope is given by the three projects such as KMMTTP, IMT trilateral

Highway. Third, the unexplored potential of the region which if utilized properly is able to create a market in ASEAN countries. The objective of the paper is to analyze the potentials and constraints of Barak Valley in the context of expanding its relationship with ASEAN economies. The paper also suggested some measures to expedite the process of economic development of Barak valley.

ASEAN and India

Association of Southeast Asian Nations (ASEAN) came into existence in 1967 to promote inter-governmental cooperation and facilitate economic integration among the member countries. At present the association has ten members which include Indonesia, Malaysia, the Philippines, Singapore, Thailand, Brunei, Cambodia, Laos, Myanmar and Vietnam. ASEAN shares land borders with India, China, Bangladesh, East Timor and Papua New Guinea and maritime borders with India, China, Palau and Australia. The importance of ASEAN countries to India has magnified after the latter's adoption of 'Look East Policy' in 1990s. Look East Policy (LEP) aims at integrating India

Table 14.1: Size of the ASEAN economies

Country	*Total land area km²* 2015	*Total population thousand* 2015	*Gross domestic product at current prices US$ million* 2015
Brunei	5,769	417.2	12,909
Cambodia	181,035	15,405.2	18,463
Indonesia	1,913,579	255,461.7	857,603
Laos	236,800	6,902.4	12,639
Malaysia	330,290	30,485.3	294,390
Myanmar	676,577	52,476.0	65,392
Philippines	300,000	101,562.3	289,503
Singapore	719	5,535.0	291,938
Thailand	513,120	68,979.0	395,726
Viet Nam	330,951	91,713.3	193,407
ASEAN	4,488,839	628,937.3	2,431,969
India	3287.3*	1295.3**	2028***

Notes: *The figure is in KM² Thousand for the year 2014. **In million for the year 2014. ***Gross National Income (GNI) in US$ Billion in Current Exchange Rate for 2014.

Source: ASEAN Secretariat.

with East and South-East Asia. The objective is to strengthen the socio-economic and cultural ties of India with East and South-East Asian countries like China, Korea, Japan, Myanmar, Indonesia, Singapore, Myanmar, Malaysia, Thailand etc. The factors that encouraged India to frame LEP include the end of the cold war, the world wide rising trend of regionalism, notable performance of East Asia, the China factor and giving a focus to NER in the development sphere. The impressive growth performance of the Southeast Asian countries has attracted the attention of the Indian policy makers and to deepen socio-economic ties with the ASEAN countries.

ASEAN's economic potential is undoubtedly impressive. If treated as a single entity, the ASEAN would rank as the third largest economy in Asia and seventh largest economy in the world. Over the past decade, trade and investment relations between India and ASEAN have continued to improve. It is clear from table 14.2 that the major ASEAN countries that intensified trade with India are Indonesia, Malaysia, Singapore, Thailand and Vietnam.

Table 14.2: Trade between India and ASEAN Countries in 2015-16

Countries	*% Share Import*	*% Share Export*
Brunei	0.001	1.48
Cambodia	0.588	0.03
Indonesia	13.50	30
Laos	0.164	0.04
Malaysia	20.03	21
Myanmar	2.436	2.59
Philippines	6.617	0.95
Singapore	29.72	27.22
Thailand	13.15	10.57
Viet Nam	13.59	6.33

Source: ASEAN Secretariat

It is clearly seen from table 14.3 that the major products exported from India to ASEAN countries are vegetables and fruits, meat products, fish products, spices, sugar, rubber, cotton, mechanical appliances, electrical and electronics and transport equipments. The composition of the exports to ASEAN countries shows that Barak Valley and NER as a whole has the comparative advantage to produce and export some of the product to ASEAN economies. These are vegetables, fruits, meat products, fish products, spices etc. The prospect for such trade is extensively explored in later part of this paper.

Table 14.3: Major commodity exports of India to ASEAN (US$ Million)

Products	*2005-06*	*2015-16*
Veg. & Fruits	76	216
Meat Products	193	2649
Fish Products	97	1089
Spices	46	499
Sugar	22	488
Rubber	88	226
Cotton	165	602
Non Ferrous Metals	469	1322
Mechanical Appliances	348	1617
Electrical & Electronics	280	798
Transport Equipments	698	2150

Source: Import Export Data Bank, Government of Ind2ia, Department of Commerce

ASEAN and NER

LEP is unquestionably beneficial for NER in many respects. It is, however, also true that due to the strategic location of NER, LEP is not practically possible without giving due importance to the former. India's north eastern region (NER) is unique in respect of providing opportunities for trade and investment. About 98 per cent of the region's borders form India's international boundaries. NER shares borders with China, Bangladesh, Bhutan, Nepal and Myanmar (NE Vision, 2020). Given its strategic location, the region can be developed as a base for India's growing economic linkages not only with ASEAN but also with other neighboring countries, viz. Bangladesh, Bhutan, and Nepal (RIS, 2011). So, the expansion of the border trade can be a feasible strategy for the economic development of the region. According to Rajiv Sikri, India's Look East Policy "envisages north eastern region not as the periphery of India, but as the centre of a thriving and integrated space linking two dynamic regions with a network of highways, railways, pipelines, transmission lines crisscrossing the regions." The discussion of LEP should begin with NER. The LEP should promote commercial links between NER and with neighbouring nations to break the economic and geographic isolation of NER with rest of India. The LEP can play a pivotal role to transform this landlocked region from a consumer to a productive region by opening up some key sectors of NER which remained underutilized due to poor expansion of trade and commerce.

Northeast India consisting of eight states, located in the NER of the country is ethnically, linguistically and culturally very distinct from the rest of India. NER as a whole represents 8.9 percent of India's geographical area 3.8 percent of India's population (45.8 million in 2011), and a little over two percent of India's GDP. Assam is the largest state of northeast representing 30 percent of the region's geographical area, 68 percent of its population, and 30 percent of northeast's net state domestic product (NSDP). NER offers plenty of energy and mineral resources such as natural gas, crude oil, coal, limestone, etc. It accounts for 20 percent of hydrocarbon (oil and gas) potential, large quantities of low ash coal resources, limestone and dolomite deposits, as well as other minerals, such as kaoline and graphite. Assam and Tripura offer high natural gas reserves; together they are estimated to have 48 billion cubic meters of natural gas reserves. Besides, northeast India also has huge reserves of coal, limestone, and dolomite. In addition, substantial amount of clay, white clay, kaoline, graphite, quartzite, sillimonite, uranium, etc. have also been mined in the region recently. The region has the potential to develop into a vibrant source of energy, oil, natural gas, coal, and limestone. Additionally, it is also endowed with India's largest perennial water system – the river Brahmaputra and its tributaries – which can help generate hydro-power based energy, transforming the region into a source of clean energy powerhouse. Potential for immense tourism opportunities exist due to the region's rich bio-diversity, rare flora and fauna, natural scenic beauty, unique performing arts, and varied cuisine and handicrafts. Geographical advantage exists due to proximity to countries in South and Southeast Asia. Northeast can emerge as a strategic base for foreign/domestic investors to tap markets of South and Southeast Asia. Opening of a border custom station between Myanmar and northeast (Moreh in Manipur) along with the possibility of a second border trading point opening at Champhai, the region is seen as a corridor for flow of goods and services between India and Southeast Asia. Northeast's internal waterway network connects the region with Bangladesh and Myanmar, giving access to the ports of Chittagong (Bangladesh), Calcutta and Haldia (West Bengal in India), and Sittwe (Myanmar).

Need for Economic Integration of NER with ASEAN

India's economic growth could benefit from developing NER and exploring areas of potential in the region. Socio-economic indicators show a high level of regional imbalance and backwardness among north eastern states. The region is lagging behind other states in terms of per capita income, industrial growth, foreign investment and infrastructure. Even after sixty years of planned economic strategy the country has not succeeded in providing basic infrastructure and resource base to this geographically isolated and ethnically sensitive region. India's approach towards a balanced and sustainable economic growth under globalization and liberalization is not expected to achieve its targeted objective unless the compelling issues of regional imbalances are tackled with effective policy framework (Singh, 2010).

Reasons for integration

- Cultural similarity with some of the ASEAN countries.
- Accessing ASEAN market for northeast people can be easier in terms of time and money spent due to geographical location.
- Scope for economic development to be enhanced post integration due to various factors: (a) increased economic activities, (b) increased exports from the region, (c) increased movement of tourists (d) increased investment by domestic and foreign companies (e) transfer of technology, knowledge.

The integration can lead to:

- Increased per capita incomes, which is presently very low compared to the national per capita income.
- Development and the creation of infrastructure in the region; and
- Enhance the productivity and efficiency of the local producers.

Moreover, the prospect for the intensification of the economic ties of the NER with the ASEAN economies becomes brighter because of three major projects of connectivity. The brief outline of the three projects is given below:

I. Kaladan Multi-Modal Transit Transport Project (KMMTTP)

This project will connect the eastern Indian seaport of Kolkata with Sittwe seaport in Myanmar by sea. Then it will link Sittwe seaport to Paletwa in Myanmar via Kaladan river boat route and then from

Paletwa on to Mizoram by road transport. This project has several routes:

- 539 km shipping route from seaport of Kolkata in India to Sittwe seaport in Myanmar via Bay of Bengal.
- 158 km river boat route from Sittwe seaport to Paletwa jetty via Kaladan river in Myanmar
- 110 km road route from Paletwa jetty to Indo-Myanmar border in Myanmar
- 100 km route from Indo-Myanmar border to Lawngtlai in Mizoram in India by road on National Highway 54 (India) (NH-54), which then continues further to Dabaka in Assam via 850 km long NH-54 which in turn is part of the larger East-West Corridor connecting northeast with the rest of India.

II. India-Myanmar-Thailand Trilateral Highway

IMT trilateral highway will connect Moreh (Manipur), India with MaeSot, Thailand via Myanmar. The road is expected to boost trade and commerce in the ASEAN–India Free Trade Area, as well as with the rest of Southeast Asia. India has also proposed extending the highway to Cambodia, Laos and Vietnam. The proposed 3,200 km route from India to Vietnam is known as the East-West Economic Corridor (EWEC). The highway's route will be Moreh (India) – Tamu (Myanmar) – Kalewa (Myanmar) – Yagyi (Myanmar) – Monywa (Myanmar) – Mandalay (Myanmar) – Meiktila (Myanmar) – Nay Pyi Taw (Myanmar) – Payagyi (Myanmar) – Theinzayat (Myanmar) – Thaton (Myanmar) – Hpa'an (Myanmar) – Kawkareik (Myanmar) – Myawaddy (Myanmar) – Mae Sot (Thailand).

III. Trans Asian Railway

TAR is a project The TAR is a project of the United Nations Economic and Social Commission for Asia and the Pacific (UNESCAP). It will integrate freight railway network across Europe and Asia. The Trans-Asian Railway Network Agreement is an agreement signed on 10 November 2006, by seventeen Asian nations as part of a United Nations Economic and Social Commission for Asia and the Pacific (UNESCAP) effort to build a transcontinental railway network between Europe and Pacific ports in China. The plan has sometimes been called the "Iron Silk Road" in reference to the historical Silk Road trade routes. UNESCAP's Transport & Tourism Division began work on the initiative in 1992 when it launched the Asian Land Transport Infrastructure Development project. The Trans-Asian Railway system will consist of four main railway routes. The existing Trans-Siberian railway, which connects Moscow to Vladivostok, will be used for a portion of the network in Russia. Another corridor to be included will connect China to Korea, Mongolia, Russia and Kazakhstan. In 2003, the president of Kazakhstan proposed building a standard gauge link from Dostyk (on the Chinese border) to Gorgan in Iran; it has not yet been built.

These three projects will definitely improve the connectivity between India and ASEAN economies along with other Asian countries. But NER stands at the focal point in all the three projects. So, these projects will open the scope for expanding the trade and commerce between NER and ASEAN. In fact, ASEAN economies are more easily accessible than the main parts of the rest of India.

ASEAN and Barak Valley

The three projects of connectivity show that NER has the huge potential in the ASEAN countries. The NER can reach the ASEAN economies more easily than other parts of India itself. The same is true also for Barak Valley. The composition of exports from India to ASEAN countries (table 14.3) shows that Barak Valley can also export some of the major items. These may be vegetables, meat products, fish and fish products, spices etc. In this light, the section discusses the potentials of Barak Valley to explore the markets in ASEAN countries and the constraints that the region has been facing.

Barak Valley

The three districts of southern Assam—Cachar, Hailakandi and Karimganj together constitute Barak Valley which in the pre-Independence period was a part of the erstwhile Surma Valley. It is bounded on the north by the North Cachar Hills of Assam and Jaintia Hills district of Meghalaya; on the east by Manipur; on the south by Mizoram and on the west by Tripura and Sylhet district of Bangladesh. The total area of Barak Valley is 6,922 sq. kms, of which Cachar district alone accounts for 57.4 percent of the total area; the shares of Hailakandi and Karimganj district being 19.2 percent and 26.1 percent respectively.

Barak Valley is basically an agriculture dependent economy as more than 70 percent of its population depends on agriculture as a source of income. However, the condition of agriculture is primitive in nature with lack of technological progress. Industrial performance of the valley is quite depressing. Contribution of tertiary sector is developing day by day which is a good sign for Barak Valley.

Potentials

The rich and fertile soil of Cachar had attracted the attention of Pemberton (1935) who was struck by the beautiful and fertile valley of Barak. He described the land on the South bank of the Barak River as "the finest plain, almost wholly unoccupied, through which the rivers Dullaseeree and Sonaee flow from South to north." In fact, Sylhat and Cachar are always known for their bountiful production of Paddy. The prospect for fisheries in this valley is immense. Several species of fishes like *Chapila* and *Bacha* are cultivated in this valley. Indian major carps like *Rohu* and *Katla* are also found in wide scale. Eel, catfish, small shrimps and even edible snail culture can have prospects in South East and East Asian markets. The small shrimp species of Barak Valley have a characteristic flavor and could be marketed as shrimp paste, especially in ASEAN countries. The valley is endowed with large floodplain lakes (locally called 'haors' or 'beels') like Chatla, jabda and Lucca in Cachar and Shonbeel and Ratabeel in Hailakandi and Karimganj districts. But the agricultural sector is still backward due to a number of reasons. It is able to enhance rural income due to poor productivity. Thus, productivity revolution in agriculture through technological advancement coupled with diversification of commercial crops, processing industries and agro-exports will generate abundant employment in the rural sector.

Quality rather than quantity matters when we think for production for export. Certain paddy landraces could be revived and marketed abroad. These include fragrant cultivators like 'Kalijira', 'Sahebshail' etc. The high starch 'Biroin' varieties could possibly find markets in South East and East Asian countries where such rice is preferred. Rice sweets and rice cakes are very popular in South East Asian countries. Horticulture development can provide another very important avenue for Barak Valley. There is ample scope for growing better known fruits like pineapple and orange, the indigenous fruits like some berries, citrus varieties like 'Satkora' and others. Thailand has also very successfully introduced its unique fruits to the western tourists. The jackfruits could possibly be marketed like the *durian* of South East Asia. Durian flavored chewing gums and boiled sweets are fairly popular in Vietnam. Wine-making from some of these fruits may also be explored.

Similarly, tea industry can also contribute a lot in the development process of Barak Valley. It is often said that there was a time when the economy of the Barak Valley was revolving around the tea industry. The soil and climate of this valley are suitable for tea cultivation and the British took full advantage of those geo-climatic conditions. Tea industry was flourishing and it brought a complete change in the economy of this valley. In the sphere of export and price realization, the performance of Cachar tea was remarkable. India was the largest exporter of tea and 'Cachar tea' was holding a dominant position among the manufacturing regions. In the price front Cachar tea were fetching very good price and was strong enough to resist any price and demand crash. John Smeal (proprietor of several tea gardens) told the then Commissioner in 1868, "...our teas have fetched a very high price, averaging last year in London, rupees 125 a maund. Rupees 60 per maund is a common average price in London for Cachar tea." (Griffth, 1967). Unfortunately, the tea industry in Barak Valley is in a precarious condition. The productivity in Barak Valley is the lowest in northeast India.

The prospect of the handicrafts and cottage industries in Barak Valley is very bright. The local availability of raw-materials, long tradition in handicrafts, weaving, carpentry, boat making, and also in the manufacture of a variety of consumer goods, availability of cheap skilled and semi skilled labour, and the prevalence of a favourable law and order situation in the valley offer favourable environment for growth of small and medium industrial units, particularly the forest and agro-based industries. Barak Valley can aspire to find a place on the eco-tourism map if it can put an immediate halt to any further degradation of its forests and wetlands and ideally undertake some eco-restoration activities. Several activities like river cruises along the upper reaches of Barak and Katakhal rivers, nature walks in the forests and tea gardens, trekking in the forests etc. Before the partition, water routes used to be an important mode of transport of goods between

Barak Valley and the rest of the world through the rivers in East Bengal. Now the volume of transport through these water ways has declined almost to zero. Some transportation by steamer takes place between Karimganj in Barak Valley and Kolkata port through the traditional water ways. But this takes place only in the summer months. The water transport system is currently operated by the Central Inland Water Transport Corporation (CIWTC). The region has good potential for revival of inland water transport route (Roy, 2009). This requires improvement of infrastructure in the form of restoration of the existing 'dak bunglows' and forest lodges and creation of new facilities wherever necessary. The folk dances and other art forms of the different ethnic groups could prove to yet another attraction. The region can become a hub for medical tourism and education tourism because of the prestigious institutions like Silchar Medical College (SMC), National Institute of Technology (NIT), Silchar and Assam University. However, all these need imaginative planning, sincere political will, efficient administrative machinery and informed and pro-active civil society.

Barak Valley has the capability to establish various food processing and fruit processing industries by utilizing its indigenous items. The production of pineapple, orange, jackfruit, mango etc. can give ample opportunity for agricultural processing industries which can easily find market in ASEAN countries. Marketing of medicinal products like *Chalmugra oil*, essence – yielding species like *agar* and *Gondhi Kochu* can make Barak Valley well known both in and outside India. The vegetation in the valley is mostly Tropical evergreen and there are large tracts of rainforests in the northern and southern-eastern parts of the valley, which are home to tiger, elephants, malayan sun bear, capped langur, hoolock gibbon, etc. The forests of Barak valley were once rich in wildlife but now vanishing due to human onslaught. Rare species found are hoolock gibbon, phayre's leaf monkey, pig-tailed macaque, stump-tailed macaque, masked finfoot, white-winged wood duck, etc. have been recorded. The Asian elephant has already vanished from most of the valley. The southern part was also recommended as 'Dhaleswari' wildlife sanctuary. Barail is the only wildlife sanctuary of the Barak valley region. It was initiated by noted naturalist Dr Anwaruddin Choudhury, who originally hailed from this region in early 1980s. This sanctuary was ultimately notified in 2004. Hailakandi have Inner line reserve forest and Katakhal reserve forest.

It is not a denying fact that the Barak Valley region is full of human resources. Since there is lack of sufficient opportunities to utilize the human resource, there is outflow of this very critical resource from this valley. But the human capital can prove to be an important instrument in the development process of this valley. This is because ideas and innovation contribute positively in the process of economic growth of any region as proved by the endogenous growth models.

Constraints

The region lacks sufficient infrastructure of all kinds. But the existence of physical and socio-economic infrastructure is the prerequisite for economic development of any region. The infrastructure in power, communications, agriculture and industry is dismally poor. The absence of state patronage through irrigation, agricultural restructuring, and agrarian reform and overall appropriate development initiative prevented the economy from the economy from a takeoff. The uninterrupted power supply is the pre-requisite of any economic activity, especially industrial development. The Valley is poor in the arena of industrial establishment due to power crisis. The up gradation of small scale industries, start up businesses depends on the uninterrupted flow of power supply. There is insufficient supply of power compared to the demand. The demand for power is growing, but the supply has failed to fulfill the demand.

Any plan for economic development would be futile without proper investment. Investment is the precondition for progress. Barak Valley has been suffering from the poor rate of investment since independence. There is meager amount of investment from the private enterprises due other associated factors. The major chunk of the investment in Barak valley comes from the public sector. Inadequate capital has been found to be the major causes of poor performance of tea industry in this valley. There is absence of political will to make this region developed and globally competitive. This will be clear if we compare the region with other regions of NER and India. There are a number of 'development deficits' in this region. The government and political leaders do not express keen desire to formulate a comprehensive plan of economic development of this region. Moreover, the region lacks entrepreneurial initiative due to sufficient confidence building measures. The intention is to stimulate 'outside the box' thinking among the planners and entrepreneurs. Entrepreneurs in Barak Valley could learn a few lessons from their counterparts in South East and East Asian countries like Thailand, Singapore, Malaysia, South Korea and Vietnam, which have succeeded in aggressively marketing their indigenous products to novelty-seeking, health-conscious consumers from the west (Gupta, 2009). The people of Barak Valley have become morally weak after staying in an inaccessible terrain for a long period of time. The partition of India into two pieces at the time of independence and thereafter the creation of Bangladesh has made this valley backward in terms of connectivity. This might be the reason that people have become less enthusiastic, inward looking and risk averse. The work culture of this valley is relatively poor compared to other parts of India. The lack of innovative practices in agriculture, the existence of mono cropping can be attributable to the worsening work culture despite the available resources. That is why the valley is unable to produce surplus in production and export. The Barak Valley has become mere the importer of major goods and services.

Conclusion

The paper discussed the potentials and constraints of the region Barak Valley to initiate its economic relationship with ASEAN economies. The discussion gets its importance due to three major projects of connectivity between India and ASEAN countries, namely, KMTTP, IMT tri-national highway and TAR. If NER has the opportunities to expand its trade and commerce with the ASEAN countries due to locational advantages, then Barak Valley will also have prospect because it is a part of NER. The need is to act upon the available resources and best utilization of the human capital.

There is a common perception that the construction of broad gauge railway and some mega projects like the Tipaimukh dam can work miracles for developing Barak Valley. The newly completed broad gauge will undoubtedly develop the connectivity of the region. But without improved production base there will be inflow of goods in this valley without an outflow. It is to be realized that improved communication and power supply are mere tools for development. They are like enzymes that can catalyze the development, but there is need for a sustainable natural resource base to act upon in order to bring about all-round, long lasting development (Gupta, 2009). Another important aspect is the recognition and utilization of the existing human resources of the valley. It is the human capital that can turn the available resources of the valley into the products which are unique on this earth and globally competitive. We must hope for the better future and continue our endeavor to establish the position of Barak Valley in the global map. The paper highlighted some of the aspects of the economy of Barak Valley which can play a role in exploring ASEAN markets given some momentum. Each of the potential sectors requires in depth research to have an insight into the area. This paper is expected to open further research avenues in some of the unexplored areas of the economy of Barak valley.

15

NER-ASEAN Connectivity and Development of Barak Valley

Subodh Chandra Das

Introduction

There is a long-standing interest in the role of connectivity in regional development. The two most critical benefits of connectivity are efficient and cost-effective mobility and reduced inequality, within and between regions. It is important for the people and communities to be connected to people and community of the wider economy to have access to the places, labor and commodity markets for the spontaneous participation in the society (Salemink and Strijker, 2015).

Therefore, investment on connectivity represents a larger share than that of the resources allocated to health, education and social services combined (World Bank, 2007). Moreover, the World Bank Report has suggested that the first step in any development strategy is to implement spatially-blind policies that ensure the supporting infrastructure is in place for local strategic investments to be successful. Therefore, in order to facilitate economic growth between lagging and leading regions, the focus should first be on investing in the infrastructure that facilitates the movement of people, goods and information across space. People seek opportunities, and providing the spatial connectivity for them to do so increase accessibility to places where their skills can be put to productive use (World Bank, 2008). However, whether a good endowment of transport infrastructure delivers greater economic development and promotes territorial cohesion remains controversial. Theoretical and empirical analyses of the returns of transport infrastructure point in different directions, making it difficult to extract any firm conclusions about the impact of transport infrastructure investment.

The empirical results suggest that there is little evidence of an impact of the transport infrastructure endowment of any given region or of its neighboring regions on economic growth. Once innovation, social conditions, and migration are taken into account, the coefficients for transport infrastructure endowment become insignificant, while, by contrast, local R&D capacity, local social conditions, and migration are much better predictors of economic performance (Crescenzi and Pose, 2012). Places without the appropriate socio-institutional capacity to absorb new ideas and transform them into economically-useful knowledge will thus not reap the benefits from targeted innovation investments and, in most cases, from infrastructure investment.

NER-ASEAN connectivity is also going to shape the region in the future. If this connectivity is not designed with care many issues may arise like inequality among the people, states and the various pockets within a state as the Barak Valley remained underdeveloped in Assam even the state as a whole has shown some signs of progress. Barak valley has been remained marginalized due to lack of connectivity and may remain so even after NER-ASEAN linkages if the region is missed in terms of connectivity. The present study intends to examine how the valley is going to benefit from the present planning scenario of NER-ASEAN connectivity. It explores the existing, proposed/planned connectivity and the gaps in the connectivity. Four modes of physical connectivity viz. roads, rail, civil aviation and waterways are considered for the study.

Socio-economic overview of Barak Valley

The Barak Valley, (also South Assam) is located in the southern region of the Indian state of Assam. The valley is surrounded by the Indian states of Meghalaya, Manipur, Mizoram and Tripura and also shares international border with Bangladesh. As it is the gateway of the two states of India viz. Mizoram and Tripura, its connectivity plays a vital role in connecting them with the rest of India. As the region is situated in the bank of the river Barak it is called Barak valley. Silchar is the main city in the region as well as an important town in Assam. The Barak valley mainly consists of three administrative districts in the state of Assam viz. Cachar, Karimganj, and Hailakandi. Among these three districts, Cachar and Hailakandi belonged to the erstwhile Cachar district in British India, whereas Karimganj belonged to the Sylhet district. Karimganj was separated from Sylhet after the 1947 referendum. The rest of Sylhet district falls under Bangladesh (erstwhile East-Pakistan) and Karimganj under India.

In fact, the valley has a multi-ethnic, multi-linguistic and multi-religious social base. Democratic system of governance holds its 3 crore population over a geographical spread of 30,285 sq miles. As 86 per cent of the population in Assam live in rural areas (Census, 2011) and about 40 per cent of them live below the poverty line (Govt. of Assam, P&RD website), various welfare schemes targeted to rural poor are being implemented through panchayati raj institution. The region remained predominantly agrarian in nature. However, there has been some indication of industrial development also. Table 1 shows the district-wise number of registered industrial units in the Barak valley. There are 1853 registered industrial units in the valley, almost all being small scale industries. And again majority of them are engaged with the production and marketing of tea. There is only one large scale industry viz. Cachar Paper Mill, Panchgram, A unit of Hindustan Paper Corporation Ltd that is too have become non functional for the past one year. In addition to these, there is one medium scale industry i.e. Barak Valley Cement Ltd, Badarpurghat, which employs near about 100 local people.

Table 15.1: Industry in Barak Valley

		Cachar	*Karimganj*	*Hailakandi*	*Barak Valley*
1	Registered Industrial Unit	665	765	423	1853
2	Total Industrial Unit	665	765	423	1853
3	Registered Medium & Large Unit	1	1	1	3

Source: Ministry of MSME

Although, the valley has number of industrial units most of them are sick, non functional and functioning with the government assistances. As there is no major industries, large share of population derive their livelihood from agriculture and allied activities. Only small chunks of people who are engaged in government services or small trading activities are in a little better off conditions. One of the major reasons for this backwardness of the valley even after 69 years of independence, while the India as a whole projecting itself to be a global super power, might be due to its disconnectedness with the mainland India in general and Assam in particular.

Partition and Disconnectedness of Barak Valley with India and world

Although, the region was well connected with the major ports, mainly through water and railway route before independence, after the partition of the country the region become landlocked. The East India Company linked Silchar with Kolkata along the Barak-Surma-Meghna navigation channel. However, with the partition of India in 1947, water transport received a serious blow as a foreign country was born between northeast India and the port of Kolkata. The Barak also has small ports at Karimganj, Badarpur, and Silchar and ferry services at several places across it. The rivers Dhaleshwari, Sonai, Tuilianpui, and Chimtuipui in Mizoram are also used for navigation with small country boats in convenient stretches.

A 150 kilometres (93 mi) rail track between Chittagong and Comilla was opened to traffic in 1895. The Comilla-Akhaura-Kulaura-mahisasan-Badarpur section was opened in 1896-1898 and finally extended to Lumding in 1903. With the partition of India in 1947, it got disconnected at mahisasan from the Chittagong port.

As the three districts of Barak valley geographically isolated from the major Brahmaputra valley of Assam and inhabited by different socio-cultural and linguistic population who are minority in number, they received less attention from the government in spite of preferential treatment which was required for its development. As a result the valley remained isolated from the mainland Assam and rest of the country in terms of connectivity. In the next section the existing connectivity options of within the Barak valley and with other neighboring states is being discussed.

Poor Connectivity of Barak Valley after Partition

Within Barak valley connectivity

The connectivity of Barak Valley within the region is very poor as compared to Assam and India as a whole. Barak Valley had a total road length of 3547 kms in 2011 of which 290.16 kms national highway, 157.5 kms state highway, 417.12kms main district highway comprises only 24.38 percent of the total roads in the valley. Others are rural, border and kachaa roads.

Table 15.2: Rail and road connectivity within Barak Valley

	Cachar	*Karimganj*	*Hailakandi*	*Barak valley*
Railways				
i) Length of rail line	87	145	83	315
Railway Route km per 1000 Population	0.05	0.12	0.13	0.08
Roads				
a) National Highway	95	97.16	98	290.16
b) State Highway	107	33.5	17	157.5
c) Main District Highway	165	153.12	99	417.12
d) Other district & rural roads	748	160.49	351	1259.49
e) Rural road/Agricultural Marketing Border Roads	NA	340.79	NA	340.79
f) Kachacha Road	441	460	181	1082
Total Road	1556	1245.06	746	3547.06
Population 2011	1,736,617	1,228,686	659,296	3,624,599
Road per 1000 population (in kms)	0.89	1.01	1.13	0.98

Source: Compiled from MSME and Census of India reports 2011

The road per 1000 population in Barak valley is only 0.98 km (Table 1) whereas the same for Assam as a whole is 7.83 kms in 2008 and for India as a whole is 2.77 kms in 2008 (MOSPI). These statistics clearly indicates the poor road connectivity within the three districts of Barak Valley. Railway Route km per 1000 Population is in Barak valley is 0.08 km (table 1) which is slightly higher as compared to Assam as a whole (0.078 km) and India as a whole (0.055 km) (MOSPI, 2008). The statistics indicates that the valley is better off in terms of railway connectivity. However, the railway serves only a portion of the transport needs of the people. Majority of the population is dependent on road networks where railway is not available. Road is also important to connect to the railway station. As the train are available on schedule times, roads complements when there is no train.

Connectivity of Barak valley with other NER states

The national highway Silchar-Shillong Road connects the Valley with the rest of the country via Guwahati through Siliguri corridor or the chicken's neck. This road is the lifeline of the valley as the major goods and passengers are commuted through this road. The valley is also connected to its three neighboring states viz. Manipur, Mizoram, and Tripura. The valley is connected to Imphal which is the capital of Manipur by Silchar-Imphal road. It is connected to Agartala the capital of Tripura and Aizwal the capital of Mizoram. These roads are shown in the following Map.

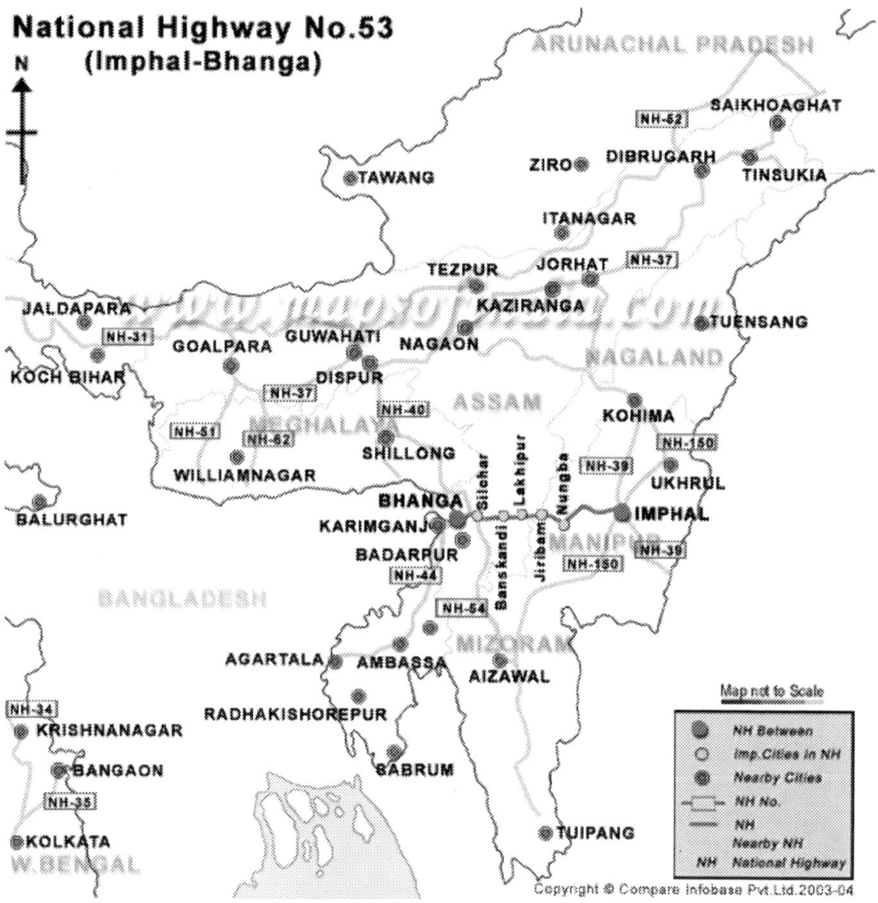

Again, there is a road from Silchar to Haflong, the head quarter of N.C. Hills. These roads are metalled and black-topped on paper only. In realty, all the roads are dilapidated in such a way that it is difficult to call them as roads by any standard definition. During the rainy season, these roads remain suspended frequently owing to landslides. Transporting necessary goods from the other region using these roads is a great challenge. As the valley is not connected with the other regions in India in general, and NER in particular, the question of connecting with neighbor countries ASEAN for example is beyond imagination. However, the present BJP led Assam government emphasized on improving the road conditions of Barak Valley and treated as one of the major priorities of the government. In the budget 2017-18, the government has earmarked Rs 2,000 crore for the same.

The Barak Valley is connected by railway with Agartala (Tripura) and Lumding (Assam), Jiribham (Manipur) and Bhirabi (Mizoram). Recently, the track has been converted from meter gauge to broad gauge in all the routes which gives partial relief to the people of the valley in terms of connectivity.

On the other hand, there is only one domestic Airport in the Valley which is located in Silchar built by the British in 1944 and is also a civil enclave airport as it is under the control of Indian Air Force. It is the fourth busiest airport of the north eastern India next to Guwahati, Imphal and Agartala. In 2013-14, Silchar Airport handled 206,000 passengers. Approximately 30 flights per week depart from the Silchar Airport for Imphal, Guwahati, Kolkata, Jorhat and Agartala. It is equipped with Instrument Landing System CAT I. Plans are on to set up a new integrated terminal which would facilitate modern passenger comfort and accommodate more passengers. On March 15, 2003, Indian Airlines (now Air India) started using ATR 42-320 (operated by Alliance Air) aircraft to Kolkata, Imphal and Guwahati routes. After a long wait for many years the runway and apron extension work finally stabilized on August 2007 and then the last Boeing 737-200 flight took off for Kolkata on 2 September 2007 which was operated by Alliance Air (present name Air India Regional) and from the next day itself Air India started operating Airbus A320 on Kolkata route as the old Boeing 737-200 aircraft were not in safety zone in terms of flying purpose. On May 2011 JetKonnect a subsidiary company of Jet Airways introduced daily flights on Kolkata and Guwahati routes using their ATR 72 aircraft. In October 2016, Spicejet introduced daily flights to Kolkata and Guwahati using its Bombardier Dash 8 Q400 aircraft. Indian Airlines maintain flights connecting Silchar with Kolkata, Imphal, Guwahati.

Although the valley was earlier connected with rest of the country through Barak-Shurma-Megna channel it is now closed after the partition. In spite of the availability of the river system the water transport is absent in the valley.

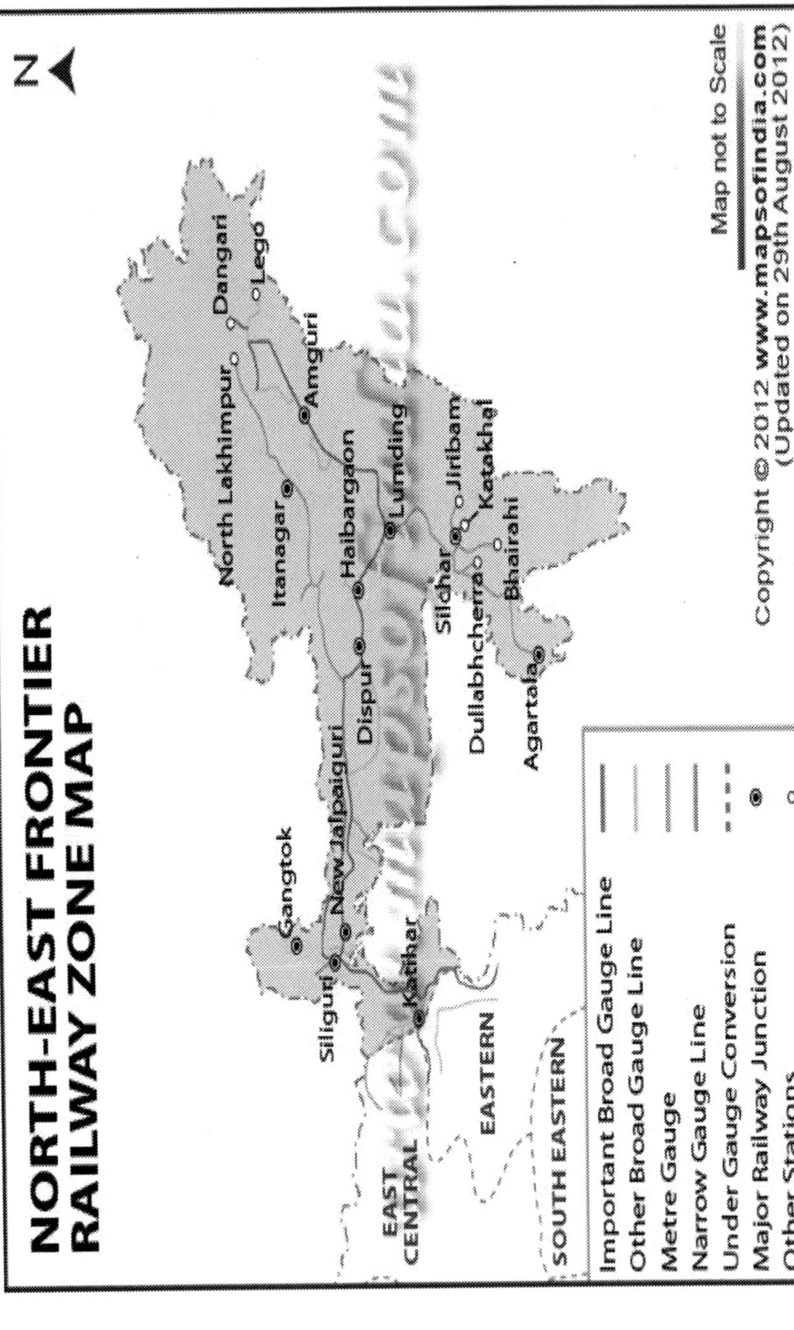
NORTH-EAST FRONTIER
RAILWAY ZONE MAP
N
Gangtok
Siliguri
New Jalpaiguri
Katihar
Dispur
Haibargaon
Itanagar
North Lakhimpur
Dangari
Lego
Amguri
Lumding
Jiribam
Katakhal
Silchar
Bhairabi
Dullabhcherra
Agartala
EAST CENTRAL
EASTERN
SOUTH EASTERN
Important Broad Gauge Line
Other Broad Gauge Line
Metre Gauge
Narrow Gauge Line
Under Gauge Conversion
Major Railway Junction
Other Stations
Map not to Scale
Copyright © 2012 www.mapsofindia.com
(Updated on 29th August 2012)

NER-ASEAN Connectivity Plans

With the initiation of act east policy, the trade between India and ASEAN has increased. Percentage Share of ASEAN in India's annual average total trade has increased from 7.40 percent in 1991-00 to 9.63 percent in 2011-14. However, the increased trade happened through the major ports like Kolkata, Mumbai and Chennai which bypassed the landlocked north eastern region as it is far from the major ports which requires huge transport cost. Connecting NER with ASEAN is imperative to deepen the India-ASEAN tie and for the development of NER. In order to deepen the India-ASEAN link the government of India has initiated a number of major projects namely. IMT Trilateral Highway, Kaladan Multimodal Transit Transport Project –Sitwee SEZ and Port and IWT, Delhi – Hanoi Railway Link, BCIM initiative etc.

IMT Trilateral Highway

The India–Myanmar–Thailand (IMT) trilateral highway will connect Moreh, India with Mae Sot, Thailand via Myanmar. The road is expected to boost trade and commerce in the ASEAN–India Free Trade Area, as well as with the rest of Southeast Asia. India has also proposed extending the highway to Cambodia, Laos and Vietnam. The proposed 3,200 km route from India to Vietnam is known as the East-West Economic Corridor (EWEC).

IMT Trilateral Highway

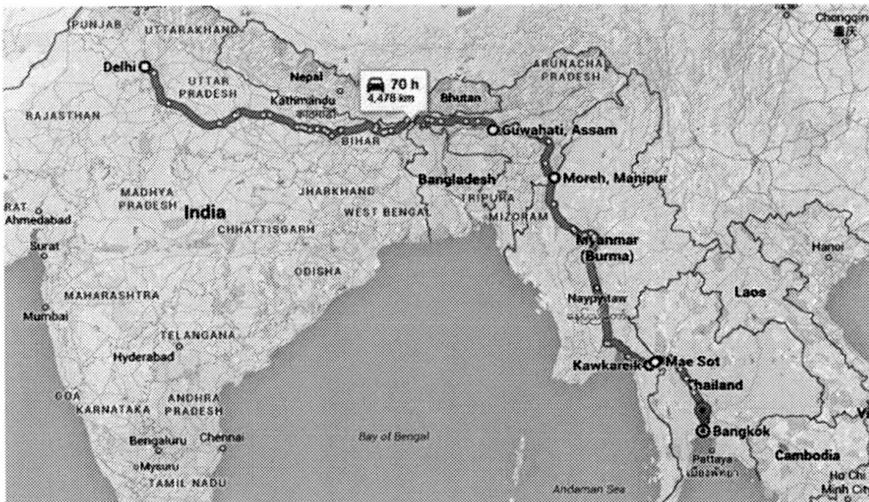

Kaladan Multimodal Transit Transport Project

The Kaladan Multi-Modal Transit Transport Project will connect Kolkata seaport with Sittwe seaport in Myanmar by sea. It will then link Sittwe seaport to Paletwa in Myanmar via Kaladan river boat route and then from Paletwa to Mizoram by road transport.

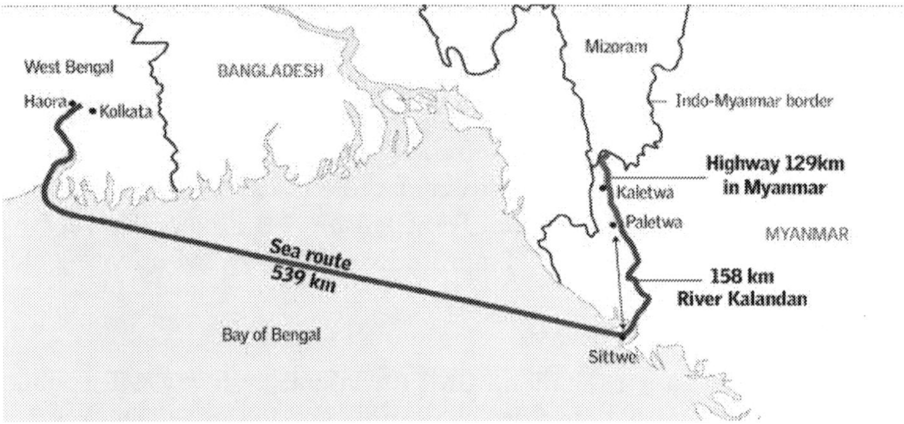

The project has several sections viz. 539 km shipping route from seaport of Kolkata in India to Sittwe seaport in Myanmar via Bay of Bengal, 158 km river boat route from Sittwe sea-port to Paletwa jetty via Kaladan river in Myanmar, 110 km road route from Paletwa jetty to Indo-Myanmar border in Myanmar 100 km route from Indo-Myanmar border to Lawngtlai in Mizoram in India by road on National Highway 54 (India) (NH-54), which then continues further to Dabaka in Assam via 850 km long NH-54 which in turn is part of the larger East-West Corridor connecting northeast India with the rest of India. Mizoram is now connected with broad gauge railway line by Silchar-Bhairabi and Bhairabi-Sairang is yet to be completed. The Ministry of Railways has prepared a Plan for New Line from Sairang to Indo-Myanmar Multi Modal Transit.

Delhi–Hanoi Railway Link

The Delhi-Hanoi Railway link aims at connecting India's Manipur with its main railway corridor, and to re-establish and renovate railway networks in Myanmar.

Indian government has extended US$ 56 million credit to the Myanmar government for the up gradation of 640 km of railway system between Mandalay and Yangon section in Myanmar. An Indian railway project Diphu-Karong-Imphal-Moreh rail line which will link India with ASEAN is in progress in Indian side. Another project, construction of a 98 km railway line from Jiribam to Imphal has already been initiated in April 2003. After completion of these projects there will be railway connectivity from India to Myanmar-Thailand-Malaysia-Singapore and India to Myanmar – Thailand – Hanoi Vietnam.

The BCIM Economic Corridor

The Bangladesh–China–India–Myanmar Forum for Regional Cooperation (BCIM) is a sub-regional organization of four Asian nations to have a greater economic integration among the four countries. The forum has conceptualized the Bangladesh, China, India and Myanmar (BCIM) Economic Corridor which will be the first multi-modal corridor that will pass through Bangladesh, India, Myanmar and China. In India the project will benefit the northeast in general and Manipur and Barak valley of Assam in particular since the proposed economic corridor will pass through these states as shown in the following maps.

In addition to the above explained initiatives India is also in cooperative dialogues to get access of Bangladesh to enhance the connectivity of the NER.

Agartala-Akhaura Railway Line

The foundation stone for a project called Agartala Akhaura railway line has been laid by the Indian and Bangladeshi governments on July 31st 2016 to ease surface transport between the two countries. Indian railway will build a 15-km railway tracks linking Agartala, the capital of Tripura, with Akhaura, the southeastern city of Bangladesh. Akhaura is an important railway junction that is connected to Chittagong port, resource-rich Sylhet and Dhaka the capital of Bangladesh.

Mahisashan-Shahbajpur Rail Link

The government of India has sent a proposal to its Bangladeshi counterpart for reviving the defunct railway link between India and Bangladesh through Mahisasan point on the Indo-Bangladesh border in Karimganj district of Assam. Mahisasan is a border railway station which is linked to Karimganj 11 km away and is near to Shahbajpur

Delhi–Hanoi Railway Link

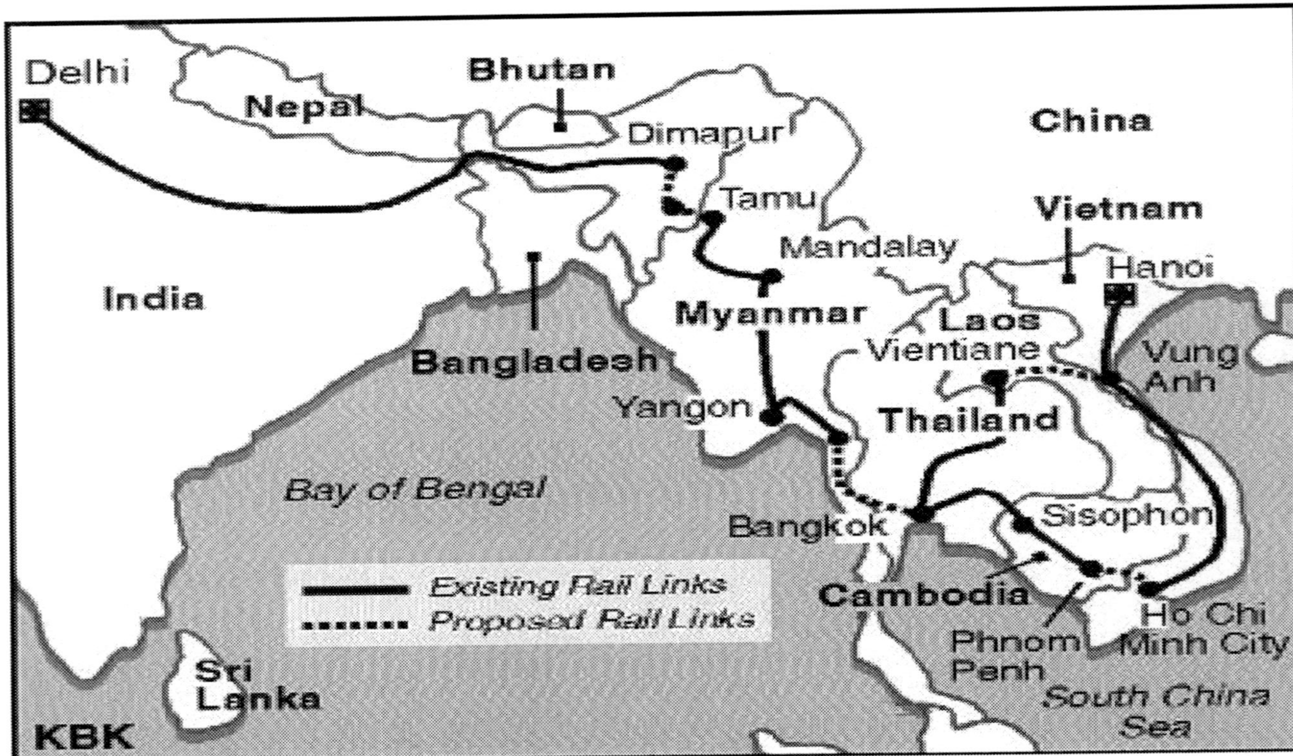

Source: http://www.tribuneindia.com/2004/20040209/edit.htm accessed 13/04/17

The BCIM Economic Corridor

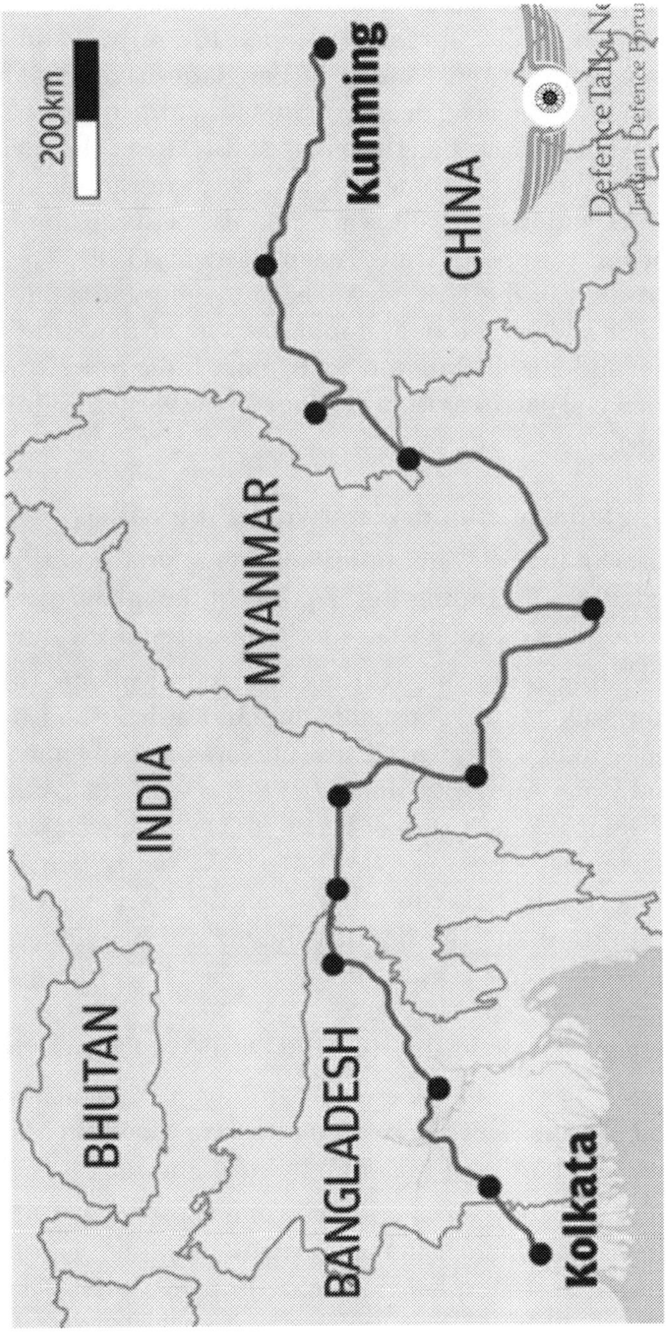

station on the Bangladesh side in Sylhet district. The Prime Minister of Bangladesh is also agreed to reopen the railway link between Mahisasan in India and Khulna in Bangladesh via Shahbajpur. To reopen the link there is no dearth of infrastructure in India. The formal positive response from Bangladesh is still waited. The revival of the link will help northeast come much closer to rest of the country and south Asian nations as well. This link also assumes importance in course of the proposed Trans-Asian Railway (TOI). The Southern corridor route 1 of the TAR is visualized to enter India through Tamu in Myanmar and Moreh in Manipur, then enter Bangladesh through Mahisasan and Shahbajpur and again enter India from Bangladesh at Gede which will enter Pakistan at Attari on the western side (Streanline supply Chain).

Indo-Bangladesh Inland Waterways Protocol

There exists an Inland water transit and trade protocol between India and Bangladesh. According to the protocol the inland vessels of one country can transit through the specified routes of the other country.

The existing routes are (i) Kolkata-Pandu-Kolkata, (ii) Kolkata-Karimganj-Kolkata, (iii) Rajshahi-Dhulian-Rajshahi and (iv) Pandu-Karimganj-Pandu. However, these routes are presently non functional. The Inland Water Authority of India (IWAI) is working to declare Barak River as National Waterways-VI. As there are well-developed terminals in Barak river, once the water way is declared and new investments to develop more infrastructure of IWT on the National Waterways-6 (proposed) are made the Barak valley could be connected to the erstwhile water transport network.

The Place of Barak Valley in NER-ASEAN Connectivity

Although the Barak valley does not share any international border with the ASEAN countries it can be connected via Moreh in Manipur and Indo-Myanmar border at Mizoram by road and rail.

The Barak valley has two major gateways to ASEAN through Moreh at Manipur and Langtlai at Mizoram. Moreh is connected by road from Silchar to Imphal via Silchar-Jiribam ; Imphal-Jiribam (NH 37) and Imphal-Moreh. From Silchar to Moreh the road Distance is 329.7 KM. It is connected by Imphal-Jiribam (NH 37) and Imphal-Moreh NH 102. It should take 10h 35 min but the road condition is

Agartala-Akhaura Railway Line

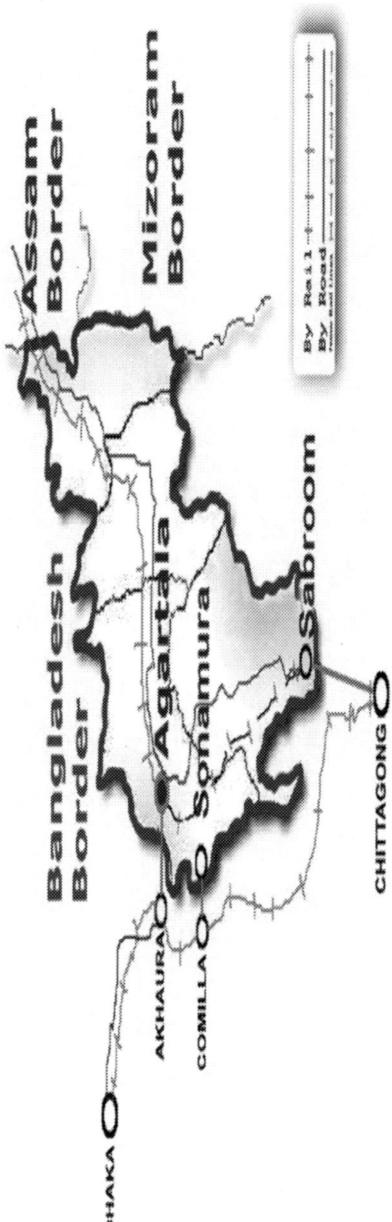

Source: http://tripuratourism.gov.in/train

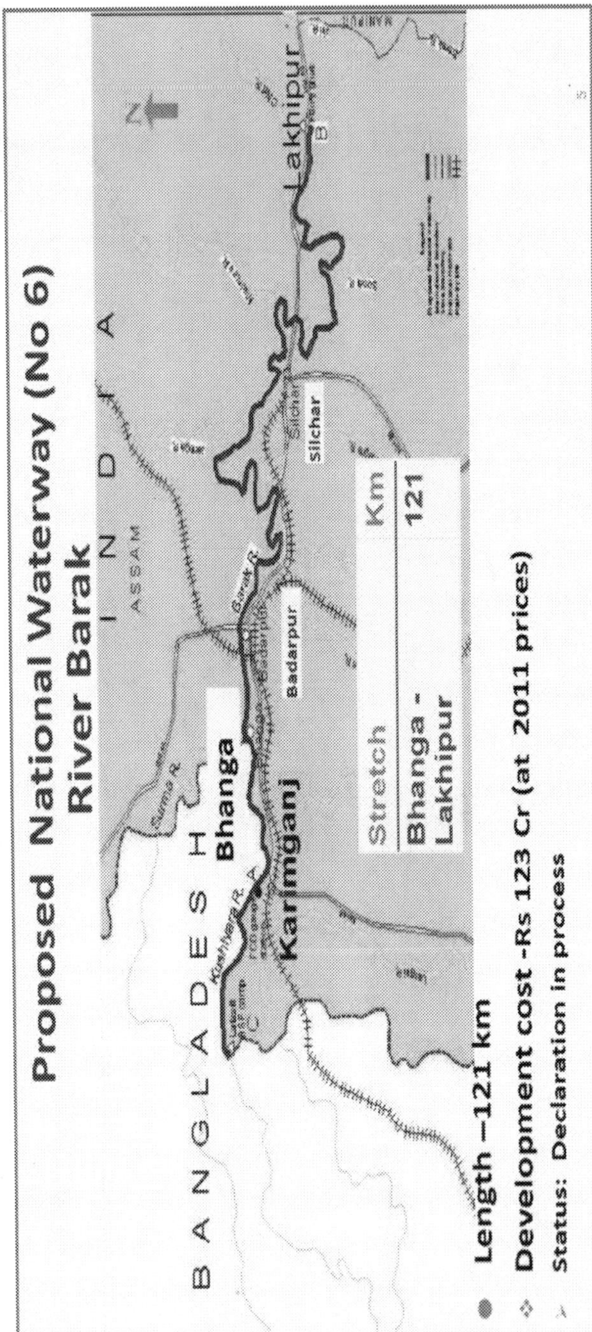
Proposed National Waterway (No 6)
River Barak
INDIA
ASSAM
BANGLADESH
Bhanga
Karimganj
Badarpur
Silchar
Lakhipur
Stretch
Km
Bhanga - Lakhipur
121
Length –121 km
Development cost -Rs 123 Cr (at 2011 prices)
Status: Declaration in process

very pathetic in most of the time during the year it remains non functional. As Imphal-Jiribam (NH 37) highway which connects to Silchar is in pathetic condition. Once it is connected to Moreh it can access the India-Myanmar-Thailand Trilateral highway.

The second route is via Mizoram. It is connected through Silchar Aizwal and Aizwal-Langtlai road. The Kaladan Multimodal Transit can be accessed once Longtlai is reached. Silchar to Lawngtlai approximate distance is 427 Kms and 100 km route from Indo-Myanmar border to Lawngtlai in Mizoram in India by road. In addition to these two short routes there are two other possibilities via Shilling-Guwahati –Kolkata and Agartala-Dacha-Kolkata. However, the quality of the roads in fact, is not dependable at all in any way because of their poor condition and difficult geographical conditions which is mostly due to poor maintenance.

The railway has the natural advantages in terms of lower cost of carriage and ability to carry bulk over long distances which can be used to connect the land locked Barak valley to the ASEAN countries via Moreh in Manipur and Indo-Myanmar border in Mizoram.

The Ministry of Railways has prepared a Master Plan for north eastern region to improve rail connectivity (a) within the region, (b) connectivity with rest of India and (c) connectivity across international boundaries. Some of the projected lines which will pass through the Barak valley are: (a) a new line from Pancharatna to Silchar, (b) a new line from Sairang to Indo-Mayanmar Multi Modal Transit, and (c) Lalabazar (Assam)-to Vairengte (Mizoram). In the near future it is visualized that Sairang will be connected to Aizwal-Lawngtlai-Indomyanmar border and finally to sitwe port. Once it is connected the Barak valley will have direct access to the ASEAN.

As the Indian Railways is engaged in harmonization of railway tracks in the north eastern India and also construction of new lines the Barak valley also has the potential to connect itself with the ASEAN countries via Moreh at Manipur. A project for the construction of a 98 km railway line connecting Jiribam to Imphal has already been taken up in April 2003 and is not been completed yet. On completion of this project Barak valley will be connected to the two large railway networks to access the ASEAN countries. These are: (i) India–Myanmar–Thailand–Malaysia–Singapore rail link, and (ii) India–Myanmar–Thailand–Hanoi rail link.

There is an alternative route from Barak valley to ASEAN via Bangladesh that will emerge once the Agartala-Akhaura railway line is completed. There will be railway connectivity of Barak valley via Agartala-Akhaura-Dhaka-Chittagong-Sabroom route which will provide access to Dhaka as well as Chittagong port. The Barak valley can also be connected to the Seaport at Chittagong, Kolkata, once the Mahisashan-Sahbhajpur rail link is reopened. If Bangladesh allows the Chittagong port, the valley can use it to transport the consignment to the ASEAN countries. As the Trans-Asian Railway network is visualized to pass through Mahisashan-Sahbhajpur link, once it realized Barak valley will be not only have direct rail connectivity with Bangladesh but also it would have connectivity across Asia, Europe and Africa.

The waterways are useful for transporting heavy consignments as it is very cheap as compared to other modes of transportation although a bit slow. The Barak valley can be connected to the Kolkata port via Surma-Magna navigation channel to access the ASEAN market through sea route.

The air connectivity is important for quick movement of passengers and cargo. If the valley is to trade with the ASEAN countries it is extremely important to have convenient air connectivity. In case of transporting light valuable and perishable commodities and movement of labor forces engaged in service industry and the movement of the business people the air connectivity is extremely important. Although, Barak valley does not have an international airport, there is a domestic airport which runs flight from Silchar to Guwahati, Kolkata, Imphal and Agartala. As there is a plan to run small flights from Imphal (Manipur) to Manadalaya (Myanmar), people from this region can have a quick journey to the ASEAN countries.

Concluding Remarks

The connectivity helps in the development of a region in many ways. Although, it is sometimes empirically found that the investment in connectivity infrastructure may not lead to the development of a region without the necessary socio-economic-political and cultural environment. Well developed connectivity is the necessary condition for the development of any region. As the Barak valley remained landlocked and underdeveloped since independence the former seems to be the cause of the later more than the opposite. In any way improved connectivity is also a part of the development process.

The look/act east policy of the government of India which aims to deepen the economic tie with the ASEAN countries by way of better physical connectivity and trade facilitation via NER for which many projects have been initiated. It is expected that the initiatives once completed will give an impetus to the development process of the NER. However, as the NER region is diverse and has poor connectivity it is very difficult to predict how the NER-ASEAN connectivity will be helpful in the overall development of the region. The present study has addressed the question as to how the NER-ASEAN connectivity help in the development process of Barak valley a landlocked region in the southern Assam.

As the valley is not sharing any border with the ASEAN countries it is not directly getting connectivity with these countries. However, India-Myanmar-Thailand trilateral highway, Kaladan Multi Modal transit and Delhi Hanoi railway link can be accessed by the valley provided all weather connectivity is available from Silchar to Moreh in Manipur and Indo-Myanmar border in Mizoram, which are presently inadequate and poor in condition. As these routes are not passed through this region and the state government usually do not pay much attention to the valley which made this region landlocked it is very early to predict the benefits from these projects for the Barak valley unless the central government takes some special initiative. Even if these roads are connected a big question remains for the maintenances.

In addition to these projects, the BCIM initiative and Trans Asian railway network will be more beneficial for the Barak Valley to connect with the ASEAN because these routes are of international importance and passes through the Barak valley, it can have direct connectivity with ASEAN as well as other parts of Asia, Europe and Africa. Once the connectivity has the national and international importance they get due importance for maintenances because of various national and international pressures.

Although, the valley seems to be having surface connectivity in the near future it also have the potential to be connected by air and water. As the Silchar airport is limited to fly only a few domestic flights with minimum facility and high passenger tariffs there is a scope for improvement. If the airport is upgraded with state of the art technology, it can run more flights carrying both passenger and cargo to domestic and international destinations at a cheaper price. As there is an agreement between India and ASEAN relating to the aviation, a flight from Silchar to Mandalay (Myanmar) can be introduced initially which will give boast to both merchandise and service trade between Barak valley and ASEAN.

The water transport facility is also not utilized in this region. The Inland Water Authority of India (IWAI) is working to declare Barak River as National Waterways-VI. As there are well-developed terminals in Barak River, once the water way is declared and new investments to develop more infrastructure of IWT on the National Waterways-VI are made the Barak valley could be connected to the erstwhile water transport network. Once this is realized, a multi modal hub at Badarpur can be developed where rail, road, inland waterways and civil aviation facility can be converged. Although, the airport is at Silchar but the other modes of transport – road, rail and inland waterways converge at Badarpur. It will give a boost to the development process of Barak valley and the entire southern part of the NER as well.

Therefore, from the discussion above, the future of the landlocked Barak valley seems to be shiny. However, it should not be forgotten the saying that 'a bird in the hand is worth two in the bush'. The condition of the existing connectivity is probably worst in the world due to lack of proper maintenances. In this condition only time can answer as to how the NER-ASEAN connectivity will deliver development to the Barak valley.

Bibliography

Acharya A (2000) *Constructing a Security Community in Southeast Asia: ASEAN and the Problem of Regional Order.* New York: Routledge

_______ (2010) Regional Integration in Asia: Why Asian Regionalism? *World Politics Review.* Retrieved from https://goo.gl/GgL5c3 Accessed on March 19, 2017.

_______ (2012) Foundations of collective action in Asia: Theory and practice of regional cooperation. Tokyo: Asian Development Bank Institute. Retrieved from www.adbi.org/working-paper/2012/02/14/4994.foundations.collective.action.asia/ Accessed on April 10, 2016.

Adhikari R (2015) Greater Tumen Region Trade Facilitation Study. Beijing, China: United Nations Development Program.

Alamgir J (2009) *India's Open Economy Policy: Globalism, Rivalry, Continuity.* London and New York: Routledge

Almond G and Powell CP (1966) *Comparative Politics: Developmental Approach,* New York: Amerind Publishing Co. Pvt. Ltd.

Allen RL (1963) Review of the theory of economic integration, by Bela Balassa. *Economic Development and Cultural Change* 11(4): pp. 449-454.

Agrawal P (2005) Foreign direct investment in South Asia: Impact on economic growth. In Graham EM (Eds.) *Multinationals and Foreign Investment in Economic Development.* Basingstoke: Palgrave Macmillan.

Agrawal RC (Undated) Present Scenario on Border Trade and Look East Policy, Northeast Federation on International Trade. Retrieved from https://goo.gl/6k1RmG. Accessed on March 11, 2017.

ASEAN-India Centre (2014) Transforming connectivity corridors between India and Myanmar into development Corridors. New Delhi: RIS, pp.4-10.

Asian Development Bank (2013) Assessment of the Greater Mekong Sub-region energy sector development: Progress, prospects, and regional investment priorities. Mandaluyong City, Phillippines: Asian Development Bank.

Association of Southeast Asian Nations (ASEAN). Retrieved from http://www.aseansec.org/about_ASEAN.html. Accessed on January 14, 2016.

Assam Population Census data (2011). Retrieved from https://goo.gl/1vvCz. Accessed on March 22, 2017.

Bagchi A (2008) Globalisation and federalism: Uneasy partners? *Economic and Political Weekly* 43(38): 41-48.

Balaji MS (2016) India-Bangladesh Relations: An Enduring Economic Partnership. Vivekananda International Foundation. Retrieved from http://www.vifindia.org/sites/default/files/india-bangladesh-relations-an-enduring-economic-partnership.pdf. Accessed on March 22, 2017.

Balassa B (1961) The Theory of Economic Integration. Homewood, Illinois: Richard D. Irwin.

_______ (1962) Economic development and integration.

Bajpai K, Basit S and Krishnappa V (2014) (Eds.), *India's Grand Strategy; History, Theory, Cases.* New Delhi: Routledge, p.1.

Barrel R and Pain N (1996) An econometric analysis of U.S. foreign direct investment. *Review of Economics and Statistics* (78): 200-207.

_______ (2005) *Durable Disorder: Understanding the Politics of Northeast India.* New Delhi: Oxford University Press

Baru S (2010) Centring States. *Business Standard*, September 13, 2010. Retrieved from http://www.business-standard.com/article/opinion/sanjaya-baru-centring-states-110091300008_1.html. Accessed on January 12, 2017.

Baruah S (2004) Between south and south east Asia: Northeast India and the look east policy, *CENISEAS Papers*, (No.4). Guwahati: OKDISCD

_______ (2005) *Durable Disorder: Understanding the Politics of Northeast India.* New Delhi: Oxford University Press.

Benz A and Broschek J (2013) *Federal dynamics: Continuity, change and the varieties of federalism.* Oxford: Oxford University Press.

Bezbaruah MP (2007) Indo-Myanmar border trade: The stakes for north east India. *Dialogue*, 9 (1).

Bhagwati J (1993) Regionalism and multilateralism: An overview. In

Melo JD and Panagariya A (Eds.) *New Dimensions in Regional Integration*. New York: Cambridge University Press, pp. 22–51.

Bhagwati J and Panagariya A (1996) The theory of preferential trade agreements: Historical evolution and current trends. *The American Economic Review* 86 (2): 82-87.

Bhagawati SH (2007) Insurgency: A hindrance to economic development of north eastern region. In Sonowal AP (Eds.) *Insurgency and Economic Development in North-East India*, (p. 183).Guwahati, Assam: DVS Publishers.

Bhatia R (2011) India's look east policy. *Foreign Policy Research Centre Journal* (Focuss: India's Look East Policy), No. 8.

Bhattacharya AK (1973) Economic regions in the context of development : Some basic considerations. *Artha Vijnana* 5(1):57-90.

Bhaumik S (2009) *Troubled Periphery: Crisis of India's North East*. New Delhi: Sage Publications.

_______ (2014) Look East through Northeast: Challenges and Prospects for India. ORF Occasional Paper 51. Observer Research Foundation June 2014.

_______ (2016) Multi-connectivity between the NER and Myanmar. Presented in an International Seminar of CENES Kolkata Chapter, on *Mizoram: the Gateway to South East Asia*, Mizoram University, 5-6 October 2016.

_______ (2016) *The Agartala doctrine: A proactive northeast in Indian foreign policy*. New Delhi: Oxford University Press, New Delhi.

Bhushan B (2016) Five fact why the Kaladan project is to crucial for India's Act East Policy. New Delhi: Catch News, 4.37 minutes. Retrieved from http://www.catchnews.com /video/five-fact-why-kaladan-is-crusial-to-india's-act-east-policy/mp4. Accessed on January 14, 2017.

Bissinger J (2012) Foreign investment in Myanmar: A resource boom but a development bust. *Contemporary Southeast Asia* 34: (1):17.

Boyer R. (1993) The convergence hypothesis revisited: Globalization but still the century of nations? Conference on "Domestic Institutions, Trade and the Pressure for National Convergence' organised by MIT Industrial Performance Center, February 22-26. Bellagio. Retrieved from http://www.cepremap.fr/depot/couv_orange/co9403.pdf, accessed on March 22, 2017.

Brada JC and Mendez JA (1988) An estimate of the dynamic effects of economic integration. *The Review of Economics and Statistics* 70 (1): 163-168.

Brook, DHF (2006) The rise of regionalism: A neo-utilitarian approach. Retrieved from https://ssrn.com/abstract=923108 or http://dx.doi.org/10.2139/ssrn.923108. Accessed on June 10, 2016.

CAREC Corridor Performance Measurement and Monitoring (2015) Annual Report, Asian Development Bank, 2015.

Chakraborty G and Ray AK (2014) *The Look East Policy and Northeast India*, New Delhi: AAKAR Books and Guwahati: OKDISCD.

Chatterjee S (1965) The gazetteer of India (Vol. 1). New Delhi: Govt. of India.

Chatterji R and Chaudhury ABR (2016) India-Bangladesh connectivity: A year after Modi's visit. ORF Special Report, June 2016. Retrieved from http://www.orfonline.org/wp-content/uploads/2016/06/ORF_SpecialReport_14.pdf. Accessed on December 22, 2016.

Chirathivat S and Cheewatrakoolpong K (2015) Thailand's economic integration with neighboring countries and possible connectivity with South Asia. ADBI Working Paper Series, Asian Development Bank Institute

Choudhary J (2016) Role of Tripura and Mizoram in India's trade relations with Myanmar. Presented in the International Seminar on *Mizoram: the Gateway to South East Asia*, Centre for Eastern and North East Studies (CENES-Kolkata), Mizoram University, 5-6 October 2016.

Chowdhury S (2014) Regional disparity in India: A study of three decades using comparable tables. Rotterdam: IARIW. Retrieved from http://www.iariw.org/papers/2014/Chowdhury2Paper.pdf. Accessed on September 12, 2016.

Chutia S (2015) Prospects of Border Trade for North East Region of India with South Asian Countries. *International Journal of Research in Economics and Social Sciences*, 5(10): 9-14.

CMI Social Research Centre (Undated). Export potential of horticultural products from north eastern states. Sponsored by Agricultural and Processed Food Products Exports Development Authority (APEDA). Retrieved from https://goo.gl/TwF4PN. Accessed on January 11, 2017.

Community Forest International (CFI) (2006) Forest sector review of northeast India. Retrieved from https://goo.gl/kIKzgH Accessed on July 28, 2016.

Cooper CA and Masselll BF (1965) A new look at customs union theory. *The Economic Journal* 75 (300): 742-747.

Crescenzi R and Pose AR (2012) Infrastructure and regional growth in the European Union, *Papers in Regional Science*, 91(3).

CUTS International (2009) Memorandum to Prime Minister regarding Indo-Bangla trade with reference to Nepal and Bhutan. September 7, 2009. Retrieved from www.cuts-international.org/Letter_to_PM_Memorandum_on_Indo-Bangla_Trade.pdf. Accessed on March 11, 2016.

Das G (2016) India's Myanmar policy: Implications for India's northeast. In Das G and Thomas CJ (Eds.), *Look East to Act East Policy: Implications for India's Northeast*. New Delhi: Routledge.

Das G, Das SC and Paul U (2016) Look east policy: Economic engagements with ASEAN and East Asian countries. In Das G and Thomas CJ (Eds.), *Look East to Act East Policy: Implications for India's Northeast*. New Delhi: Routledge.

Das G, Paul U and Mathur T (2017) Making "Act East Policy' work for the development of North Eastern Region of India. In Jha P and Mishra R (Eds.) *Integrating North East in India's Act East Policy*. New Delhi: ICWA, pp44-45.

Das G and Singh G (2010) Development of national peripheries through mobilizing cross-border synergies : A case for Sino_Indian cooperation for the development of India's northeast and China's southwest. In Das G and Thomas CJ (Eds.) *India-China: Trade and Strategy for Frontier Development*. New Delhi: Bookwell.

Das HN (2011) Beyond north-east insurgency-history-development. New Delhi: Manas Publications, p.250.

Das SK (2010) India's look east policy: Imagining a new geography of India's north-east. *India Quarterly*, 66(4): 346.

Das SK and Barua A (1996) Regional inequalities, economic growth and liberalization: A study of the Indian economy. *The Journal of Development Studies* 32(3): 364-390.

Das SK and Tewari R (2010) India – ASEAN free trade agreement and development of north east: Prospects and challenges. Draft Paper for CDS – IIFT-RIS-UNCTAD National Seminar on India – ASEAN Free Trade Agreement & Way Forward 5–6th February, 2010 Centre for Development Studies, Trivandrum.

Das UR (2016) Enhancing India-Myanmar border trade: Policy and implementation measures. Department of Commerce, Ministry of Commerce and Industry, GOI.

Devlin R and Estevadeordal A (2001) What is new in the new regionalism in Americas? Buenos Aires: Institute for the integration of Latin America and the Caribbean, Working Paper No. 6, p. 19

De P et. al (2011) Expansion of north east India's trade and investment with Bangladesh and Myanmar: An assessment of the opportunities and constraints. RIS, New Delhi.

Dey S (2009) Tripura fast becoming investment hotspot in NE. *Business Standard*, July 9. Retrieved from http://www.business-standard.com/article/finance/tripura-fast-becoming-investment-hot-spot-in-ne-109070900021_1.html. Accessed on March 16, 2017.

Dikshit, S (2008) India, Burma ink pact. The Hindu, 03 April 2008. Retrieved from http://www.thehindu.com/todayspaper/tpnational/IndiaMyanmarinkpact/article15196703.ece?test=2&textsize= small. Accessed on March 31, 2017.

Eapsirimetee P, Suthikarnnarunai N and Harnhiran S (2013) Balancing canned pineapple supply chain in Thailand. *European Journal of Business Management* 5(4): 32–39.

Elwin V (2007) A philosophy for NEFA, Directorate of Research: Government of Arunachal Pradesh.

Elazar DJ (1987) *Exploring federalism*. Alabama: University of Alabama Press.

Engagement of Indian states in external affairs (2014) *Indian Foreign Affairs Journal* 9(1): 33-45.

ERIA Study Team (2010) Current status of ASEAN transport sector in ASEAN Strategic Transport Plan 2011-2015. Jakarta: ASEAN Secretariat and ERIA. p.3.1-3.4-6. 95.

FICCI (2014) Gateway to the ASEAN India's northeast frontier, 27 Nov, 2014.

Food and Agricultural Organisation (FAO) (2007) World bamboo resources: A thematic study prepared in the framework of the Global Forest Resources Assessment 2005. Retrieved from http://www.fao.org/3/a-a1243e.pdf Accessed on June 22, 2016.

Fukuyama F (1992) *The End of History and the Last Man*. New York: The Free Press.

Ganguly S (2015) *Indian Foreign Policy*. New Delhi: Oxford University Press.

Gerston LN (2007) *American Federalism: A Concise Introduction*. New York: M.E. Sharp

Ghosh M (2013) *Liberalization, Growth and Regional Disparities in India*. Springer.

Godbole M (2001) Management of India's international borders. *Economic and Political Weekly* 36(48): 4442-4444.

Gordon S (1995) *India's Rise to Power in the Twentieth Century and Beyond*. New York: St. Martin's Press, p. 299.

Goswamia C and Saikiab KK (2012) FDI and its relation with exports in India: Status and prospect in North East Region. *Procedia - Social and Behavioral Sciences*, 37: 123 – 132.

Government of Assam (2014) Industrial and investment policy of Assam, Retrieved from https://easeofdoingbusinessinassam.in/Industrial%20and%20Investment%20Policy%20of%20Assam%202014.pdf. Accessed on March 24, 2017

Government of Assam, Department of Panchayat and Rural Development. Retrieved from http://pnrdassam.nic.in/bpllist.html#2SUM. Accessed on May 21, 2016.

Government of Manipur (2011) Draft industrial and investment policy of Manipur, 2011. Retrieved from http://www.dcimanipur.gov.in/documents/Draft%20IIPM%202011.pdf. Accessed on March 24, 2017.

Griffith P (1967) *History of Indian Tea Industry*. London : Weidenfold and Nicolson.

Greater Mekong Sub-region Economic Cooperation Program (2015) Asian development Bank.

Greater Mekong Sub-region Statistics on Growth, Infrastructure, and Trade (Second Edition) (2016) Greater Mekong Sub-region Eighth Economic Corridors Forum, Cambodia: Asian Development Bank.

Gupta A (2009) Development of Barak valley: Question of sustainability. In Bhattacherjee JB (Eds.) *Development Strategies for Barak valley (Assam)*. New Delhi: Akansha Publishing House.

______ (2013) Role of states in India's foreign policy. IDSA Keynote Address delivered at National Seminar on, *Federalism, Foreign Policy and Border States: Dynamics from North East States of India*, at Sikkim University, 22-23 March 2013, Retrieved from http://www.idsa.in/speech/SikkimUniversity_agupta. Accessed on April 2, 2017.

Gupta R (2011) India's look east policy. *Foreign Policy Research Centre Journal* (Focuss: India's Look East Policy), No. 8.

Haokip T (2010) India's look east policy: Prospects and challenges for northeast India. Paper presented at the North East India Council of Social Science Research's national seminar on India's Look East Policy and North East India: Achievements and Constrains, Shillong, 26-27th March 2010.

_______ (2015) *India's Look East Policy and the Northeast*. New Delhi: Sage Publications India.

_______ (2015) India's Look East Policy: Prospects and Challenges for Northeast India. *Studies in Indian Politics* 3(2): 198–211.

Harvard Kennedy School. (2011). Myanmar agriculture in 2011: Old problems and new challenges: Prepared for proximity designs Myanmar. Retrieved from http://ash.harvard.edu/files/myanmar1111.pdf. Accessed on October 18, 2016.

Hazarika OB (2014) Evolving dynamics of federalism and foreign policy. Retrieved from https://www.researchgate.net/publication/311614624_Evolving_Dynamics_of_Federalism_and_Foreign_Policy. Accessed on April 12, 2017.

Heierstad G (2016) Foreign affairs and federal actors in the Indian democracy. Retrieved from https://www.idunn.no/indias-democracies/6-foreign-affairs-and-federal-actors-in-the-indian-democracy. Accessed on March 12, 2017.

Hettne B (1999) The new regionalism: A prologue. In Hettne B, Inotai A and Sunkel O (Eds.), *Globalism and the New Regionalism.* Basingstoke: Palgrave Macmillan, p. 51.

IANS (2015) Cabinet clears revised cost for KMTTP. *Business Standard,* New Delhi: Author. Retrieved from http://www.business-standard.com/article/115010400905_1. Accessed on August 8, 2016.

Indian Chamber of Commerce (2016). Augmenting bilateral trade between India & Myanmar: Case for enhancing India's exports. Retrieved from www.indianchamber.net/new/INDIA-MYANMAR_Sept12.pdf. Accessed on January 06, 2017.

International Trade of Bamboo and Rattan (INBR) (2012) International trade of bamboo and rattan. Retrieved from https://goo.gl/XAMb0z Accessed on August 2, 2016.

Isard W (1955) Value of regional approach in economic analysis. Studies in income and wealth 21. Retrieved from http://www.nber.org/chapters/c7601.pdf. Accessed on February 22, 2017.

Johnson A (2005) The effects of FDI inflows on host country economic growth. Retrieved from https://static.sys.kth.se/itm/wp/cesis/cesiswp58.pdf. Accessed on March 11, 2017

Jacob H (2016) *Putting the periphery at the centre: Indian States' role in Foreign Policy*, Carnegie India, October 2016.

Jangu SL (2016) India's Look East Policy: The energy security perspective. in Das G and Thomus CJ (Eds.) *Look East to Act East Policy: Implications for the India's North East* New York and London: Routledge (South East Asia Edition), pp 131-140.

Jenkins R (2003) India's states and the making of foreign economic policy: The limits of the constituent diplomacy paradigm. *Publius* 33(4): 63-84.

Josling T, Anderson K, Schmitz A and Tangermann S (2010). Understanding international trade in agricultural products: One hundred years of contributions by agricultural economists. *American Journal of Agricultural Economics, 92*(2): 424-446.

Kahnert FP, Richards ES and Thomopoulos P (1969) Economic integration among developing countries. Paris: Development Center of the Organization for Economic Co-operation and Development (OECD).

Karmis D and Norman W (2005) *Theories of Federalism: A Reader*. New York: Palgrave Macmillan.

Khanna S (2002) Trade and investment in the South Asia sub-region for economic cooperation: Barriers and opportunities. Unpublished Paper, Kolkata: Indian Institute of Management, Calcutta.

Kreinin, M (1963) On the dynamic effects of a customs union. *The Journal of Political Economy* 72 (2):193-195.

Koo C-Mo, Hyun-Hoon L and Donna Y (2011) Northeast Asian economic cooperation: Assessment and prospects of the Greater Tumen Initiative. *Asia-Pacific Cooperation Academy Kangwon National University (August 2011.*Retrieved from http://www.akes. or. kr/eng/papers. Accessed on April 14, 2015.

Kumar N (2002) Towards an Asian economic community: The relevance of India. Discussion Paper no. 34, Research and Information System for Non-Aligned and Other Developing Countries (RIS), New Delhi.

Kumara S (2005) Burma visit highlights India's "Look East" Strategy. *World Socialist Web*, Retrieved from http://www.countercurrents.org/kumara070405.html. Accessed on October 12, 2015.

Lalthanfeli R (2010) Kaladan multi-model transit transport project,

Document of Trade and Commerce Department, Government of Mizoram.

Lawrence PW (2017) *Act East and India's North-East*. India: Pentagon Press, India, p. 52

Lipsey RG (1960) The theory of customs unions: A general survey. *The Economic Journal* 70 (279):496-513.

Max F (2016) The south china sea; Explaining the dispute. New York Times, July 14 2016, Retrieved from https://www.nytimes.com/2016/07/15/world/asia/south-china-sea-dispute-arbitration-explained.html?_r=0. Accessed on February 14, 2017.

Machlup F (1977) *A History of Thought on Economic Integration*. New York: Columbia University Press.

Majumdar M (2016) India's act east policy: Whiter Northeast India? The Shillong Times. p. 6.

Mc Lean I and McMillan A (2003) *The Concise Dictionary of Politics*. New York: Oxford University Press.

Ministry of Development of North-Eastern Region, Government of India, (1873) Bengal Eastern Frontier Regulations. Retrieved from https://goo.gl/QidHHt. Accessed on July 10, 2013.

_______ (2008) North-eastern region vision 2020, pp.1-4. Retrieved from http://www.MDONER.gov.in/sites/default/files/silo2_content/ner_vision/Vision_2020.pdf. Accessed January 14, 2013.

_______ (2011) Look east policy and the north-eastern states. Retrieved from, http://www.mdoner.gov.in/sites/default/files/silo2_content/Look%20East%20Policy/Aspects%20of%20Look%20East%20Policy.pdf. Accessed on June 18, 2014.

_______ (Undated) International Border. Retrieved from http://mdoner.gov.in/node/202. Accessed on January 14, 2015.

Ministry of External Affairs, Government of India (2007) Discussion holds the Kaladan project in respect of investments. The press released of meeting of then the Foreign Minister Pranab Mukherjee and Myanmar's Minister for Planning and Economic Development. New Delhi: Author. Retrieved from http://www.mea.gov.in/outgoing-visit-detail.htm?2246/External+Affairs+ Minister+ visit+ to+ Myanmar. Accessed on December 21, 2016.

_______ (2014) India and Myanmar sign memorandum of understanding on border cooperation. Retrieved from http://www.mea.gov.in/pressreleases.htm?dtl/23315/India+and+

Myanmar+sign+Memorandum+of+Understanding+on+Border+Cooperation. Accessed on November 22, 2016.

______ Annual Report 2015-16, Government of India, pp. 81-85, http://www.mea.gov.in/Uploads/PublicationDocs/26525_26525_External_Affairs_English_AR_2015-16_Final_compressed.pdf. Accessed on November 27, 2016.

______ (Undated) About Mekong Ganga cooperation. Retrieved from http://www.mea.gov.in/aseanindia/about-mgc.htm. Accessed on July 24, 2016

Ministry of Home Affairs, Government of India (2016) Insurgency in north east. Retrieved from http://mha.nic.in/sites/upload_files/mha/files/InsurgencyNE_052016.pdf. Accessed on August 16, 2017.

Ministry of Law, Government of India (Undated) Sixth schedule. Retrieved from http://www.constitution.org/cons/india/shed06.htm. Accessed on October 11, 2015.

Mishra L (2016) Government plans major boost to water transport. *The Hindu*, 23 September. Retrieved from http://www.thehindu.com/news/cities/mumbai/business/Govt.-plans-majorboost-to-water-transport/article13998276.ece. Accessed on December 21, 2016.

Mohan CR (2012) *Samudra Manthan: Sino-Indian Rivalry in the Indo-Pacific*. Washington, D.C: Carnegie Endowment for International Peace.

Morris S (2005) Explaining foreign direct investment in Gujarat: A study base on an opinion survey of persons involved in the foreign direct investment process. Retrieved from https://web.iima.ac.in/assets/snippets/workingpaperpdf/2005-02-01morris.pdf. Accessed on August 8, 2016.

Mujtaba SA (2007) India, Burma ready to finalize Kaladan project. Retrieved from www.mizzima.com Accessed on April 9, 2017.

Mukherjee JK (2016) Kaladan multi-model transit transport project. Paper presented in an International Seminar of CENES Kolkata Chapter, on *Mizoram: A Gateway to ASEAN*, Mizoram University, October 5-6, 2016.

Mukhim P (2013) Sixth schedule and tribal autonomy. The Statesman, 15 July.

Muni SD and Chadha V (2014) *Asian Strategic Review 2015: India as a Security Provider.* New Delhi: Pentagon Press.

Naidu G V C (2008) India and Southeast Asia: An analysis of the look east policy. In PV Rao (Eds.) *India and ASEAN: Partners at Summit.* New Delhi: KW Publishers.

Nayyar D and Sen A (1994) International Trade and the Agricultural Sector in India. *Economic and Political Weekly, 29*(20): 1187-1203

Neog R (2014) Northeast India: Where is the Chinese investment? Retrieved from http://www.ipcs.org/article/india/northeast-india-where-is-the-chinese-investment-4750.html. Accessed on March 27, 2017.

North D (1955) Location theory and regional economic growth. *Journal of Political Economy* 63(3): 243-258.

Panagariya A (1998) *The Regionalism Debate: An Overview.* University of Maryland.

Pattnaik JK (2015) Act east through the India's North-East. *Mainstream,* 53(16): 6-9.

_______ (2016a) Look east policy and India's north eastern region: Status of cross border trade and connectivity. In Das G and Thomas CJ (Eds.), *Look East to Act East Policy: Implications for India's North East.* New Delhi: Routledge, pp.213-224.

_______ (2016b) Should the Stilwell Road be Reopened? *Economic & Political Weekly,* 51(15):1-6.

_______ (2016c) BCIM Corridor: The Road Map for Northeast. The Sangai Express, 4 December.

Paul M and Lesley W (2014) U.S. call for south china sea 'Freeze' gets cool response from China. Retrieved from http://www.reuters.com/article/us-asean-southchinasea-idUSKBN0G904O20140809. Accessed on August 15, 2014.

Paul U and Das G (2017) Reaping Dividend from India's Act East Policy: What North-East Can Offer? In Thomas CJ and Sarda K (eds.) Act East and India's North-East. New Delhi: Pentagon Press.

Phanjoubam P(2013) Inner line demand: The horseman must think faster than the horse. *Dialogue,* 15(1): 22.

Planning Commission of India (1997) Transforming the north-east. High level commission report to the Prime Minister. Retrieved from http://planningcommission.nic.in/reports/genrep/ne_exe.pdf. Accessed on October 16, 2014.

Press Trust of India (PTI), (2014) Navy gets facility for uninterrupted communication with ships. Retrieved from https://goo.gl/V9b90N. Accessed on March 10, 2017.

_______ (2016) IWAI inks pact with IPGPL for Kaladan project. *Economic*

Times, New Delhi. Retrieved from http://economictimes.indiatimes.com/news/economy/infrastructure/iwai-inks-pact-with-ipgpl-for-kaladan-multimodal-transit-work/printarticle/52837295.cms. Accessed on November 14, 2016.

Priyoranjan C (Undated) Border trade in Manipur ground level survey and status report. Draft Report. Department of Commerce and Industries Project, GOM. Retrieved from http://economics.manipuruniv.ac.in/SAP/Reports/IndoMyanmar%20 Dorder%20 Trade%20Report.pdf. Accessed on April 10, 2017.

Pudiate LT (2010) *Mizoram and Look East Policy*. New Delhi: Akansha Publishing House, p.175.

Pye LW (1966) *Aspects of Political Development*. Boston: Little Brown.

Racioppi L (1994) *Soviet Policy towards Asia since 1970*. New York: Cambridge University Press.

Rajshekhar M (2015) Travelling down the Kaladan Highway. *Scroll.in*. Retrieved from https://scroll.in/roving/27/travelling-down-the-kaladan-highway. Accessed on May 27, 2016.

Ramesh J (2005) North east India in new Asia. Retrieved from http://www.india-seminar.com/2005/550/550%20jairam%20 ramesh.htm. Accessed on July 3, 2013.

Ranganathan CV (2011) India's look east policy. *Foreign Policy Research Centre Journal* (Focuss: India's Look East Policy), No. 8.

Ravenhill J (1995) Competing logics of regionalism in the Asia-Pacific. *Journal of European Integration*, 28 (2"3): 179"199.

Ray A (1992) New economic policy and federalism. *Economic and Political Weekly* 27(4): 147-150.

Reddem A (2016) Singapore NRIs have big Plans for the State. *The Hindus*, April 15, 2016. Retrieved from http://www.thehindu.com/news/cities/Vijayawada/singapore-nris-have-big-plans-for-state/article8478322.ece. Accessed on March 24, 2017.

Research and Information System for Developing Countries (RIS) (2011) Expansion of north east India's trade and investment with Bangladesh and Myanmar: An assessment of opportunities and constraints. New Delhi: RIS.

Rios AR, Masters WA and Shively GE (2013) Linkages between Market Participation and Productivity: Results from a Multi-Country Farm Household Sample.

Rochhamliana (2007) Sittwe Port: The port of hope for Mizoram. The Scribed, online newspaper. 9 October. Retrieved from http://

www.scribd.com/mobile/document/16361304/port-sittwe-port-of-hope-for-mizoram/htm. Accessed on April 8, 2017.

______ (2008). Port Sittwe: Port of hope for Mizoram. In Patnaik JK (Eds.) *Peace and Development in Mizoram: Role of the State and Civil Society*. Aizwal: Department of Political Science, Mizoram University, p248-259.

Roy N (2009) Exploring economy of Barak valley for development strategy. In Bhattacherjee JB (Eds.) *Development Strategies for Barak valley (Assam)*. New Delhi: Akansha Publishing House.

Roy N and Bezbaruah MP (2002) *Agricultural Growth and Regional Economic Development*. New Delhi: Mittal Publications.

Salemink K and Strijker D (2015) Regional development and connectivity: A digital perspective. An ITRACT project funded by the Interreg IVB North Sea Region Programme of the European Union.

Sarkar S (2007) India sealed Kaladal deal as Myanmar bled. Retrieved from www.merinews.com, October12, 2007, Accessed on April 7, 2017.

Sarmah GN (2015) Look east policy and north east India: Challenges and Opportunities. *International Journal in Management and Social Science*, 3(4): 247.

Schiff M and Winters AL (1998) Dynamics and politics in regional integration arrangements: An introduction. *The World Bank Economic Review*, 12 (2):177-195.

Sen R Asher MG and Rajan RS (2004) ASEAN India Economic relations: Current status and future prospects. Discussion Paper no. 73, Research and Information System for Non-Aligned and Other Developing Countries (RIS), New Delhi.

Shahin S (2003) India's 'Look East' Policy pays off. *Asia Times*, 11 October 2003.

Sharma A and Bezbaruah MP (2009) Industry in the development perspective of North East India. *Dialogue*, 10 (3).

Sharma K (2000) Export growth in India: Has FDI played a role? Economic Growth Center, Discussion Paper. Yale University.

Siddhanta G (2014) FDI in northeast India. *The Thumb Print*, September 14. Retrieved from http://www.thethumbprintmag.com/fdi-in-northeast-india/. Accessed on March 27, 2017.

Singh A (2011) South china sea dispute and India. SAEA Group Research, 25 September 2011. Retrieved from http://

saeagroup.com/articles/2011/sept/south-china-sea-dispute-and-india.html. Accessed on May 29, 2015.

Singh BE (2014) Looking east from the north east: Noises from the ground. Retrieved from https://goo.gl/kwjHeP. Accessed on February 18, 2017.

Singh CP (2012) Implications of border trade barriers vis-a-vis connectivity between India and Myanmar with special reference to north east India in the advent of look east policy. *Radix International Journal of Research in Social Science, 1*(8): 58-91.

Singh M (2006) Prime Ministerial speech at the 16th Asia Society Corporate Conference, Mumbai: March 18th 2006

Singh MP (2011) Political Economy of Federalism in India: Economic and Regional Disparities, September 2011, http://socialsciences.in/article/political-economy-federalism-india-economic-and-regional-disparities. Accessed on April 12, 2017.

Singh NB (2010) Border Trade at Moreh-Tamu Sector: Bane or Boon for Manipur. In Bijoy Kumar Singh and Damodar Nepram (Eds.), (2010). *Perspectives on the Economy of Manipur* (236-251). New Delhi: Akansha Publishing House.

Singh N and Srinivasan TN (2004) Indian Federalism, Economic Reform and Globalization http://citeseerx.ist.psu.edu/viewdoc/download?doi=10.1.1.453.7845&rep=rep1&type=pdf. Accessed on February 12, 2017.

Singh S (2007) Mekong-Ganga Cooperation initiatives: Analysis and assessment of India's engagement with Greater Mekong Sub-region, (Occasional Paper No. 3) Bangkok: Research Institute on Contemporary Southeast Asia.

Singh SP (2010) ASEAN: A potential export destination for products from northeast India, CUTS CITEE, Jaipur.

Sinha A (2004) The changing political economy of federalism in India: A historical institutionalist approach. *India Review* 3(1): 25-63.

Sinha V (2017) How Federal is the Indian Foreign Policy? February 16, 2017, Retrieved from https://www.youthkiawaaz.com/2017/02/how-federal-is-the-indian-foreign-policy/. Accessed on December 12, 2016.

Sinha Y (2003) Resurgent India in Asia, Speech at Harvard University. Retrieved from http//www.meaindia.nic. in/speech/2003/9/Harvard lecture29ss01.htm. Accessed September 29, 2016.

Staley CE (1977) Review of A history of thought on economic

integration, by Fritz Machlup. *Annals of the American Academy of Political and Social Science* 434:242-243

Sundaram A (2013) Look east policy. *International Journal of Advancements in Research and Technology* 2(5).

Suryanarayan V (2014) Federalism and foreign policy: Regional inputs in India's neighbourhood strategy. Retrieved from http://www.ipcs.org/article/india/ipcs-debate-federalism-and-foreign-policy-regional-inputs-in-indias-4283.html. Accessed on March 22, 2017.

Tewari F and Pant HV (2016) Paradiplomacy and India: Growing role of states in foreign policy. Retrieved from http://www.orfonline.org/expert-speaks/paradiplomacy-and-india/. Accessed on March 18, 2017.

Thakuria N (2007). Waiting for a Sea Port. Burma Digest.

______ (2014) Northeast India Anticipates Seaport. The Diplomat.

Tochkov K (2015) Regional integration and economic convergence in Northeast Asia: Evidence from the Greater Tumen Initiative. *Journal of Northeast Asia Development* 17: 85-108.

Umezaki S (2012) ASEAN-India connectivity: The comprehensive Asia development plan (CADP), Phase-2. Paper presented in an ICRIER Seminar on *India-Japan Relations: Trends and prospects*, New Delhi, February 29, 2012.

Uninathan S (2011) Gunrunners of north-east. India Today, 6 June. Retrieved from http://indiatoday.intoday.in/story/chinese-agents-smuggle-arms-to-spread-militancy-in-north-east/1/139538.html. Accessed on February 24, 2015.

United States International Trade Commission (USITC) (2015) Trade and investment policies in India, 2014-15, September 2015. Retrieved from https://www.usitc.gov/publications/332/pub4566.pdf. Accessed on February 12, 2017.

Vajpayee AB (1998) Joint effort for economic development of north eastern region, Speech at the meeting with Chief Ministers of North Eastern states in New Delhi, May 8, 1998.

Ward A and Ward L (2009) The Ashgate Research Companion to Federalism. Farnham: Ashgate.

Weigall D (2002) *International Relations-A Concise Companion.* Great Britain: Arnold Publishers, p. 191.

Win ZawKhin (2017) Federalism, ethno-linguistic identities and minority rights: Perspectives from India and Myanmar. Speaking in an International Seminar at Mizoram University, April 27-28, 2017.

World Bank (2007) *Evaluation of World Bank support to transportation infrastructure*. Washington DC: World Bank Publications.

_______ (2008) *World development report 2009: Reshaping economic geography*. Washington DC : World Bank Publications.

Yang KR (2012) The new great game: ASEAN's balancing act? RSIS commentaries. Retrieved from http://www.rsis.edu.sg/publications/Perspective/. Accessed on December 26, 2015

Index